Dream Life

Dream Life

An Experimental Memoir

J. Allan Hobson

The MIT Press
Cambridge, Massachusetts
London, England

For information about quantity discounts, email special_sales@mitpress.mit.edu.

Set in Stone Sans and Stone Serif by Toppan Best-set Premedia Limited. Printed and bound in the United States of America.

Library of Congress Cataloging-in-Publication Data

Hobson, J. Allan, 1933–
Dream life : an experimental memoir / J. Allan Hobson.
  p. cm.
Includes bibliographical references and index.
ISBN 978-0-262-01532-5 (hardcover : alk. paper)
1. Hobson, J. Allan, 1933– 2. Neuroscientists—Biography. I. Title.
QP353.4.H63A3   2011
616.80092—dc22
[B]

                                        2010030562

10 9 8 7 6 5 4 3 2 1

Contents

Preface

In 1961, appalled by the arrogance and ignorance of my psychoanalyst teachers at Harvard Medical School, I left my psychiatric residency to seek training in brain science. This book tells what led up to that decision and what has happened since. It is not a simple memoir. In addition to the usual psychological details about my life, it emphasizes important biological forces that are generic but no less important. Out of this mix emerges a new concept of dream consciousness that transcends Freud's Dream Theory. Thus, the book is both an autobiographically structured critique of psychiatry and a selective historical review of sleep and dream science. In it I celebrate the biological findings of the past 60 years and show how they constrain and shape psychology. I also seek to demonstrate why I see sleep and dream science as fundamental to the study of consciousness and how I arrived at that conclusion. I go on to describe the first fruits of the endeavor.

I claim that dreaming is not so much an unconscious mental process as a state of consciousness occurring in sleep. It is difficult to access dream consciousness via memory in the awake state because of sleep-related amnesia. But dreaming is not unconscious, and dream amnesia can be overcome. Laboratory studies and home-based studies reveal dreaming to be a virtual-reality state with features that may be useful to the emergence of waking consciousness.

Although sleep and dream science was at first dedicated to proving Freud's 1900 Disguise-Censorship hypothesis, it was evident by 1977 that a new paradigm was needed. The neurobiology of REM sleep, whose trajectory I helped to plot, has now led to a new theory of dream consciousness. Dream Life details the evolution of this new theory.

Among the consciousness-enhancing features of the physical substrate of dreaming are (1) the sense of agency (I dream, therefore I must be), (2) agency-initiated movement (I move in my dreams, therefore I am capable of movement), (3) an imagined space (in which I move in my dreams and therefore must be capable of movement in actual space), and (4) an integrated set of emotions (accompanying my self-initiated movement in the fictive space).

All these formal features of dreaming are relevant to the development of consciousness because they represent automatic, endogenous, and spontaneous contributions to the solution of the famous binding problem, which the brain must achieve if it is to integrate the multiple cognitive functions that are the several components of consciousness. The new theory holds that the preponderance of REM sleep in utero and in early postnatal life enables the human brain to actively prepare for its most ambitious achievement: waking consciousness.

I maintain that dream consciousness and waking consciousness continue to interact positively throughout life so as to mutually enhance one another. This idea transcends Freud's Disguise-Censorship hypothesis—a hypothesis that was dominant in 1961, when I began my psychiatric training. Not only was Freud's Dream Theory wrong, but psychoanalysis has systematically warped psychology and delayed the development of psychiatry. A century later, and not a minute too soon, we can begin to reconstruct psychology and psychiatry on the more secure foundations of brain science—foundations that Freud lacked.

Of course, the ideas expressed in this book, though mine in their details, are the distillate not only of my research but also of my interactions with many other scientists. Among the many inspiring teachers that I have met along the way are Frederick Snyder, Edward Evarts, Michel Jouvet, Elwood Henneman, and Vernon Mountcastle. I thank my students and co-workers for stimulation and support. Of these, none has been more constant and more helpful than my long-term collaborator Robert McCarley, now a successful sleep scientist in his own right.

To protect them from potential embarrassment, I have changed the names of the three people who inspired my accounts of the characters referred to in the book as Serena Valverde, Sebastian Bonanno, and Daniella Davis. Because I wish to give credit where credit is due, all other names in this book are veridical, except that the initials N.H. conceal the identity of my most important patient-teacher.

This book was five years in the making. For some of this delay, which permitted me to showcase my new protoconsciousness theory, I am grateful to Tom Stone, my first editor at the MIT Press. But I am even more grateful to Philip Laughlin, who finally agreed to publish this odd memoir. Paul Bethge tried, with some success, to curb my hyperassociative verbosity. My friend and assistant Nick Tranquillo cheerfully and competently incorporated my endless tweaks of the manuscript.

My basic research was generously supported by the National Institutes of Health, the National Science Foundation, and the National Aeronautics and Space Administation. My integrative efforts were encouraged by the John T. and Catherine D. MacArthur Foundation, in whose Research Network on Mind-Body Interactions I basked during the last decade of the twentieth century. My biological conception, my growth, and, most important, my freedom were given to me by my father, John Robert Hobson, and my mother, Anne Barnard Cotter, to whom I lovingly dedicate the book.

I Biologically Speaking: An Experimental Autobiography

1 Brain Birth: A Non-Immaculate Conception

"I'm coming!" my father may have cried. Continued pelvic thrusting and vigorous prostatic pumping delivered a myriad of gene-laden sperm into the welcoming warmth and wetness of my mother's vagina. He felt good. She was satisfied too, though in a less ecstatic, more enduring way. She had always wanted to be a mother, but her first pregnancy had ended sadly in a miscarriage. Although apprehensive, she had wanted to try again. Here was a chance.

And what a chance it was! Made more efficacious by the lubricity of their new environment, millions of tiny sperm cells made their way through the mouth of the uterus. Virtually weightless and invisibly small, some of the wiggly creatures entered the tube running from one of my mother's ovaries to her uterus. There one of them met its match, an egg.

My conception probably occurred in September of 1932, just before Franklin D. Roosevelt's election to his first term as president. The country was in the depths of a fearsome economic depression, and the young Hobsons were understandably apprehensive about bringing a child into such an uncertain world. But despite their misgivings, the combination of his lust and her maternal yearning set the stage for chance to play its part.

Why did one sperm cell, and only one, fertilize that particular egg? What identity did these two entirely non-conscious biological entities confer upon the future person? And how was this formidable constructive process realized? What little we know about these matters is all the more precious. The sperm and the egg that found each other in September of 1932 each contained the genetic material that would become an embryo, then a fetus, and then me. My father contributed half of the genes, my mother the other half.

In 1932 nothing was known about the molecular biology of the gene. Charles Darwin had enunciated his theory of evolution, which posited that the survival and propagation of each species was a functional adaptation of the particular genetic foundation of that species to its environment. The first laws of heredity had been established in the late nineteenth century by the famous pea-cross experiments of Gregor Mendel.

It was not until 1953 that the molecular structure of DNA was successfully modeled by Francis Crick and James Watson. By then, the being that was conceived in 1932 had become me, and I was, biologically, 21 years old. I would come to know Francis Crick later, when we both became convinced that the brain was dynamically active in sleep and that such brain activity was functionally significant for learning.

In 1932, there was a meeting of one sperm cell and one egg. Each of these two germ cells was chock-full of DNA molecules. Those DNA molecules combined to form an entity who, with time, would become a new person. It is likely that many of the characteristics of that new person were predetermined by chance, since the genetic structure of each of the millions of sperm cells that fertilized that egg was different from all the others.

It is this rich and unpredictable molecular diversity that determines many of the traits that we later evince as persons. The conjunction of the stars at the time of my birth (or at the time of my conception) probably has little or nothing to do with my personality or my behavior. Being skeptical about such thought systems as astrology—or any other faith-based theory of genesis—may be one of the traits that I developed at any early age. I may have been born skeptical. I will certainly die that way.

Of course, astrological analyses, like other forms of psychoanalysis, can become self-fulfilling prophecies as soon as practitioners begin to use the teachings or texts of such systems as guides to life. Then circularity becomes complete, because individuals act as if the predictions were both accurate and binding. Is one any less credulous to believe in biological predestination? I think the answer to this question is Yes, because biological predestination lends itself to experimental refutation. The other belief systems cannot fulfill this criterion and are properly regarded as religions or as pseudosciences if they have any scientific pretense at all.

The man and the woman who made love in September of 1932 were both from long lines of Anglo-Saxon people. On my mother's side, which was better-researched than my father's, was Roger Williams, the rebel and reformer who founded the Providence Plantation. My familial (and presumably genetic) lines went back to the king of Scotland who was called Robert the Bruce. As myth has it, Robert the Bruce decided his battle strategy by closely observing the behavior of a spider. Was he aware that chance might have been as good a guide as a spider in making important life decisions? Or did he believe that the spider was a messenger conveying the orders of some higher power, perhaps God or the stars? Other great kings appear in the medieval period of my family tree, as they do in the well-researched genealogy of almost any English-speaking person. That is because there are many more descendants than ancestors.

In noting the presence in my genealogy of such a historically important character as William, the Norman Conqueror of England, I do not mean to suggest that the person conceived in September of 1932 behaved as he did because he carried the genes of his forebears. It is far more likely that the superficial resemblance is either a complete coincidence or a consciously learned piece of mimicry. Rigid belief in heredity is every bit as unjustified as rigid belief in anything else.

Whatever the history of my family, and whatever the local circumstances in which my parents struggled for survival, everything I know about myself derives in some way from the biological script of that particular sperm and that particular egg. This should be emphasized because we are as tempted to attribute causes to local and proximal events (when generic and remote causes are at work) as we are to attribute aspects of our behavior to our mind (ignoring our brains and organic factors of which we are still, for the most part, in the dark). We must learn to be more cognizant and appreciative of our ignorance. This seems perverse, but saying "I don't know" leaves the door open to novel explanations. By contrast, the strong conviction that one has an explanation that is correct closes that door and decreases the probability of discovery. I am talking about the difference between faith and skepticism, and the difference between religion and science. Because that difference was not explicitly taught to me, it is possible that an innate brain function related to genetic and hereditary factors as well as to the local conditions was the proximal cause of a particular path of development. How did my brain develop?

The most rapid multiplication of brain cells took place between 8 and 15 weeks after conception. The dramatic growth of what would become a brain began around January 4, 1933. In the spring of that year, my neurons, which had begun to migrate from the center to the burgeoning surface of my brain in December, sprouted their spider-like information-collecting processes and readied my developing brain for functional activity. By March, my neuronal development was impressively advanced and capable of generating the electrical activity that activates the brain in sleep.

By the time I was (biologically) 30 weeks old, I was able periodically to activate my still-tiny brain. I did so reliably and enduringly. I was floating in the amniotic fluid of my mother's uterus, connected to her circulatory

Me and my parents (1934). I was about one year of age when these photos were taken during a family outing to Mount Greylock in western Massachusetts. In the photo at left, my mother is beaming at me and I offer my father, the photographer, a tentative smile. In the photo at right, my father is less happy, perhaps because he is about to carry me up the mountain but also because he was always less demonstrative of positive feelings. I look at my mother a bit apprehensively.

system by an umbilical stalk from which I received oxygen (enabling me to respire without breathing) and glucose (enabling me to grow without eating).

Between March and June of 1933, the weight of my little brain doubled twice. This was a much faster rate of growth than any stock market rally and one that certainly put to shame the country's slow economic recovery from the Great Depression. In the best of times, an economic recovery would take several years to match what my brain accomplished in those three months.

Thanks to work by many people who are my friends and colleagues, we now know that the primordial brain-activation state of the fetus is analogous to the REM sleep that is so prominent in the neonatal period. Together with electrical activation of the fetal brain, writhing trunk and limb movements appear, as does deflection of the eyes. The being conceived in 1932 was very active by March of 1933, when my mother began to detect the unmistakable signs of my life. She felt good about the kicks and punches that her child-to-be unknowingly delivered to her. They were sure signs that I was alive and well inside her.

Thus, the being conceived in September of 1932 was capable of primitive behavior by March of 1933. The genetic program conferred by the sperm and the egg had constructed a body (including arms, legs, a trunk, and a head) and internal body parts (including a heart, two lungs, a digestive system, and a brain). The believer in us might say "God works in wondrous ways," explaining everything and nothing at once.

How does the fetus activate its own little brain, and to what end? Does it possess a clocklike mechanism in its tiny but already elaborate brainstem? I now think that a possible goal of prenatal brain activation is to implement a virtual-reality program that is used to guide subsequent brain development and to help meet the sensorimotor challenges of life after birth. At what point did that fetus become sentient? When did it first feel sensation, experience emotion, and attribute agency to its movements? Certainly sensation and emotional expression are present at birth. It is therefore reasonable to suppose that such primordia of consciousness are present in utero. Obviously we can't really know, because a fetus cannot speak. But because it can cry as soon as it begins to breathe, the basic brain mechanisms for emotional expression must have developed in utero, perhaps as early as 30 weeks after conception. We can make this guess with informed confidence because babies born as much as 10 weeks early (and are, biologically speaking, 30 weeks old) show definite cycles of sleep and waking and an impressive range of awake-state behaviors.

One inference is that from March to early June of 1933, between the biological ages of 30 and 40 weeks, I was not just floating in my mother's womb; I was simulating waking, and I was, in a primitive sense, also simulating dreaming. Why persist in calling this being a fetus? Why not call it a person and assume that it was conscious? This question has great relevance to scientific and philosophical models of ourselves.

To say that the fetus may experience a primary form of consciousness is to invite unwelcome debate about the intentional ending of its life. Where do we draw the line? How early does the primitive consciousness, consisting of sensation and emotion, arise? How old were this mother's two spontaneously aborted fetuses? Were they sentient? We cannot know. But we can suppose that our newborn creature, on whom his parents conferred the nominal identity of John Allan Hobson, was not capable of the full consciousness that probably arose sometime during the first two years of postnatal life. My consciousness may be said to have begun in utero with a primitive sense of volition about the agency of my early motor behavior. It then continued to evolve until the age of 4 or 5 years, when my memories became truly autobiographical.

In other words, the creature that became me spent 5 years developing its brain to the qualitative level of adult human consciousness. And, of course, I still had a long way to go before I would write my college thesis (22 years) and my first book (53 years). I began writing this book when I was 40 years old, when I began keeping a journal, but the manuscript did not take its present form until I was 70 (and my brain was nearly 71). At this writing I am 77 and still making changes in my story. My progress, you will agree, has been very slow but also very continuous.

In the early morning hours of June 3, 1933, my mother was struggling to push me out into the world, hoping I would survive. Had I then been capable of thought, I might have wondered why my peaceful sleep was being disturbed by such violent pressure. I had been jostled before, largely by my own kicks and twists. This was quite different. I didn't initiate the pushes, and I had no idea why they came at such regular intervals. In fact, I had no idea what was going on. As far as I know now, I had no ideas whatsoever. Cognitively, I did not yet exist.

I accept the story that, on the day I was born, I was forced out of the warm bath in which for nine months I had floated, virtually weightless and not having to breathe, eat, or excrete. As I floated, did I do anything, consciously speaking? Did I dream? If I did, what was the nature of my dreams? Protoconscious dreams are hard to imagine without reference to the sort of consciousness that, once we have grown up, ensues when we wake up from sleep. By now I have developed waking consciousness and can describe the dreams I happen to remember. When I am awake I do not feel that I am dreaming, but I am now fairly sure that my dreaming brain continues to function in an important way. I have even thought that we cannot have waking consciousness without dream consciousness. This is a speculative hypothesis, but it is certainly true that we can't have either waking or dreaming consciousness without more brain development than we have when we are born.

Enter, nervously, my new concept: protoconsciousness. By 'proto' I mean both prior to and foundational of. To imagine the subjectivity of proto-consciousness is a challenging thought experiment. Let us first subtract the content of what we have good reason to believe derives from awake-state consciousness, and see what might be left over. First and foremost is some primordial sense of self. My brain is activated, therefore I am? But is it reasonable to assume that I am only the activation state of my brain cells jabbering away to one another in the dark, afloat in my mother's belly? What does that I feel like? The mind boggles at the question.

Is there any sentience at all in utero? The query is fraught with moral weight. Since the answer is unknowable, the situation appears to be in favor of the right to life. But the likelihood of any sentience worthy of the name is so improbable as to ease the conscience of those women who decide that they do not wish to be mothers just yet.

When my brain was activated, I moved. As my mother's pregnancy entered its third trimester, I was capable of significant movement. My arms moved, and I could even suck my little thumb. My eyes moved, and sometimes their movements occurred in REM-like clusters. And my legs could kick hard enough to awaken my mother, whose own sleep was becoming more fitful as June 3, 1933 drew near. Did these movements resemble instinctively meaningful fixed action patterns, or were they simple mass reflexes? The question is moot, but an answer is now obtainable with the use of non-invasive imaging technology in humans and through direct observation of animal fetuses.

Whatever the answer about movement, we can assume it possible that I perceived myself to be the agent of the movement. Consider the twitches that often occur at the onset of sleep. I feel that I make those twitches, and I convey my sense of agency to you in giving my account. Because I often twitch violently, I may say "I must have been falling asleep." I do not say that the excitability levels of reflex circuitry in my brain were changing rapidly because I was falling asleep, although that might be a better way of putting it. The point is that as I developed I took responsibility for actions that may have been entirely reflexive. A self, an I, emerged from this process. It may at first be an illusion (and some scientists say it is always an illusion), but protoconsciousness theory insists that the sense of self as agent emerges slowly and gradually during early development.

Whenever I (or my activated brain) generated a twitch, the movement produced showers of sensory data that were incorporated into my perception of the twitch. I may have had a sense of falling (as I often do at the onset of sleep), or I may have simply jumped without really changing body position at all. And it is not uncommon for me to see something, to hear a voice, or even to perceive an external noise as a vision. I am often surprised by such experiences. Occasionally, I am fearful. Rarely, I am pleased. These emotions, seemingly consequential, are usually folded into the perceptions.

I cannot resist the temptation to back-project these phenomena onto the dark screen of pre-conscious existence. Knowing that this assumption cannot be tested directly (since protoconscious beings, such as I imagine myself to have been, cannot, by definition, give us an account of their experience), I must ask myself whether it is at all appropriate to indulge in such speculations. I answer that it is appropriate, because many implications of the theory are testable and because others are plausible.

Human development is lifelong. Its earliest stages are poorly understood because developmental neurobiology is still underdeveloped. And the science of consciousness is still in its own infancy. But the science of sleep and dreaming has now come of age, and I believe it can come to the rescue of both consciousness science and developmental neurobiology. The goal, of course, is to elaborate testable hypotheses to guide our research.

The dawn of consciousness must be gradual. By the time I was a year old, my mother was convinced that I was conscious (when awake) even if she never dreamed that I was dreaming when I was asleep. David Foulkes asserts that adult-type dreaming begins between the ages of 6 and 8 years. I think it may begin between 5 and 7, but that is still quite late. My point here is that the individual evolution of awake-state and dream consciousness is a long, gradual process that cannot be precisely demarcated. In this sense, the origin of consciousness is analogous to the origin of species, which has a long, ill-defined history.

The scientist who is interested in the development of consciousness has the great advantage that this process repeats itself over and over again before his very eyes.

But can we see into the heart of things? We must admit that we have not done a very good job. How could we do better?

A first step is to conceptualize the problem in a novel and tractable way. I will try to do this as I tell the story of my biological and psychological life. I will try to create a model with the following features: full operation of a protoconsciousness platform by the third trimester of pregnancy, damping of protoconsciousness beginning at birth, completion of the damping as the awake state increasingly takes its place and dynamic interaction between its residua (dreaming and primary consciousness) thereafter, progressive enrichment of waking (or secondary) consciousness for at least five years, a parallel development of dreaming consciousness, lifelong communication of content issues between the two states of consciousness, relatively fixed interactional dynamics between ages 15 and 60, and gradual deterioration of both systems after age 60.

At first, I thought that to tell this story it would be sufficient to write a typical autobiography. But many intelligent people persuaded me that I was not sufficiently famous to make such a book interesting to others. In response, I then thought I could spice it up by interspersing discussions of my dreams with an account of my life. Other intelligent people told me that, although the discussion of my dreams was indeed interesting enough to make a book, such a memoir would still not be up to snuff. Inspired by my recent theorizing, I attempt a neurobiology-based autobiography. In contrast with the psychobiography-based form inspired by psychoanalysis, this is a biopsychography. Think about that awkward word for a moment, then read on.

2 Brain Growth: The Illusion and the Reality of Being

My brain, already formed and functioning when I was born, began to absorb and react to information of a very elaborate and particular world at the moment of my birth. Recollections of that world constitute the subject matter of most autobiographies. In part II of this book, I recount in detail what I consciously recognize to be historically significant events in my life. That part of the book is written in the traditional form of psychobiography.

But it is equally important to emphasize the many generic and particular developmental factors that are not now accessible to conscious recollection. These include many of the preconscious and unconscious forces that Freud thought could be brought to light by psychoanalysis. Although Freud was certainly right in insisting that many formative interactions occurred in early postnatal life, both his theoretical model and his method of investigation were in serious error. Like all other human infants, I have only dim and suspect memories of life events before the age of 2 or perhaps even 4 years.

When did I first experience consciousness, and what was it like? I have no clear answer to either of these important questions, but my scientific work discussed in part III of this book has implications that form part IV. Those implications are properly foreshadowed here. If consciousness is graded, componential, and state dependent, as we can now be quite sure it is, then my awake-state consciousness probably was constructed very gradually as my brain interacted with other parts of my body and with the outside world. It seems reasonable to propose that awareness of my bodily sensations came first. As the creature that was to become me first moved, it generated both a primordial sense of agency and a primordial sense of feeling.

This primordium is the basis of what Gerald Edelman calls "primary consciousness." If it can be ascribed to animals, it can be ascribed to us humans. It is the consciousness that is a meld of sensation, emotion, and action. Humans, and probably only humans, later become aware of their awareness and can then describe this secondary form of consciousness by means of language. We have primary consciousness long before we develop secondary consciousness. And secondary consciousness develops throughout our lifetime. Movement and sensation of the fetus may have given rise to the foundation of consciousness when the creature that became me was, biologically, about 6 months of age. It seems likely that visceral and emotional sensations were elements of that early awareness. Without memory I can never be convinced of this, but memory is not a good gauge of conscious experience. It's just the best gauge we have for standard autobiographical accounts. Biology allows us to go further. By trusting inferences from third parties, we can supplement memory and go beyond its reach.

By the time the creature that became me was born, a remarkably rich repertoire of capabilities had developed. With the help of consciousness I was then taught to gain control of them. To help me develop consciousness of a self, I was given a name. It is my tendency to believe that I was John Allan Hobson even before I was born, but a moment's thought will convince any sensible reader that the particular sense of self that I so thoroughly associate with my name developed only gradually, and relatively late in comparison with other important building blocks of my consciousness.

What really happens to the brain in the uterus, where it is so warm and snuggly? I have already mentioned that sleep in general, and REM sleep in particular, increases with prematurity, and that fetuses are active in a way that suggests the occurrence of REM in utero. Direct proof of these conjectures has been achieved by recording from animals in utero. This technical tour de force was accomplished by G. S. Dawes and his colleagues using sheep, which are large and relatively docile. Dawes and colleagues were able to exteriorize the uterus of a pregnant ewe and implant a Plexiglas window in its wall. Through the uterine window, Dawes was then able to observe the fetal lambs twitching and moving their eyes as they floated in the amniotic fluid. He even managed to insert electrodes into some of lambs-to-be and recorded the muscular, ocular, and cerebral electrical activities of a very REM-like brain-activated state. Whether or not the fetal lambs were really in REM, it was clear that intrauterine life is anything but tranquil. Instead it is animated, indicating that mammalian brain development is an early and active process.

Fetal Alcohol Syndrome

Fortunately for me, my mother was temperate in regard to alcohol. She had an occasional cocktail with my father in the evening before supper, but I never saw her drunk on wine or beer. Her temperateness probably was related to her horror at her father's addiction to alcohol and her awareness of the hardship it had imposed on her mother and her four sisters. I vividly remember her distress when, after she picked up her father at the Hartford train station, he insisted on going to a package store to buy a case of beer.

About 1 percent of the population is not so lucky. When it is said, in jest, that you should choose your parents carefully, it could be specified that you should not have an alcoholic mother. Alcoholic mothers not only run health risks of their own; they expose their offspring to the risk of severe developmental defects.

Fetal alcohol syndrome is a lifelong disability resulting from exposure of the developing brain to alcohol in utero. Since alcohol is a powerful suppressant of REM sleep, it is fair to speculate that some of the deleterious effects of fetal alcohol syndrome are due to interference with the normal contribution of intrauterine brain activation to protoconsciousness.

That adult humans exposed in utero to alcohol suffer from a disorder of consciousness was recently suggested to me in a personal communication by Fred L. Bookstein, an expert on the syndrome:

The classical clinical descriptions of what heavy fetal alcohol exposure does to the person sound remarkably like alterations of consciousness. I extract here from two main sources, a published clinical vade mecum for neuropsychologists (National Center for Birth Defects and Developmental Disabilities, "Fetal Alcohol Syndrome: Guidelines for referral and Diagnosis." US Department of Health and Human Services, 2004) and a checklist for parents and teachers (AP Streissguth, FL Bookstein et al. "A fetal alcohol behavior scale," Alcoholism: Clinical and Experimental Research, 22:326–333, 1998). The current United States federal guidelines describe persons with these disorders, as manifesting, among other behaviors, concrete thinking, lack of inhibition, difficulty grasping cause and effect, inability to delay gratification, difficulty in changing strategies or thinking of things in a different way, inability to apply knowledge to new situations, easily distracted, difficulty completing tasks, naiveté, gullibility, superficial interactions, inappropriate sexual behaviors, difficulty understanding the perspective of others, poor social cognition, tactile defensiveness, alexithymia (difficulty reading facial expression), and lack of stranger fear.

And the checklist for parents that we published a decade ago finds all of the following, along with some two dozen other traits, to be reported in more than half of a large sample of children and adults with diagnoses in this range: impulsive, stubborn, unaware of the consequences of actions, poor in attention, "throws tantrums" (unusually distractible by rage), unable to take hints, too easily led, overly reactive, showing poor judgment, liking to be the center of attention, very active opinionated, overly friendly, manifesting superficial friendships.

We cannot know if all (or any) of these devastating effects are specifically due to REM sleep suppressants in utero, but it is not unreasonable to hypothesize such a mechanism. It is clear that alcohol causes other brain defects, and these may be enough to account for the clinical symptoms. Bookstein goes on to say:

There is a general shortage of neural mass all over the cortex, particularly in the region of the corpus callosum with its left-right interwiring specializations. At the same time, there are serious heterotopias, wires crossed or never getting to their destinations, leading to a complementary failure of some regions to be properly pruned for efficient computation.

Clearly alcohol is a potent CNS drug. That is why it is so popular! It affects cortical functions in anyone who drinks it. Especially for those of us who think too much, are inhibited by fear of social disapproval, and need to relax, a little alcohol goes a long way to help. But the dose-response curve is steep, and the "buzz" that we value after drinking two ounces of 86-proof gin becomes intrusive, hyper-aggressive, obnoxious drunkenness if we consume six ounces.

At the six-ounce level, suppression of REM sleep is certain. The resumption of REM sleep that follows the cessation of drinking is a welcome relief to a hangover. When my colleagues and I were testing our Nightcap home-based sleep-recording system (illustrated on page 162), we were surprised to find that some Harvard undergraduates showed complete suppression of the posture shifts that normally punctuate sleep at a rate of two per NREM-REM cycle. When we questioned those "sleep-dead" subjects, we learned that heavy social drinking was the cause of their sleep-related postural immobility. Alcohol had shut down their REM-sleep generators.

Exposure to alcohol during pregnancy can lead to sleep abnormalities in female rats. It is not surprising to learn from Fred Bookstein that humans suffering from fetal alcohol syndrome also show disturbance of the cycle of sleeping and waking. Of course sleep could be one of many brain functions disrupted by alcohol, but since we have good reason to suppose that sleep is beneficial to brain development (especially in early life), we can hypothetically invoke sleep disturbances as causal of brain dysfunction rather than a mere effect of alcohol overdosage.

A case in point is the contribution of REM sleep suppression by alcohol to the ultimate development of delirium tremens in alcohol-addicted persons. Alcohol suppresses REM sleep until alcohol intake stops, at which time REM rebound takes over. REM sleep percent may thus increase to 100 percent of sleep time, and, as it does so, the syndrome of visual hallucinations, memory loss, disorientation, and confabulation begins.

In previous writings, I have argued that this delirium tremens syndrome shares with dreaming its four formal features: visual hallucinosis, disorientation, memory loss, and confabulation. Put another way, dreaming is a normal delirium. When dreaming is prevented by alcoholic REM suppression, there is an increased probability that delirium, normally confined to sleep, will disrupt waking.

In any case, I'm glad my mother was temperate. She granted my REM-sleeping brain freedom from suppression and, in that respect at least, guaranteed its normal functioning. Should any woman drink at all during pregnancy? My guess is that an occasional cocktail or glass of wine (up to, say, two ounces a day) will probably not have dire consequences. But if I were a pregnant woman, I would switch to ginger ale or some other alcohol-free drink.

Infancy

The creature that became me waked and slept enough to allow its caretakers to get some rest. When awake, the baby, now called Allan, could make its needs known by insistent crying. My cries entered my mother's brain and caused her to appear, to give solace with her face, to give milk from her breasts, and to change my diaper when it was wet or soiled. It was in this innocent and helpless state that I was taught how to be. The me that emerged from this two-to-three-year process was a joint product of all the genes that happened to combine in October of 1932 and the behavior of my caretakers, principally my mother, between 1933 and 1936.

During my first year outside the womb, I slept a lot. And in that sleep my brain self-activated, as I will show in detail in chapter 3. When did I first have a dream in the sense of consciously recollected subjective experience? Probably not at all during that period. Not until I had learned to talk, to answer to the name Allan, and to converse could I have had a dream worthy of the name—as I noted in chapter 1, probably not before age 5.

Before age 5, I could not recollect a primary consciousness dream or any other form of consciousness, because memory and language were not yet fully available to me. Important early life experiences are thus as unremembered as most dreams in adult life. An important difference, of course, is that adult dreams can be remembered if an awakening occurs and the brain memory system of waking is promptly reinstated.

This is not to say that the preverbal and preconscious infant cannot learn. It can. Learning is strongly associative, and the brain can process associations without the help of memory. Abundant experimental evidence supports the idea that even very primitive nervous systems can learn. When two stimuli are paired, the nerve cells that mediate their processing become more excitable or less so. The pairing of the stimuli thus triggers a change in the excitability of the cells such that the subsequent presentation of one of the stimuli can evoke a response that previously depended on the other stimulus.

This "classical conditioning" was first described by Pavlov early in the early twentieth century, when my parents were young. Understanding the dissociation of learning from memory is important in thinking about how I came to be me and about how I did not come to be someone else. My conditioned learning began in earnest at my birth and may even have antedated my birth. Because I have no memory of my early conditioning, I am doomed to speculate about it. I cannot recover early experiences, however important they may be, by means of memory, because memory is a function that develops very late in my life—in childhood rather than in infancy.

The point of all this is to emphasize that my ability to reconstruct my development through the use of memory is severely limited. Not only is my genetic determination unknown; much of the functional training of the brain that fabricates my "self" is also unknown to my first-person recollections. Just how much of "me" is a function of structurally preprogrammed brain function is also unknown. Moreover, a significant chunk of my brain function was interactive with the environment in ways that are unknowable to me as an autobiographer. Until recently, it was assumed that early experience was engraved in memory and buried deep in the unconscious. Such memories were thought to be recoverable via free association (in psychoanalysis) and via age regression (in hypnosis). Doubt has been cast on these assumptions. The recognition of false memory construction has also contributed to scientific skepticism regarding testimonial accounts of recall of early life experience.

Classical conditioning is just one robust form of learning. Operant conditioning is another robust form of learning, and one more easily understood as relevant (at least by parents). The probability of a certain behavior by a child is changed by altering the parents' response it. If praise or other tangible rewards follow certain behaviors, those behaviors increase in frequency. A good example is the reward of my own communicative efforts by my mother's smiling.

I have entertained the speculation that my mother was so pleased to have me survive that she evinced pleasure at whatever I did. That made me feel that everything I did was OK. That's not a good way to instill moral discrimination. My father, on the other hand, was so glum and gloomy that I felt I could never please him. That's not a good way to instill comfort with male authority figures. These speculations are supported by robust parental behaviors and attitudes that I can consciously recall. That they antedated the acquisition of my memory and that they exerted their force on me as powerful unconscious learning mechanisms seem to be reasonable hypotheses.

Developmental Neurobiology

To complement our curiosity about human development and to enrich my understanding of my own biological history, it is useful to look at animal models.

Mammalian systems are generally eschewed by basic scientists interested in cellular-level and molecular-level analyses of the developing brain. The scaffold for an enlightened approach to the early organization of brain systems is in place, however, since we know a great deal about neuronal birthdays, chemical identities, and migratory pathways to brain addresses. But what those neurons do when they arrive at their destinations is a complete mystery. Do they fire spontaneously? Are they are at first like pacemaker cells, and do they develop synaptic dependency only later? Or do they influence one another only trophically, via the secretion of as-yet-unidentified neuronal substances? In connection with these questions, the now-classical studies of Peter Huttenlocher are not encouraging. Focusing on the midbrain reticular formation, which in his day was thought to be the major activating system of the brain, Huttenlocher reported scant electrical activity in the reticular neurons of kittens. Because it was uninformative and difficult, this line of work was dropped. It must be noted that the microelectrode is capable of recording only relatively large neurons in adult animals. If immature neurons are small, perhaps they were missed altogether. Now that we have other means of measuring activation, such as early gene expression, this approach should be tried again. Maybe the decade of the 1960s was just too early to investigate the birth of brain activation.

Me swinging between my parents (1941). I loved my swing, which was made of iron pipes and chains and sat in the back corner of our yard at 1902 Asylum Avenue in West Hartford. On the summer evening in 1941 when this snapshot was made, my mother (then pregnant with my sister Harriet) and my father (shirtless because he had just cut the grass) were joined by our neighbor Jack Winter (in cap), who was one of several businessmen who urged me to go to Yale. I went to Wesleyan instead and became a physician instead of the trapeze artist I imagined becoming when this picture was taken.

It is also difficult to trace early activation by studying the origin of electrographically defined behavioral states. Daniele Jouvet showed that baby rats, newborn guinea pigs, and kittens all entered REM-like states (albeit with differing manifestations and timetables), which suggested that REM sleep was a universal form of early brain organization in mammals.

Because (as I said earlier) consciousness is componential and graded, it is reasonable to suggest that the consciousness components Edelman calls primary are well developed in utero and continue to function in parallel with the growth of secondary consciousness networks in the first two years of life. Thus, the infant that would become me (and was already named John Allan Hobson) was capable of sensation, perception, attention, emotion, instinct, and movement. Gradually, through conditioning and learning, the infant that became me acquired the capabilities of language, orientation, volition, and thought that are the hallmarks of secondary or "higher" consciousness, the kind of consciousness that Edelman proposes to be uniquely human.

It was with the development of these capacities in the third, fourth, and fifth years of my life that a sense of self emerged. During that time I was able to begin to formulate an operational "me" that was the functional arm of John Allan Hobson. All that development depended on my brain function. But it didn't feel that way. How it really felt I can never know, but I can be reasonably certain that it never felt like a brain function. My brain is insensitive to itself—so much so that even as an adult I cannot directly perceive that my awareness is dependent on my brain. Instead, I experience my awareness, my consciousness, and my self as disembodied subjectivity. This deep dissociation of mind from body is at the heart of the dualism that has held philosophy back since the time of Plato. It is also the source of the philosophical malaise that has plagued us since the time of Descartes. Can we ever move beyond this impasse?

Recognizing just how expensive our dualism illusion is may help to motivate us to try to be more realistic. Unfortunately, our vanity and our hopes for a life beyond this physical one will continue to hold us back.

My conviction that I am really a self that is independent of my body is very strong. In fact, I am constantly tempted to believe that I am an essentially free agent who, by exercising my reason, can choose a school, a profession, friends, and a spouse. I may even go so far as to suppose that my self is, in fact, a soul that inhabits my body only temporarily and then goes on to another body or, depending on my earthly behavior, enjoys the tortures of hell or the pleasures of heaven for all eternity. Of course there is no scientific evidence for this scenario, but that makes it no less appealing to me.

From day to day, it feels as if the self who is known to the world as John Allan Hobson is an immaterial agent who runs my body and my behavior from some privileged position within my head. But let us suppose, for just a minute, that this is a wondrously constructed illusion, and that my apparently disembodied self is really a brain function that is unaware of its deep physicality. No one today really doubts that sensation, perception, attention, emotion, and movement are brain functions. Their disruption following lesions of specific brain areas makes this conclusion inescapable.

We know that even primary consciousness is an illusion when we take it to be non-physical. It becomes a little more difficult to perform the same reductio ad absurdum argument on abstract thinking. Abstract thinking includes imagination, poetry, and spirituality, but here again the evidence that even such high-flown talents are brain functions is very strong, and hard evidence against the physicalistic view is non-existent. I conclude that even transcendent, inspired, and illuminative states are brain functions. So, of course, is "mental" illness.

The mounting experimental evidence is that my self is a continuously evolving state of my brain. This hypothesis implies that the notion of the self as an independent structure is an illusion. Mounting in parallel is experimental evidence that much of the will that I experience as free is an illusion too. When awake subjects are asked to signal their first conscious awareness of the will to move, they do so long after brain potentials signal that upcoming intent. Furthermore, their conscious experience is projected backward in time so that the subjects feel as if their conscious decision to move antedated their automatic and apparently spontaneous brain impulse to do so. This is what the psychologist Daniel Wegner calls "the illusion of conscious will." When I first read of experiments performed by my late friend and colleague Benjamin Libet, I was incredulous. Now that I am aware of Libet's findings, I have become much more self-observant. Every morning I notice that I decide to get up only after I have swung my feeble legs over the side of the bed. My conscious intention to take the decisive step to start my day thus follows my brain's commandment to do so.

The conscious experience of an upcoming willed act can be translated into a cancellation of that act. This is what Richard Gregory called "free won't." It is a scientifically robust equivalent of free will. This state of affairs allows me to conceive of my self as an automatically impulsive creature who learns to take responsibility for his impulsiveness and to make important decisions not to act on impulses when these are concealed in the emperor's new clothes of conscious will.

In order to retain a thoroughly physicalistic view of these experimental facts, it is necessary to suppose that the conscious evaluation of any automatically impelled act evokes a conscious awareness of the potentially deleterious consequences of that act. Conscious awareness is itself a brain state. As such, consciousness can have causal consequences. Behaviors can be allowed, or can be canceled, if the circuitry instantiating that decision is placed between the neuronal impulse generator and the neuronal movement effector. As we will soon see, that place is very likely to be in our dorsolateral prefrontal cortex, and thus to be interposed between the subcortical impulse generator and the cortex (which must be recruited if voluntary movements are to be performed).

My self is thus a dynamic construction of my brain. I often have the illusion that my self is fully in charge of my life, and I am tempted to believe that my self is somehow different—or even separable—from my brain. Giving up this illusion does not mean that my sense of self is an illusion. The illusion that my self is not my brain springs from my inability to see how my conscious experience could be physical. But my conscious experience must be physical. Otherwise it could not be causal. And I am sure that my consciousness is causal. Whether or not my will is truly free (as I still suppose it must sometimes be), I know that my will is efficacious, and I know that I often decide, whether rightly or wrongly, between two alternatives.

So consciousness—like the constructed self that appears to have it—is not wholly an illusion either. It is real. Like my self, it is a dynamic and physical state of my brain. This means that when I (a dynamic state of my particular brain) think (enter a dynamic state of my particular brain), it is really my brain that is doing the thinking.

The Unity and the Multiplicity of Self

When I dream (and when I wake), I am always convinced that it is the self-same me that is conscious. And that me is always enveloped in a world of my or its own devising. When I am awake, the outside world takes over. But I say that my brain is prepared to read it by the practice it had while I was asleep—when "I" was dreaming.

Why do I never change my first-person identity? One answer is that I am not afflicted with either schizophrenia or multiple-personality disorder. Conversely, it is the durability of my activated self that protects me from those dysfunctional states. A robust and reliable sense of self is important to adaptation. My brain worked long and hard to generate this fabulous illusion. By emphasizing these points in a chapter on my own brain's development, I am suggesting that my early days asleep in my mother's womb and in my crib were not time wasted. On the contrary, I was making up my brain so that I could make up my mind.

One reason I am so persuaded that I am me is that my actions always seem to flow from my will: I am the agent who causes them, or so it seems. When I dream, I have the same illusion: I will my dream actions, or so it seems. Careful reflection indicates that I take responsibility even for my dream acts. In fact, in a dream it is difficult to will action. If successful in doing so, I may, in fact, wake a part of myself up. This is called "lucid dreaming." When I become lucid, I become aware that I am dreaming because a part of my brain has escaped from the thrall of REM sleep and split itself off from the dream so that "I" am two mes, one of whom watches the dream and one of whom dreams it. Now I am dissociated, like a person with multiple-personality disorder.

The me that becomes lucid does not perceive the outside world. The elaborate sensory surround of my dream continues to hold sway. If, when lucid, I decide that I want to fly, I may command running movements, flap my arms like a bird, and just avoid the telephone wires when I take off. My self, my actions, and my perceptual content are all manufactured by my brain, which is also capable of witnessing this extravaganza.

We have good reason to believe that my lucidity, my second self, and my secondary consciousness all depend on frontal-lobe activation, while my dream experience is mediated in the occipital and parietal areas. From a developmental point of view, I would predict that the frontal lobe acquires its power later than more posterior brain structures. Because the peak of spontaneous dream lucidity occurs at about age 9, I can further predict that frontal-lobe development must reach a critical level by that age.

It is tempting, also, to see my lucid dream experience as undergoing functional brain splitting. When a brain is split surgically, by cutting the corpus callosum, the right and left hemispheres are definitively separated. The right brain doesn't know what the left brain is doing, as each half-brain has its own identity and awareness. When the brain is split functionally and frontally, as in lucid dreaming, the front end does know what the back end is doing, and can even influence what it does. The usual integrity of my self is all the more amazing in view of these potential vicissitudes.

Brain science, and especially developmental neurobiology, still has a long way to go before it can explain my dream consciousness and its dynamic interaction with waking. Next I will take up what we have learned about that dynamic interaction.

3   Brain State: A Self-Organizing Process

That the being that became me was subject to powerful and automatic forces was suspected, but such forces were not specified until long after I was born. In fact, I was 30 years old before the patterns of fetal, premature, and postnatal sleep that I discuss in this chapter were first recognized. Thus, I can only speculate that my little brain was self-organizing as a sequence of states both before and after my birth. I came into this world capable of sleeping in a brain-activated state very much like the REM sleep that would later support my dreaming.

Like many other biological phenomena, the order that shaped my emerging wake-sleep-dream behavior was innate. Of course, my developing brain interacted with the environment (and it very much needed that interaction to develop normally). But it is the intrinsic organization of my vigilance states that I will emphasize here.

No one could get an objective fix on these dramatic developmental processes before the discovery of the electroencephalogram (EEG), which came in 1928—the year my parents married, and five years before I was born. Using the string galvanometer that had allowed Willem Einthoven to record the electrical activity of the heart, Hans Berger—a psychiatrist working in Jena, Germany—attached electrodes to the scalps of his subjects and observed voltage changes, which he correctly assumed were of brain origin. The scientific world was skeptical of Berger's interpretation, but by 1933 the English neurophysiologist Edgar Adrian had found other evidence for the brain origin of the signals that composed the EEG.

If electrodes had been attached to my delicate scalp, it would have been possible to record the electrical activity of my newborn brain. The patterns would not have been exactly like those I have now, but they would already have demonstrated an equally marked state dependency. That is to say, my EEG would have changed when I went to sleep, which was then, of course, quite often. It was the tendency of the EEG to change at the onset of sleep that helped to convince Berger and Adrian that the EEG signals they recorded were not simply muscle potentials but arose within the brain.

I was a normal baby, born at full term (40 weeks). After coming home from Hartford Hospital on June 8, 1933, I slept about 16 hours a day. Sometimes I fell into a state of "quiet" sleep, with some slowing of my EEG waves, but just as often I passed directly into a state of "active" sleep. At such times my EEG did not change much, but I might then become quite limp and evince animated facial expressions, twitches of my limbs, and rapid eye movements despite being clearly asleep. In both active and quiet sleep, my brain was intrinsically energized. Never did I turn off, like the light bulb on my bedside table, even though I was quite dead to the world.

Quiet sleep is so called because the sleeper breathes slowly and regularly. I looked unperturbed, restful, and peaceful. My EEG then was of relatively high voltage and relatively low frequency, but just after birth I had neither the EEG spindles nor the high-voltage slow waves of non-REM sleep.

"Non-REM" (abbreviated NREM) is a curious label for quiet sleep because it is negative. It honors REM (active) sleep, a state that was surprising when first discovered. Until that time (1953, when I was 20 years old), nearly everyone assumed, wrongly, that the brain turned off, or at least turned down, during sleep. NREM sleep is relatively quiescent, but even during that relatively quiescent state the brain does not turn off completely. In non-REM sleep, the brain remains at least 50 percent active. In fact "non-REM" is a misnomer, because adult quiet sleep contains about one-third as many eye movements as REM itself. The main point here is that the brain continues to work while we sleep. Consciousness must ride at the very top of the process of brain activation. It is thus a very poor indicator of what is going on in the brain, because quite a lot is going on even in its complete absence.

Rapid eye movements were directly observable in my active sleep, but my mother never told me that she had seen them. One reason for this common oversight is that the REMs are associated with smiling, grimacing, and other attention-getting facial expressions that please mothers like mine, who probably thought I was thanking her for a job well done—as perhaps I was, too. About half the time, REM sleep came first, often when I was still trying to suck milk from my mother's breast. As my sucking efforts became less and less efficacious, my brain switched from the eyes-closed awake state directly to REM. Not only did I stop sucking as I fell asleep; my muscle tone suddenly collapsed, and my mother had to catch me to keep me from falling off her lap.

My mother didn't know that my immature brain was still nearly as active in those sleep-onset REM periods as it was in the awake state. After all, she too was tired, and she hoped that my sleep would continue long enough for her to catch a well-deserved nap. My mother's own sleep began to improve around September of 1933.

The improvement in my mother's sleep in that September of 1933 was associated less with Roosevelt's New Deal than with my increasing ability to sleep through the night. With the maturation of my hypothalamus, I was acquiring a circadian rhythm of sleep and waking. At about the same time, my NREM sleep deepened as I began to produce EEG spindles and high-voltage cortical EEG waves, which signaled that corticothalamic circuits were being established. I needed those circuits to become more conscious when I was awake, and I suspect I also needed them to develop dream consciousness in series and in parallel with the awake state.

Subsequently, when I opened my eyes, I was not just awake but already a little bit conscious. I was significantly more responsive, playful, and competent. My mother dandled me, played with me, and even talked to me during my longer and longer waking hours of the winter of 1933 and the spring of 1934.

When I slept during that first year of my life, my REM and NREM sleep states alternated within 50-minute periods. About half of each 50-minute period was one or the other kind of sleep. The fact that I then slept as much as 16 hours a day means that I was spending 8 full hours in each kind of sleep. That was about as much of each kind as I would get of both when I grew up.

By 1956, when I married at the age of 23, the amount of REM sleep I needed had decreased from 8 hours to 2. That momentous fact alone is sufficiently impressive to give credibility to the hypothesis that sleep in general, and REM sleep in particular, played an important role in the development of my brain. What might that role have been, and how might we conceptualize it so as to facilitate its scientific investigation?

The Connection between REM Sleep and Dreaming

The fact that I had REM sleep long before I could have a narrative dream indicates that the physiological and psychological states, as they are now defined, are dissociable. This does not mean, however, that they are independent of each other. By 1953, when I was 20 years old, my sleep had achieved its adult pattern. If I had gone to a sleep lab then, awakenings from REM sleep would have yielded long, detailed dream reports in about

80 percent of cases. Roughly half of the awakenings from NREM sleep would also have been followed by reports of antecedent mental activity. This fact has led to a controversy about the exclusiveness of the connection between REM sleep and dreaming that must be discussed.

The first point to be made is that in both REM sleep and NREM sleep there is often enough brain activation to support mental activity. Recall that even in stage IV, the stage in which sleep is deepest, the brain is still at least half as active as it is when the person is awake. This indicates that the brain has not ceased its activity absolutely, only relatively. Any relationship between brain and mind would, therefore, necessarily be quantitative, not qualitative.

The mental activity of REM sleep *is* quantitatively different from that of NREM sleep. REM-sleep dreams are more perceptually vivid, more bizarre, and more emotional than NREM mental activity. In contrast, NREM mental activity is more thought-like and more perseverative. NREM-sleep thinking may go on and on without significant change and without definitive resolution. Some would say that these differences are so great as to be qualitative, but we need not take that extreme position to profit from the quantitative difference.

To make the science described in this book relevant to dream theory, it is enough to assert that the distinctions among awake-state consciousness, NREM consciousness, and REM consciousness are robust, quantitatively measurable, and psychophysiologically understandable. There is no reasonable doubt that REM sleep is the most favorable substrate for dreaming. That's all I need to carry on my effort to say why this is so.

Protoconsciousness and Virtual Reality

As an active phase of sleep, REM offers, at the very least, an opportunity to instantiate a functional program for the development of brain circuitry. The activation of my visual system, for example, could have been quite useful when that system was off line and therefore not processing external visual inputs from my eyes. Instead of processing internal inputs, my visual system probably was readying itself to see when I was awake and I looked into my mother's eyes. The truth of the matter is almost certainly more complicated and more interesting than any mere theory of circuit testing would imply. I may well have been integrating my visual system with other systems in my brain so that I could not only see my mother but also perceive her, bond with her, and begin the long process of acquiring a language.

With the enrichment of my thalamocortical circuitry (made manifest in sleep by the appearance of EEG spindles and slow waves in NREM sleep), my ability to communicate behaviorally, emotionally, and verbally increased slowly but surely. The first words I uttered were dutifully recorded by my mother's hand.

By June 3, 1934, my first birthday, I had learned to crawl and was beginning to stand and to walk. Think of it. In only a year, I had progressed from a state of total helplessness and primitive responsiveness to a proto-person who responded to his own name and smiled at his mother contentedly. I knew, somehow, that I was Allan. I perceived and moved. I recognized and interacted socially with my mother. I communicated with her by means of gestures, emotions, and even proto-words. This is all the more amazing in view of the fact that for about two-thirds of that year I had been asleep.

How did all that maturation occur? By learning, you say? By instructing me while I was awake? Yes, certainly. But almost as certainly, something important was also going on while I was asleep. By consolidation of my awake-state learning, you suggest? Yes, certainly, lots of REM favors lots of

The Hobson twins nursing (1995) on a cushion built to facilitate simultaneous breast feeding by my wife, Lia Silvestri. When sated with milk, both twins passed directly from waking into a state of sleep with muscle atonia, eye movements, and emotional facial expressions. They slept 16 hours instead of the 8 they now enjoy. Their infant sleep was 50 percent REM. As newborns, they thus evinced a 400 percent preponderance of REM sleep, which, I now theorize, enhanced their brain development.

procedural learning, and no one learns more procedures faster than a human infant. My new protoconsciousness theory proposes that I became me because a genetic script was elaborating my brain in such a way that I was able to learn and to build that learning onto my behavioral repertoire. What other evidence can we adduce for this theory?

Prematurity

I was patient and waited to be born as long as I could. If I had been born on May 3 instead of June 3, I would have weighed as much as 2 pounds less than my full-term birth weight of 7 pounds and 6 ounces. Such prematurity would have been associated with an increase in my postnatal sleep and an increase in the amount of REM in that sleep. The increases in REM are proportional to the degree of prematurity and approach 100 percent as the 30-week mark of fetal age is reached. This implies that a brain-activated sleep state is a hallmark of the third trimester of pregnancy and that there is a continuum between fetal and infant brain development in sleep. At first, sleep is all there is. Waking arises out of it.

Was the fetus that became Allan dreaming? Almost certainly not if our definition of dreaming involves language, narration, and plot. Propositions (the essence of awake-state thought) and narration (essential to both dream construction and reporting, as well as to awake-state discourse) were not in my repertoire before age 5 at the earliest. I did not even begin to speak in the most rudimentary fashion until the end of my first year of life. So what was happening when my little brain was buzzing away during sleep in so much of my early life?

Protoconsciousness theory holds that I was activating and sculpting the neuronal circuits that would later be used to support consciousness in my awake state and in my dreams. In other words, the intrinsic activation of my brain *in utero* and in early infancy fostered the neuronal connectivity and the synchrony that were essential to my becoming more and more conscious. My capabilities for awake-state consciousness and dream consciousness arose together as my brain slowly prepared me for life as a sentient human being.

It is not difficult to recognize the utility of activity-dependent neuronal maturation. Action potential generation, synapse formation, and neurotransmitter release are three fundamental processes known to depend on activation. Thus, it makes sense for the developing brain to have a way of turning itself on. It also makes sense for the system to be turned on in a way that simulates external reality. It is the boldest claim of protoconsciousness theory that the brain does just that. From this assumption, it follows that the genome has the capacity to create a brain with a built-in model of the world.

As soon as my neurons were able to create the loops that were the substrate of my sensation and my movement, I tied the two together as a reflex arc. Soon my brain was capable of cranking out such primordial acts as the sucking, grimacing, and smiling that surfaced in active sleep after my birth. These motor programs, established automatically, allowed me to take nourishment and to express discomfort or pleasure. These simple but crucial capabilities may well have been the fruits of the impressive amounts of intrinsic brain activation between weeks 30 and 40 of my intrauterine life.

Does this mean that as I floated in my amniotic hot tub I smiled, frowned, and sucked? Yes, it means just that. What was I smiling at? My future, of course. I was getting ready to be born.

Just as Noam Chomsky asserts that a universal grammar is innate, I now propose that the protoconscious state of brain-activated sleep, better known as REM sleep, is innate. It is not only genetic but also prophetic. Prophetic? What do I mean by that? By protoconsciousness, I mean a state that is both prior and causally essential to the development of consciousness, and hence prophetic. I REM, therefore I will be. I REM, therefore I will think. I REM, therefore I will talk. I REM, therefore I will wake. And I REM, therefore I will dream. It is all given, as if it were a prophecy.

Consciousness, I say, is my awareness of the world, of my body, and of myself—including my awareness of that awareness. Consciousness develops slowly in a long progressive process that proceeds by accretion in a step-by-step fashion, much of it occurring during sleep.

Consciousness is not, like the soul in Eastern philosophy, implanted whole. Consciousness is not pre-existent, nor does it survive brain death (as even Western philosophy may sometimes suggest). Instead, consciousness emerges, we know not exactly when or how, from the high-frequency synchronous firing of billions of brain cells, each of which reports, to many others, its own excitatory or inhibitory state according to its chemical flavor. My brain was already protoconscious by the third trimester of my mother's pregnancy, in early 1933. Protoconsciousness was very prominent in the first year of my life. I now have hints of the nature of that state when I dream.

By my first birthday, to the delight of my mother, I had begun to evince some of the features of adult awake-state consciousness. My mother spent a great deal of her time marveling at my consciousness and imagining that she had more to do with it than she really did. Oh yes, she was giving me both social reinforcement and moral cues, which became integral to my being. By emphasizing genetic and automatic aspects here, I do not mean to deny or denigrate environmental influences. But I do believe that environmental factors have been grossly overemphasized. The traditional memoir, as its name implies, recounts only the part of life that the author remembers. If many of the important things that happen to me are not remembered, I must have a very lopsided and incomplete picture of myself.

False Memory

It is precisely the overemphasis on memory that I hope to transcend in this book. It has dominated and distorted dream theory for more than a century. It has deformed psychiatry by its unscientific and non-biological character. I am, of course, alluding to my bête noir, psychoanalysis, which, as will be made clear in subsequent chapters, deceived even me for many years. I resent the fact that so much of my time and energy was spent on trying to escape from the shackles of *a priori* Freudianism.

Thus, I hasten to point out that protoconsciousness is not the Freudian pre-conscious. It does not sit like a gatekeeper at the door of consciousness, letting only bowdlerized information out of the unconscious jail. And it is not the Freudian unconscious either. It is not the impulsive motor for all behavior. As conceived by me, protoconsciousness is pre-verbal, and it shares that property with what Freud called "primary process." But I do not mean to imply an arrogant and demanding id-like entity that threatens to overcome and subdue consciousness. For me, protoconsciousness is instead an essential building block of the mature mind. The term denotes the earliest efforts of the brain to achieve the daunting goal of binding the many parts of cognition into a whole that profits from the continued operation of protoconscious processes throughout life.

Brain activation *in utero* and in my early infant sleep led to the integration of sensorimotor data with an agent: my proto-self, who initiated movement (or at least supposed that it did so). My proto-self moved in a fictive way, in a fictive world, all the while feeling the cardinal emotions: fear, pleasure, and anger. The off-line brain activation that became my REM sleep was a very early sign of my self-organization.

In my theory, self-organization has two closely related meanings. My brain organized itself, and in so doing it elaborated me—the self that became the agent of my behavior and my thoughts and my feelings. The self, for me, is akin to Freud's ego, but its much earlier origin in my model is an important difference. It is not so much that the primordial self arises out of the id as that protoconsciousness encompasses the id and greatly abrogates its power. In my protoconsciousness model there are certainly elemental emotions which are built in and therefore rightly considered to be instinctual. I consider those emotions an essential component of cognition, not a symptomatic reaction to intolerable wishes.

I regard protoconsciousness as the helpmate of consciousness, not its competitive adversary (as Freud assumed). Dreaming is my subjective awareness of my sleep-related brain activation, not the disguise and censorship of unconscious infantile wishes that have been banished from consciousness by my ego. When I dream, I meet an important part of my self, and therefore I may learn a great deal by paying careful attention to my dreams. I tried to make this clear in my book *13 Dreams Freud Never Had*.

To stretch a point, it could be admitted that dreams are, after all, infantile wishes, revealing primordial desires or, better put, basic behavioral goals. Every night, my brain reactivates those impulses and attempts to integrate them with the brain traces of my day's awake-state experience. This is what Freud meant by "the day residue," but I do not view the recent memory content of some dreams as residual in a Freudian sense. Rather, I view dream memory as important to functional integration of past, present, and future experience.

My brain performs a double check: it asks that its fundamental needs be recognized and it examines my new experience in terms of its basic priorities. In this sense, too, the protoconscious brain is prophetic. It decrees what it takes to be important, and it reprograms itself for tomorrow.

Animal Models

How, you may wonder, could protoconsciousness theory be tested?

When I was about 8 years old, my parents succumbed to my persistent requests for a pet. I wanted a dog but was happy to get a cat. The fact that the cat was black didn't bother me. By then I was already skeptical about superstitions. In fact, black cats have always brought me good luck. I learned a lot in 1941–1945 from my cat, named Kitty, and a lot more in 1980–1984 from my first family's cat, named Maggie. With the exception of language and abstract thought, everything I have said about my own early sleep is also true of subhuman mammals. That includes cats. They all have REM sleep as adults, and they all have much more REM sleep when immature. Besides indicating that REM sleep has more importance to life than the support of dreaming, this fact is compatible with the idea that

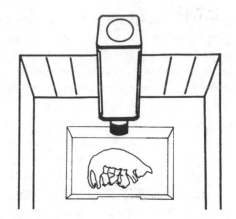

A. MOTHER PRESENT IN BOX

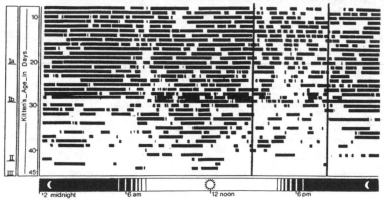

B. BOX EMPTY

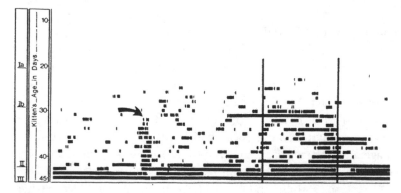

REM is linked, perhaps causally, to the development of sensorimotor integration and primary consciousness.

Maggie delivered fifteen kittens in three litters and raised them in a box in our cedar closet. We recorded the sleep and other behaviors of the mother and her kittens with an infrared time-lapse video set-up that was then cheaply and commercially available as an anti-theft device for stores and banks. We took pictures of the box of the box at a rate of one per minute, around the clock, for five weeks. We also made intermittent direct observations of Maggie and her kittens. The dynamic evolution of the kittens' sleep and their developing motor behavior was dramatic.

Analysis of the video records revealed three distinct phases of postnatal development: phase I (days 1–18), during which the kittens never left the box and Maggie left it only rarely; phase II (days 18–30), in which Maggie and her kittens were out of the box for half of the time or less; and phase III (days 30–45), in which all the animals were out of the box more than half the time. At the end of phase III, they abandoned the box altogether.

As anyone who has ever witnessed the development of a pet knows, the process unfolds with astonishing speed and regularity. There are no books, like Dr. Spock's, to help cats be good mothers. But cats don't need such books, because the system is so reliably automatic.

The eyes of Maggie's kittens remained closed throughout phase I; the kittens did nothing during that phase but eat and sleep in close proximity to Maggie, and about 75 percent of their sleep was REM sleep. We could easily see the telltale eyelid movements and body twitches. The transition from phase I to phase II was very sharp. It was associated with eye-opening, an easily observable event. When in the box, the kittens nursed and slept as they had during phase I.

Our pet cat, Maggie, bore three litters of kittens in a box in our cedar closet. The three phases of developmental behavior described in the text can be identified in this graphic analysis of time-lapse video data collected continuously from birth to five weeks, at which point the kittens left the box altogether. They were by then quite independent. The arrow in B indicates the morning time of onset of daily out-of-box activity. The vertical lines delimit an evening activity period. In addition to the time-lapse photo analysis, we measured behavior and found that as REM sleep decreased, patterned motor behavior increased, suggesting that REM and waking are functionally reciprocal. The take-home message is that newborn sleep was every bit as preponderantly REM as that of our twins. The kittens' sleep plummeted more precipitously together with eye opening and the increase in waking during their very early life.

When out of the box, initially at Maggie's insistence and later more spontaneously, the kittens learned to stand up, to walk, and to avoid objects as they (presumably) began to see. During phase II, their REM sleep plummeted from 75 percent to 25 percent, roughly the same magnitude of decline as I experienced between birth and age 15. The reciprocity between the amount of off-line brain activation (in REM sleep) and on-line brain activation (in the awake state) was progressive, as if the kittens were switching from an exclusively internal program to a predominantly external one. Something important happened to Maggie's kittens in those five weeks.

We need to know more about what happened, why, and how. Why hasn't more research been done? There are several reasons, not the least important of which is that working with such tiny, helpless, and fragile animals as kittens isn't easy—and it isn't for everyone, especially in today's animal-rights-conscious atmosphere. Two of the pioneers in this field, Constance Bowe Anders and Joelle Adrien, were young women whose personal and professional lives led them away from the study of sleep in the newborn. But before that happened, we learned that cellular activity could be electrically detected in the brainstem, and that modulatory neurons were influential in shaping sleep-state and awake-state behavior. Joelle Adrien insisted that serotonergic neurons in kittens' raphé nuclei were more active in sleep than in the awake state. That claim ran counter to the observations of several groups (including mine) that were studying adult cats. Mature serotonergic cells were most active in the awake state, less active in NREM sleep, and virtually silent in REM sleep. The discrepancy cries out for resolution, but controversy does not invite new looks by younger investigators.

It probably is safe to say that we do not yet know the detailed developmental history of brainstem modulatory neurons. I would expect that they are certainly major influences by the time that protoconsciousness would be most important—in the first five years of human life. But we do have an animal model, and it should be looked at more carefully. In addition to whole anesthetized animals, brainstem slices could be studied. At the cost of physiological integrity, a slice confers both moral high ground and great technical finesse. The initial expense of developing such an approach would be rewarded handsomely in time.

It seems safe to conclude that vision was instantiated in phases II and III. This conclusion fits well with David Hubel and Torsten Wiesel's classic observations indicating that neurons in the lateral geniculate body, which relays signals from the retinae to the visual cortex, and cells of the cortex itself, do not develop properly in the absence of light stimuli. This conclusion, in turn, supports two aspects of protoconciousness theory: that the brain is actively prepared to see and to perceive and that the acquisition of visual perception is not associated with a termination of REM sleep. Instead it is clear that vision depends on sleep. The internal visual stimulation of REM continues throughout life. We experience it as dreaming and may use it to update our brains.

Did Maggie's kittens dream? Did baby Allan dream? Did Maggie dream? Was she conscious when awake? These questions cannot be answered with anything like scientific confidence. But we can ask "Why not?" and be sure that our speculative answer is immune to scientific refutation.

Maggie, her kittens, and I all woke up and saw. Our visual behavior denoted perception. We humans all learn to answer to whatever name is assigned to us. I burbled (and the kittens purred) when held and stroked. In this way we signal our pleasure and our approval. We may all even close our eyes when we are cuddled. Is this not strong evidence for what Gerald Edelman calls primary consciousness? Edelman defines primary consciousness as the integrated sense of awareness comprising perception, emotion, sensation, movement, and memory (or at least learning). There is something going on inside our heads that accounts for this integration. I call it protoconsciousness. I say that it arises, early, in REM sleep, and that vestiges of it continue throughout life.

Edelman's concept of primary consciousness has much in common with what I call protoconsciousness. Edelman assumes that primary consciousness occurs only in the awake state, and that it is a state of awareness exclusively felt by sub-human animals. I say that protoconsciousness may be experienced by all mammals, including humans, on their way to differentiating their primary and secondary conscious awake states. Mammalian animals all share with us humans the prenatal and postnatal brain activation of sleep that we experience as dreaming. Brain activation in sleep provides the physical substrate needed to experience primary consciousness off line. Why not assume that subhuman mammals dream?

If a cat can see, perceive, feel, and play when awake, why can't it experience these things in its imagination when asleep? And might it not be helpful for cats to do so? It could just be that, like humans, in sleep cats are not just reflecting on previous waking but actively preparing for subsequent arousal. According to this principle, dream fiction is not just a piece of psychic trash to be flushed down the cognitive toilet. Dreams may, rather, be simulacra of awake-state reality to come. As such they are the subjective aspect of brain activation, and as such they are of inestimable value if our goal is to prepare ourselves for real life.

Fortunately, whether cats or babies are ever at all conscious hardly matters. The main point of looking at their perinatal sleep behavior is to appreciate the complex and elaborate aspects of early brain life. Because parents invest so much time and so many resources in caring for infants, they tend to exaggerate their contributions to development. Maggie did work hard, and she was as devoted to her offspring as was my own mother. But nowhere in my baby book is there any recognition of the role of biological mechanisms in the production of my sensorimotor or social achievements. Yet much of what happened must have been built into my brain as I slept.

Another Look at Prematurity

My twin sons, 14 years old at this writing, were born 6 weeks early. Matthew, now a strapping youth, was born weighing only 4½ pounds—less than Andrew, who had enjoyed a much more favorable intrauterine position. Because he was tender and frail, Matthew spent the first day of his extra-uterine life in an incubator.

Incubators were used to sustain the cats that were studied in Michel Jouvet's lab in Lyon in the early 1960s. Jouvet, a trained neurosurgeon, was able to remove all of a cat's brain anterior to its brainstem. The term for a feline that has undergone this procedure is "pontine cat." Like our little Matthew, Jouvet's pontine cats were REM-sleep machines. When he was being fed his mother's breast milk with an eye-dropper, Matthew slept, and most of his sleep was of the active REM kind. He twitched, grimaced, smiled, and scowled as his eyes darted back and forth behind his closed lids in the incubator.

The incubator kept Matthew warm, just as Jouvet's incubator kept his pontine cats warm. If ever they got cold, their REM sleep stopped (cold); it did not resume until external heat was supplied. This strong temperature dependence should have alerted us to two important facts of which we learned only much later. One is that REM sleep is normally linked to the circadian clock in the hypothalamus, which also regulates body temperature, thus assuring Matthew and me of entering REM sleep only when we are warm enough. We need this protection for the second and more profound reason: temperature control is abandoned in REM sleep. Even as adults, we need the warm environment that is guaranteed by central heating and/or ample bedcovers to enter REM sleep.

The temperature dependence of REM sleep could be a good reason why my mother bundled me up whether I was sleeping in my crib or outdoors in my baby carriage. Pictures of me at the age of 6 months suggest that I wore a knit woolen cap whenever I was exposed to the elements during the winter of 1933–34. My vulnerability to cold was related to my small size. Small size is, paradoxically, a contributor to a much larger ratio of body surface to mass, so a baby radiates and loses heat faster than an adult. Because my immature brain needed REM, I was always on the verge of heat loss as a baby.

Central temperature control is essential to growth and development, and later to body maintenance. This adaptation is found only in mammals and birds. All other animals lose heat when they are cold. Lower animals are likely to turn off their bodies, including their brains, and enter torpor-like states from which they only emerge when it gets warmer. Torpor is not like the hibernation in which some mammals escape the rigors of winter by setting their brain thermostats at just above freezing. However, both torpor and hibernation require wise nest selection to be successful survival strategies.

It would seem that larger brains require control of temperature to function properly. Indeed, humans are cognitively competent only in a very narrow temperature range. If we have a fever, we take to bed and may not even be able to read let alone think creatively. If we wake up cold, we get up and do something about it: get more blankets, check the thermostat, change the furnace fuses, or call the emergency service of our heating company.

It must be no coincidence that only mammals and birds, with their large, complex brains and their capacity for body-temperature control, are the only animals that have REM sleep. Other animals have non-REM sleep states but not REM. Consciousness is not imputed to those smaller-brained animals that, lacking temperature control, are likely to enter torpor in the cold. Consciousness is thus a temperature-sensitive brain function. A moment's thought brings hot summers and siestas to mind to confirm our suspicion that consciousness, sleep, and body temperature are related.

A functional inference is that sleep, especially REM sleep, facilitates the temperature control on which higher brain activity depends. At first glance puzzling, the abandonment of temperature control in REM sleep may serve to make that control more efficacious in subsequent wake episodes. It is in the awake state, after all, that our temperature-regulating talents are most severely tested. It is then that we are most likely to go outdoors. Think, again, of a hot and humid summer day, but now add the threat of a bitterly cold winter day (or night). As adults (especially in New England, where I live), we have learned to bundle up tight when we go out in the cold or go to bed. This is exactly what my mother did for me, even if she had no idea that her precautions had anything to do with my brain function.

A Neuronal Model for Protoconsciousness

To drive my REM sleep as a fetus and as an infant, I must already have been capable of generating endogenous brain activation. To be useful, this activation process would have to have been centrally directed so that more and more circuits could be recruited and synchronized. For this job, the large neurons of my pontine brainstem (described in detail in subsequent chapters) would seem to be ideal candidates. If this hypothesis is correct, then their neuronal birthdays should long antedate those of the inhibitory elements that hold them in check during the awake state. The end of phase I in Maggie's kittens may have signaled the installation of REM inhibition, which allows the brain to wake up and perform its behavioral agenda by day.

Inhibition itself depends on excitation. It is therefore not surprising that the brain first turns itself on and then, increasingly, turns itself off, thereby regulating its excitation. A similar rule is followed with respect to neuronal structure. The brain is initially populated by many neurons, some of which are eliminated by a process called "pruning." Like a successful garden, my brain once grew wildly but was gradually refined by the thinning out of elements that were no longer needed. My first brain state was active sleep. Over time this state was curtailed in favor of the awake state. When I began my brain odyssey, I sailed the dream ocean in my mother's uterus and prepared myself for life on the dry land of the awake state. It was only when I woke up that I became conscious of myself as a self and gradually came to recognize that I had thoughts and feelings and could act upon the world. But all the while there was an inner world to which I could retreat whenever I slept.

Over time, progressively strong inhibition has reduced the span of time spent in my inner world about tenfold. When I was a fetus, my brain was internally activated for at least twelve hours a day. By the time I was born, that had decreased to eight hours. Now, I'm lucky to get an hour and a half.

One possible cause of this functional suppression of my REM sleep is the maturation and increased synaptic efficacy of my brainstem aminergic neurons. I will explain how we discovered those cells and how they might work anon, but take my word for it and suppose with me that these neurons support the awake state and undermine REM. When I was an infant, my brain and my sleep-wake behavior probably were already controlled by an automatic oscillator in my brainstem.

As I grew up, the time I spent in sleep kept decreasing. My brain was trading one form of consciousness (dreaming) for another (the awake state).

II My Experimental Nature

4 The Genesis of My Experimentalism

When I was growing up, it never occurred to me that I would later have a stroke and be able to observe, with as much interest as horror, the stroke's effects on my physical and mental life. My boundless curiosity about the brain extended even to myself. I realized that I was afflicted, grievously, by the stroke. At the same time, I saw that I was being given a chance to observe, at first hand, an insult to my own brain. I will tell that story in detail in chapter 11. Since my rehabilitation, I have had the pleasure of developing the functional theory that forms the central scientific message of this book.

I had previously thought a lot about the diseases to which I was genetically predisposed, including my mother's Alzheimer's disease and my father's cardiovascular disease. Of these two, I much preferred to die of cardiovascular disease, which could be apoplectic and sudden whereas the slow brain degeneration of Alzheimer's would be more painfully progressive. Now it turns out that I have both undesirable outcomes: my stroke was apoplectic but my subsequent disability has been slowly and painfully progressive. This is a "Hobson's choice" with a vengeance. Instead of either of two bad fates, I was given both.

I wrote this memoir as much to trace the development of my scientific mind as to analyze how genetic and environmental factors contributed to my falling apart. I wanted to better understand how I became an experimentalist, and to share that understanding with the world. Therefore, I begin this part of the story with a discussion of problematic personality traits that helped direct me to science and shaped my scientific life in significant ways.

I have three character traits of which I am not proud. They must be acknowledged and understood in any account of my life and my work. I am ambitious, stingy, and irritable (as well as humble, generous, and convivial). For all these reasons, I have had my share of friends but never been very popular with many other people.

My ambition is out of all proportion to my accomplishments. It is palpable to my colleagues, many of whom spend a great deal of their time and energy cutting me down.

My stinginess is a related trait that makes me seem selfish and ungenerous to colleagues and even to my family and intimate companions.

My most unpleasant trait is anger, which seethes constantly in me like a smoldering volcano, constantly threatening to erupt and annihilate the neighboring villages. This trait is especially problematic for my intimate friends and, above all, for my family.

Where do these traits come from? With what other more admirable traits are they mixed? How have they affected my life and my work? Do they appear in my dreams? If they do, what form do they take? Can I take steps to overcome them, or at least practice damage control so that their effects are less damaging to me, to my goals, and to my friends? Is the close attention I have paid to my dreams helpful in self-understanding and self-improvement?

Before I begin to try to answer these questions and present evidence that these negative traits may have been learned as well as innate, let me say that I do not really know why I am this way. But I am nonetheless certain that I *am* this way. And I am fairly sure that I always will be, no matter how hard I try not to be. As my psychiatric mentor Jack Ewalt said: "Before my psychoanalysis, I thought I was a son of a bitch. But after my psychoanalysis I knew that I was."

Nature and Nurture

My three unattractive traits appear to be deep aspects of my nature that defy both analysis and eradication. They are as deep and ineradicable as are my enthusiasm, my curiosity, and my affection, which are easier for most people, including me, to acknowledge and accept. The contextual details I will present will make it seem that these traits have been learned and will show that they all have been shaped by experience. But I have no doubt that they are also innate, which helps to make them both enduring and ineradicable.

If, as I suggested in part I, my very self is a continuous brain function, then it must also be true that my ambition, my niggardliness, and my anger are likewise brain functions. They don't feel like brain functions, but they must be. How could that be? We have little difficulty imagining that brains generate negative emotions such as anger. Why, then, can they not also emit more complex and apparently social traits, such as ambition and stinginess?

Ambition can be reduced to getting the most for the self, and stinginess to paying the least for it. It is not hard to see how a brain might be wired to advance the self as efficiently as seems possible. In fact it is likely that such traits are innate and that society's job is to tame them to acceptable levels. In describing my own case, I will try to show how my social interactions failed to tame these traits completely and may even have intensified them. At the same time, I will insist that all three traits have contributed in important ways to my scientific success.

Ambition made it hard for me to be a follower. I wanted to lead even if that entailed rebellion. I wanted to lead on my own, a kind of stinginess that made it hard for me to collaborate and to acknowledge co-workers. My anger was quickly turned on my critics, and that made them all the more critical.

Causality and Casuality

What is the point of emphasizing geneticism in a work designed to review the interpretability of the mind in relation to the lives we live? One of my goals is to caution the reader about the danger of confounding casuality of association with causality. It is true that I am like my father in some ways—especially the stinginess and the irritability. But my father was the contributor of half my genes as well as the difficult person I lived with from birth to age 18. And it is true that I am like my mother; my enthusiasm and my affection are like hers. She, too, contributed half my genes, as well as carrying me to term and lovingly raising me from infancy to adolescence. My stinginess made me realize, early, that I needed to invest my time and energy efficiently. I needed to focus. Anger made me see red when I felt I was being hoodwinked or deceived by my psychoanalyst teachers, and anger has fueled my rebellion against psychoanalysis.

The same caveat applies to dreams. It is easy to see a connection between many details of dream content and details of the life of the dreamer. But such associations do not account either for the presence of the content or for the way that content is organized in dreams. Likewise, associations of important aspects of my personality with those of my parents cannot account for the deep persistence of those traits. They are almost as certainly inherited as they are learned. The incontrovertible evidence for this claim is that identical twins reared apart show remarkably similar personalities.

What is at stake here is nothing less than a scientific theory of becoming and being—of how we come to be the persons we are. Historical review (the approach we use in analyzing the contents of dreams) must recognize its limitations in the face of genetic determinism (which informs our formal analysis of dreams). In other words, identical twins—or even non-twin siblings—will have formally similar dreams whenever their brains are activated in sleep. One of the goals of this book it to demonstrate that dreams and lives can be discussed and understood only up to a point by taking the historical, experiential tack. This leaves much still to be explained by the determinist-formalist paradigm. Simply stated, the determinist-formalist paradigm says that the form of mental content, including dreaming, has a strong genetic predisposition that expresses itself in the universality of the activated brain state of REM sleep.

The determinist-formalist paradigm relieves the historical approach of responsibilities it cannot and should not undertake. We need to be comfortable with the limits of both the genetic and environmental models of explanation even as we use both to maximize our understanding. Far too often, we stretch one paradigm or the other too far in our effort to complete a theory whose time for completion has not yet come. No one, I hope, would ascribe the changes in my sleep and my dreams that followed my stroke to my personal history.

As an illustration of the distinction between the determinist-formalist and the content-analytic approaches to understanding dreaming and dreams, consider the following dream report. recorded in my journal on June 18, 1984:

The overall theme was a quest. I was looking for something or perhaps just a way (in both the geographical and strategic senses of the word).

One scene was in a restaurant/hotel with the usual confusion of rooms, levels, and people. In the dining room, it seemed like a reunion was taking place because there were some people that I knew were from Harvard there (though not one of them was identified). My job was to find the back door so as to exit directly to the street and not back-track to the lobby. I opened several doors only to find that there were in fact windows which had been closed, by carpentered panels, from the outside. I noticed that wooden wedges had been inserted between the window frames and the panels, an elaborate contrivance for which the function was not apparent. It seemed odd that the panels would be so spaced rather than fitting flush.

I gave up on the shortcut exit plan and started back to the lobby.

The scene then shifted to a classical temple, perhaps Greek or even Egyptian. There was a narrow stair passing below a stone arch with a prominent keystone. I remarked how one of the pleasures of working at Harvard was exposure to beauty. This curious conceit seemed adequate to explain the strange scene shift.

Abruptly, I was walking on a Vermont hillside, covered with snow, looking for an old woman. The snow was slightly off-white making me wonder if there was fresh manure just under the surface. Despite the risk, I decided to eat some of the snow to quench my thirst. It was tasteless.

I was then talking with a Vermonter (like my farmer-neighbor, Marshall Newland), about the old woman whom I had not yet found. He offered an aphorism that seemed, in typical Vermont fashion, to sum up the situation: "I may be hard to find, but when you get there, you can count on my presence." Even in the dream, this remark seemed to mean that reliability was the reward of persistence.

I woke up needing to urinate and did so. On returning to bed, I kept myself awake long enough to record these impressions in memory. I thought to myself, "Well that is typically dream-like, and unlike anything I experience when I am awake."

This dream lends itself nicely to both formal and content analysis.

From the formal point of view, the dream is typically bizarre; discontinuities abound. At first I am in a hotel, then I am in a Greek temple, and finally I am on a Vermont hillside. Even within a scene there are incongruities: the hotel has windows instead of doors; the windows are blocked; the temple has numerous architectural details that I attribute to Harvard's concern with aesthetics. In this, and in other dream thinking, I am limited to *ad hoc* explanations that don't make much sense to my awake mind.

The examples of orientational instability and cognitive uncertainty are manifestations of those universal properties of dream consciousness that I attribute to the altered mode of brain activation in sleep. They are thus not to be interpreted using content analysis.

In my journal, I noted that the hotel scene may have been related to my experience of driving around and around the block looking for a parking space before my 25-year medical school reunion dinner at the Meridien Hotel in Boston.

The Greek temple may have reflected my growing interest in classicism inspired by a recent visit to Sicily. But maybe the temple was Egyptian, a loose association within the category of architectural antiquity.

The Vermont hillside is a familiar landscape—I have a farm in Vermont that serves as a second home. The man in the dream may have been my next-door neighbor Marshall Newland, and the old woman I was looking for may have been Neil Purcell's mother. But all these interpretations are speculative. The only content-analytic interpretation that I find interesting is the idea that the dream reflects my questing. I look everywhere for adventure, for knowledge, and for social contact. I am deeply and incurably curious. But is this really an interpretation, or only a truism? And is questing in dreams really a formal quality? We are often lost and looking for our way in our dreams. This quality arises naturally from a combination of our perception of motion and our disorientation. What is left for content analysis to explain is the choice of these scenes and my action in them.

As a demonstration project, this book is dedicated to the simultaneous use of genetic and environmental approaches as I try to connect my life and my mind to my brain. I want to show that each approach informs the other even as their combined use still fails to answer certain important questions about the brain and the mind and about the content of my dreams and my life.

My inevitable failure to provide a complete and convincing analysis of my dream should not be either surprising or discouraging. On the contrary, the fact that in only half a century we have made such significant progress as we have in dream science should help us to see that more is to be gained from admitting defeat and carefully examining the still egregious short-comings of our science.

Francis Crick and the Laboratory of Neurophysiology staff on the occasion of his visit in 1983. The discovery, by Francis Crick and James Watson, of the molecular structure of DNA, was reported in 1953, the same year that Eugene Aserinsky and Nathaniel Kleitman discovered REM sleep and reported its relationship to dreaming. I was then 20 years old and totally ignorant of DNA and REM. After being awarded the Nobel Prize for Physiology and Medicine in 1962, Crick turned his attention to the science of sleep and the neurobiology of consciousness. He and Grahame Mitchison advanced the theory, first suggested by David Hartley in 1804, that we dream in order to forget. The Crick-Mitchison theory was based on the Hopfield model of reverse learning which was applied to REM sleep neurophysiology. From left: Robert McCarley, Ralph Lydic, Helen Baghdoyan, Francis Crick, me, Peretz Lavie, Stephen Denlinger, Rita Helfand, Anthony Monaco, Stephen Hoffmann.

This self-critical process can suggest what questions remain to be answered and how we might expect to answer them. We must be supple, flexible, and plastic in jumping from one paradigm to another. One thing is clear: until recently, psychiatry has failed, just as the humanities have failed, to take adequate account of biology—of genes that act through brains to cause a range of mental states whose mechanism and function we are only beginning to understand.

In 1933, the year of my birth, Sigmund Freud published the revised version of his 1900 dream theory. In fact this was nothing but a reiteration of his view that dreaming was a psychological defense process designed to protect consciousness from disruption by the alien impulses of repressed wishes released by the uncensored id during sleep. Also in 1933, Edgar Adrian and his colleagues at Cambridge were becoming interested in the claim, made in 1928 by the German psychiatrist Hans Berger, that the electrical activity of the brain could be recorded by attaching electrodes to the scalp. The electroencephalogram was to become the basic scientific tool of sleep and dream research. Within the first 20 years of my life, it led to the discovery of the brain activation in REM sleep in 1953 and set the stage for the new theory of dreaming that Robert McCarley and I would develop 24 years later. As this book illustrates, I and that dream theory grew up together, and the new dream theory informs our thinking about consciousness and about both its normal and its pathological vicissitudes.

The Great Depression

It was certainly unlucky for a person of my father's disposition to come of professional age at the beginning of the Great Depression. In 1929, the year after the EEG was discovered, the stock market crashed. My father, John Robert Hobson, was 27 years old. Just married, he was working in the Patent Office in Washington, seeking his fortune as a young attorney. By the time I was born, he had moved to Connecticut to serve as the corporate patent attorney of the Hartford-Empire Company. The Depression had by then settled on all Americans like a black cloud.

In 1932, just after I had been conceived and had begun to develop my brain in my mother's womb, Franklin D. Roosevelt had been elected with a mandate to turn the economy around and to punish big business for its economic excesses. Before long, my father was engaged in helping to defend his company from the federal government.

The Department of Justice had decided to prosecute the Hartford-Empire Company for restraint of trade under the Clayton Act of 1910. It had good

reason to do so. The Hartford-Empire Company invented and manufactured glass-making machines. It leased the machines to Libbey-Owens,
Corning, and other companies, which then paid a royalty to Hartford-
Empire for every bottle that was sold. That was clever, but it may well have
been unfair, as the government claimed. The antitrust trial dragged on for
20 years, and the combination of economic uncertainty and corporate
embattlement had a powerfully negative effect on our family life.

I don't think either my father or I ever felt economically secure. No
matter how much money we had, we were always sure that it wasn't
enough, or that what we had would be lost. We were always sure that we
needed to scrimp and save in order to survive. As the antitrust case went
from appeal to appeal, my father—who could be quite a lot of fun when
he relaxed—became more and more tense, more and more irritable, and
more and more likely to explode in anger.

For the first 12 years of my life, my sister Harriet (born in 1941), my
brother Bruce (born in 1943), my mother, and I walked on eggs, hoping
not to set off a burst of temper from Dad. By that time, the cloud of war
had joined the cloud of economic depression to further darken the skies
in which my father read gloomy weather reports. My mother, who had
known a far worse climate early in her life with her own father, was a sunny,
optimistic, and accommodating counterpoint—a bright, airy *L'Allegro* to
Dad's gloomy *Il Penseroso*.

Engineering and Invention

Creative activity at Hartford-Empire continued to thrive in spite of the
lawsuit. Through my father, I met Edward Lorenz, an inventor, whose own
son, whom we called "Young Edward," would go on to win the Crawford
Prize for Mathematics.

The Lorenzes were smart, economically comfortable, and fun. They had
a house in New Hampshire's Waterville Valley. Their getaway cabin near
Granby, Connecticut was called Betelgeuse in honor of the constellation. In
those two settings the Lorenzes introduced us to pleasures of outdoor New
England. Hiking, fishing, and skiing were among the activities my father
and I enjoyed together courtesy of the Lorenzes. The Lorenzes also loved
solving the double-crostics in the Sunday *New York Times* and putting
together thousand-piece picture puzzles. I became adept at those pastimes.

Sidney Parham, a lawyer and colleague of my father, was my godfather.
Sid was an important part of a cultural model that constituted a powerful
alternative to Hartford's insurance and aircraft engine manufacturing

executives. He and Edward Lorenz represented the inventiveness and the playfulness that can transcend economic hardship.

Love and Celebration

I remember wonderful Christmas Eve parties with the Lorenz and Parham families. They came to our house for drinks, dinner, tree-trimming, and Sid's annual reading of "The Night Before Christmas." My mother made all this run smoothly by dint of innocent good will and weeks of preparation in the kitchen. When there were too many people for our small dining room to accommodate, a card table was set up in our small den for the children. Young Edward Lorenz said hardly a word but was visibly thinking while Sarah Parham regaled us with stories of her adventures in the theater in New York. I was thus treated to personal evidence of a lifestyle that appealed to me more than conventional careers of provincial Hartford.

Later in life, as a Christmas present for my finicky and hard-to-please father, I bought a copy of James Gleick's book *Chaos*. I had heard of chaos theory but had no idea what it really was. I liked the cover image and wanted to read the book even if Dad didn't. But Dad did read it, and he thanked me profusely because, unbeknownst to me, one of the heroes of the book was Edward Lorenz—our own Young Edward. And I was amused to read Gleick's account of his interview, because it revealed that Edward Lorenz, at age 60, was still the same man of few words that Young Edward had been at age 16. According to Gleick, Lorenz said very little, but his blue eyes still twinkled as he thought. This is convincing evidence of enduring and intrinsic brain activity. The 16-year-old Young Edward, who appeared shy and introverted, was doing math in his head to stave off boredom and unwanted discourse with us adolescent ruffians. Perhaps he had some relatively mild variant of Asperger's Syndrome. At age 60, having achieved worldwide fame through his discovery of the mathematical description of the unpredictability of complex systems, he avoided Gleick's questions by attending to the music of his own cerebral spheres.

I am embarrassed to admit that as an adolescent I had written Young Edward off as a weirdo. When I learned that he had been recruited by the Navy to serve as a weatherman, I thought to myself "That's an appropriately dead end for him." In fact he had been sent to the Massachusetts Institute of Technology to model weather forecasting. It was at MIT that he showed, in two rather simple differential equations, that knowing the initial conditions of a complex system such as weather does not allow prediction of its subsequent states. Minor perturbations, such as the beating of the mythical butterfly's wings, can cause very significant departures from expected outcomes. This intuition is the basis of chaos theory, which now informs physiology and medicine as well as meteorology.

The brain is a complex system. Because its vicissitudes are unpredictable, modeling the content of its states is difficult. We learn this through the unpredictable content of our dreams—we are not very good at predicting the future content of our minds. From Young Edward's brain we get an important message about our own brain-selves: we are both complex and unpredictable.

Through my father's colleagues at the monopolistic Hartford-Empire Company, I was exposed to intellect, to inventiveness, and to an engineering variety of experimentalism. Even though my father was economically anxious and constitutionally angry, I learned at a very early age that careers rewarding experimentalist traits were possible. As Dad became more and more immersed in New England life, I was increasingly exposed to the natural world. I believe that this exposure propelled me toward anatomy and physiology. My native curiosity responded strongly to environmental stimuli. I enjoyed looking at life all through my career, and when I was brought down by a stroke it was inevitable that I would regard even that disaster as a natural opportunity.

Freedom and Playfulness

My mother had an equally large part in encouraging my curiosity about living things. In 1939 we moved from an old two-family house on a built-up street on the wrong side of West Hartford to a new single-family house in an upscale suburban neighborhood on the edge of farmland fields and woods. My parents were both supportive and laissez-faire in ways that helped me indulge my investigative nature. As is true many boys, I wanted to see, to feel, and to understand the many natural phenomena that lay just outside my door.

I was naturally fascinated by the amazing anatomical differences between boys and girls. At age 5, I already conducted experiments, playing "doctor" and other sexual games in neighbors' bathrooms, cellars, and barns. Many mothers would have quashed this behavior. In the light of my later romantic indiscretions, perhaps my mother should have been more controlling. But I'm glad she wasn't.

There is a story about my youthful skepticism that may be apocryphal. I recall it only because it was repeated over and over again by my proud parents. I could not have been older than 5, and I may have been as young as 4, when I tested the hypothesis that Santa Claus came down the chimney on Christmas Eve. I was at a neighbor's house that had a fireplace large enough for me and a portly Santa to get into. But I quickly discovered that the iron damper was too narrow to admit much more than my hand, even when it was completely open. Covered with soot, I emerged from that fireplace and announced the physical impossibility of the Santa Claus fable. Instead of punishing me for going beyond the limits of childhood curiosity, my parents simply helped me wash off the soot.

Without being able to decide between the role of genetics and environment in this story, I believe that both contribute in important ways. My child-like curiosity was native. I always wanted to see more, to understand more, and to know more. As I have noted, this kind of ambition probably is a brain function. It was no coincidence that I was called "a brain" when I excelled in school. I was already "a brain" at age 4, and my investigative spirit was a natural expression of my awake state of cerebral activation. So up the chimney I tried to go. If I couldn't fit up, how could Santa Claus fit down? The logic was simple. But most parents wouldn't allow their child to go into a fireplace. The child would get sooty, as I did, and might find out that his parents were having him on, as mine were. My parents must have been very liberal to overcome two conventional prohibitions—"Thou shalt not get dirty" and "Thou shalt not challenge popular belief systems"— at once.

Like the Santa Claus myth, the idea that dreams are smoke that goes up our psychic chimney was later exploded by finding the dream damper in the brain. It is the condition of nerve cells, not the pressure of unacceptable wishes, that causes dreaming. This means that most of our myths about dreams may be wrong—or, rather, misleading stories designed, like the Santa Claus myth, to mystify and play upon our childlike imaginations. I have nothing against imagination. Imagination is itself a brain function, and an admirable one. While imagination fuels creativity (including scientific creativity), science helps us check the veracity of our imaginative myth-making by means of critical experiments. When imagination fuels religious myth-making, it becomes as dangerous as it is comforting.

The Woods as a Laboratory

Our move to a new house in 1939 seemed like the end of the world to me, but in fact it was an important beginning. At 1902 Asylum Avenue, we had a whole and wholly new house, whereas at 32 Vera Street we had been renting one half of a shabby two-family dwelling. Our new house had a lawn, trees, and a garden. It was on a bus route to a good school named for one of the New England Sedgwicks. Most important, it was the last house on a street that was scheduled for development at the expense of woods, brooks, and hayfields. By 1941, only two more houses had been added to our street. When the United States entered World War II, the building of new houses stopped altogether for four years. I lived next to the woods from my eighth birthday to my twelfth, and the woods became my laboratory.

I could run out the door and cross the road, with no danger of traffic, and could be in the woods in seconds. I cannot remember my father or my mother ever telling me that I shouldn't go into the woods, or that it was dangerous to do so. I ran wild in those woods. I built huts and dams. I chopped down trees. I led a merry band of four younger friends in elaborate fantasy archery tournaments. I captured—and dissected—fish, frogs, birds, and snakes.

Early Sleep and Dreams

I have always slept well. As my brain-self developed, my sleep changed. I remember lying on a rug and trying to nap in nursery school. Sometimes I dozed off, but usually I just lay still, simulating sleep. I gave up napping entirely by age 6 but slept deeply from 9 p.m. to 7 a.m., presumably with two or three hours of deep non-REM sleep and about the same amount of REM sleep. These two kinds of sleep occur in 90-minute bouts. As the night wore on, there was less and less NREM sleep and more and more REM.

From recent research results, we know that motor learning benefits from both sleep phases. After age 6, I was constantly involved in intense and demanding motor activities, including roller skating and biking (no hands) at top speed down the hill to our house. With my father's help, I learned tumbling and acrobatics. I could hang upside-down from a trapeze by my toes or by my heels. Until late adolescence, I astonished my peers by doing running forward somersaults in the air. My friends and I played baseball, football, and basketball, resisting parental calls to meals or bed until the last possible moment.

I don't recall dreaming at all during my early life. If I had any recollections of dreams, they were not discussed with my parents or my friends. As time went on, I went to sleep later and later, often listening to my radio surreptitiously until 10 o'clock.

My sleep, especially my REM sleep, was both a preparation for and a reaction to the intense motoric agenda of my childhood.

When I was delivering the *Hartford Courant*, at ages 12–14, I was able to awaken automatically five minutes before 6 a.m., the time for which my alarm clock was set. This experience later helped me recognize that sleep was both plastic and partial in its pleasant takeover of my young brain. My self-awakening also tipped me off to the continuous activity of my brain during sleep. My brain was, among other things, a very reliable clock. I am still able to anticipate alarm-clock awakenings for important work and social obligations.

Instinct and Learning

I was terrified by snakes. I also knew that my fear was irrational. To the extent that it wasn't learned, it wasn't easily unlearned. There were copperheads near our brook and rattlesnakes on the mountain beyond our fields, and I learned how to recognize and avoid them. But my fear was equally great when I came upon the harmless black snakes that lived in the swampy dump that thoughtless builders had created on the edge of our woods. My approach to dealing with this fear—an early instance of cognitive-behavioral therapy—was to talk myself into going into the dump over and over again. After numerous trials I learned to kill snakes, but I never learned how to pick them up alive.

I felt fine—and safe—in these adventures because I knew that my mother was always at home. If I described an experimental exploit or a mishap to her, she was always calm and reassuring.

A Little More About My Mother

My mother had been raised, with four sisters, on a hardscrabble farm bought and later lost by her ne'er-do-well father, Lewis Fairchild Cotter. Grandpa Cotter was a Georgia cracker. He was the grandson of William Jasper Cotter, a circuit-riding Methodist preacher who in his autobiography extolled the government's removal of the heathen Seminoles from northern Georgia. And, as I have already noted, Grandpa Cotter was addicted to alcohol. According to my mother, he sat on the farm porch with a flyswatter while his wife and the five daughters worked the farm.

None of the Cotter girls graduated from college, but all four of their husbands were graduates. My uncles on my mother's side included a chemist, a machinist, an architect, and a dental technician. They were all solid and skillful men. But they were also fettered by their limiting circumstances, and uninspired as a result of their resignation. Through their

Dr. George Stone, my great-grandfather, and the horse and buggy in which he made medical house calls in Savannah, Georgia in the late nineteenth century. When I took a side trip to Savannah from Atlanta in November 1979, I found this lovely old Victorian house, in which Dr. Stone lived, on the corner of Oglethorpe Avenue and Habersham Streets. I had arrived for a meeting of the Society of Neuroscience in 1979. The Society had grown from 250 anxious-about-survival refugees from FASEB at its first meeting in Washington to an anonymous mass of 2,500 members in Atlanta. Put off by such success, I went off in search of my roots and I found some of them in Savannah. I now live in a surprisingly similar house in Brookline near the Harvard Medical School, a house that I had found and bought ten years before my visit to Savannah.

husbands, the Cotter girls were clawing their way back up the social slope to the level their mother had occupied before her marriage.

My grandmother, Clara Stone, had been born in Savannah, Georgia, where her father, a graduate of Albany Medical College, had gone as a surgeon in the U.S. Public Health Service to work against the importation of yellow fever from the tropics.

My great-grandfather, George Stone—a Yankee who had become a beloved and prominent family doctor in Savannah—had sent his daughter Clara to St. Margaret's, an exclusive girls' school in then-fashionable Waterbury, Connecticut. In the 1890s, when Sigmund Freud was hatching his dream theory in Vienna, my grandmother had roomed, at St. Margaret's, with one Florence Miriam. Known to me as "Aunt Florence," she was my godmother.

My mother had a number of charming assumptions about how I might advance socially. She thought that I should be allowed to develop as a natural left-hander, but that I should at least be taught to eat with my right hand so as to not compete for space with the woman on my left at the elegant dinner parties she was sure I would be invited to attend. She sent me to art school to learn oil painting, an activity that her own mother and other southern gentry affected. I already loved to draw and to paint, and I still do, but art school on Saturday mornings was too confining for me.

One of my mother's schemes for my upward social mobility really did work, though, and it was the one I opposed most vigorously: dancing school. In the 1940s, a paradigm shift from ballroom dancing to the Lindy Hop (or Jitterbug) was going on, and I wanted to be on the crest of the new wave. I therefore wanted to join my trendy friends who attended the O'Connell Dancing School. My mother thought otherwise. She enrolled me in Mrs. Godfrey's old-fashioned ballroom dance class, where we boys wore white gloves and black bow ties.

Mother got a discount at Mrs. Godfrey's because there were twice as many girls as boys. Once I got over my petulance about this conscription, and mastered my fear of Mrs. Godfrey's cane, I loved dancing school, and I loved dancing. This was not only because of the movement but also because of all the touching and intimacy it permitted. When it came to body pressing, the foxtrot turned out to be much better than the Lindy Hop.

It was in the touchy-feely intimacy department that my mother really excelled. My mother was genuinely, spontaneously, unselfishly affectionate, despite the examples of her social inhibition I have recounted. Deep down, she probably was a tomboy. My mother played baseball with us when we were short of players. And during my early years she was always fun to be with. Through her I became convinced that even a life of hard work should be fun and that my native playfulness was to be my key to enjoyment. I have always regarded science as socially sanctioned playfulness. It was only under the open conditions of play that I was able to make the modest discoveries I describe in part III of this book.

Skepticism, Politics, and Religion

I believe that I was skeptical, apolitical, and atheistic by nature. My experience with the church shows how deeply I resisted, and how strongly I opposed, religious and political conventions—even those of my parents. To their everlasting credit, my mother and father not only allowed me complete freedom of thought; they even went along with some of my heresies.

The first of these heresies occurred in Sunday School when I was about 7. Asked to color the angels in pictures of the Nativity, I balked. I colored the grass green, the sheep white, and the shepherds' clothes beige, brown, and gray. But, as I announced to the class, it was impossible to color the angels. I had never seen an angel, and as far as I knew neither had anyone else, so how could I know what color they were? Sunday School was obviously not for me, and vice versa.

As a boy of 8, I had a fair soprano voice and loved to sing. So when it was suggested that I join the choir of St. John's Episcopal Church—and was told I would be paid the then-princely sum of $1.80 a month for doing so—I readily assented. The choir was semi-professional, and the music was technically superb. We tackled such difficult pieces as Bach chorales and Handel oratorios as well as simple hymns. In addition to the Sunday 11 a.m. service, singing in the choir required three rehearsals a week: two for the boys, on Tuesday and Thursday afternoons, and one for the whole choir, on Friday evenings. I did this with great diligence and pleasure between ages 8 and 13. During the last two of these years, I sang falsetto because my voice was changing.

As I sat in the choir of the church, I could hear the minister, Harold Hand Donegan, droning on and on about this or that biblical text and what it meant to us as Christians. It all sounded hollow and insincere to me. The Reverend Mr. Donegan's presentation was bloodless, pretentious, and self-serving. I was convinced that most of the parishioners were materialists coming to get reassurance that their souls had not been lost in their quest for mammon. This conviction was reinforced by observing the luxurious dress and mask-like facial expressions of the parade of insurance company executives and their wives as they as they passed by me on their way to the communion rail. I swore then and there that I would never be confirmed. But in fear of offending my mother I went back on this oath and took confirmation classes, passed by keeping my fingers crossed, and then faked communion for two years. Recognizing my hypocrisy, I suddenly declared my lack of faith and my decision to quit the church. I was 15 years old and about to change my life quite radically by taking my secular education seriously and beginning my commitment to the science of mind and brain.

My trepidation about declaring my religious dissent was immediately allayed by my father. He had become one of the vestrymen who ushered parishioners to their pews and passed the collection plate. To my astonishment and relief, he said "I never much believed in that stuff either." Soon Dad was spending his Sunday mornings in the garden. My mother continued to attend church for a couple of years, but then she too stopped going. I don't know if she had a deep faith in God or not. Certainly she was a genuine Christian in her moral structure and behavior. And she never questioned me or Dad about our lack of credence in God or in the church.

Like my father, I was a naturalist. Like him, I wanted to become a scientist. All I needed was the chance. And I got that chance because Dad helped me achieve what he could not. My father's brain must have been wired in favor of linear logic, mathematics, and rationality. These traits were fueled by ambition and a slowly brewing anger, which made him tirelessly determined, committed, and critical. I am that way, too. My mother's brain was different. She was an avid reader and a prolific writer who had a native affection and sociability. Her ability to believe was related to her ability to get along and to enjoy life in spite of hardship. Her brain, like a part of mine, was psychological, clinical, and synthetic. I have inherited my parent's specific brain traits as well as their generic brain states. But I never heard either of them recount a dream.

My sister Harriet is very much like our mother: sunny, long-suffering, and devoted to family. She speaks four or five languages, has a Ph.D. in comparative literature, and keeps up with all our relatives. My brother Bruce, despite his efforts to the contrary, is like our father: single-minded, focused, and a would-be jokester. He is a creative composer who works alone, has no children, and stars at stunt skiing. We all like one another.

The Work Ethic

Much of what I have accomplished has come from dogged work. Certainly my parents had a lot to do with this. My father worked so hard, both on the job and off, that I often wondered if he was having any fun at all. When we climbed mountains together, we never stopped at the top to have a conversation or enjoy the view. Instead, he ate his bag lunch as quickly as he could and started down again. I think of this now, having written three books in a year despite my stroke.

Sometimes, when I read these books, I cannot remember ever having written what I read. The same is true of my journal. The journal now runs to 150 volumes. In them are more than 600 dream reports. As I read them, I wonder whether they are really mine. I can recognize the handwriting, but I have no recollection of dreaming the dreams or of recording them.

Much of what seems special to us at the time of our experience is lost rather quickly! This is an important corollary to the problem of false memory. We normals are thus not unlike patients with Korsakov's psychosis. We confabulate when asked about events we think we should remember. I'm sure my father couldn't remember more than a few of his climbs of the 46 4,000-foot New England peaks or the 46 4,000-foot Adirondack Mountains he struggled to summit. (He did each of the New England peaks twice, once in summer and once in winter.)

Although my father's salary was reliable, his job certainly was not richly remunerative, and his modest means were carefully conserved. I think he paid all of $12,500 for our Asylum Avenue house (with a 30-year mortgage). Throughout my childhood my allowance was 10 cents a week, just enough for either a mug of root beer at Kottenhof's Drug Store or an afternoon at the Center Theater, but not both. I earned this allowance by helping with the chores at home, especially watering, weeding, and cutting our lawn. We had the finest lawn on the street, as anyone standing at the top of the hill could plainly see. It was thick and verdant, while the neighbors' lawns were brown with bald spots or choked with crabgrass.

Dad did everything in our garden, including digging, planting, and trimming trees. He selected, hauled, cut, and carefully fitted flagstones for a patio. He repaired, improved, and painted the house. Most of these activities he did alone. This was because he was both a perfectionist and unpleasant to work with. But his example was clear: stick to a task until it is done and you will get a good result and deep satisfaction. You will also save money.

August of 1945

In August of 1945, we were in Silver Springs, Maryland (near Bethesda, where I later would get my scientific training). On August 7, knowing that President Truman's announcement of the war's end was imminent, we took the Georgia Avenue trolley to Washington to join the victory celebration. I will never forget that evening. Even though I did not write down my impressions at the time, emotional salience soldered in the memories. It was a party, and the behavioral norms were altered in ways that appealed to me enormously. On the city streets, sailors joined hands, creating a human barrier through which a women could pass only by giving up a kiss. Near Lafayette Square, just north of the White House (where we waited in vain for Truman to appear), we saw men and women frolicking nude in a fountain. As wartime depression yielded to hypomania, we were on the edge of a cultural paradigm shift that was to culminate in the sexual revolution of the 1960s. I loved it in part because my brain was just then undergoing its own sexual revolution.

Law and Harvard

Dwight Eisenhower was elected president in 1952, and shortly thereafter the antitrust case against Hartford-Empire was thrown out of court, no final judgment having been reached. I was as puzzled as I was relieved by this news. Wasn't the law the law? No, my father said, the law was a matter of opinion. And, he added: "You can be whatever you want to be when you grow up, but please don't become a lawyer. Lawyers prey on the misfortune of others." And he had a related caveat: "You can go wherever you want to college as long as you don't go to Harvard." "Why not Harvard?" I asked. "Because Harvard was President Franklin Delano Roosevelt's school." According to Dad, FDR had been a traitor to his class.

Limoges and Lemon Pudding

Working in our tiny kitchen with my mother was always a great pleasure for me. Mother liked to talk and was a patient teacher. She dealt out emotional and gastronomic rewards with an easy generosity. She was not a great cook, and she felt bad about that. When we entertained guests at rare sit-down dinners, she obviously knew nothing of sophisticated food preparation or of wine drinking, which for me would soon become habitual activities. I will never forget her chagrin when, asked by a better-educated person if the dessert dish was Limoges, she replied "No, it's lemon pudding." Of course, her guest meant the china—which in fact was Limoges, a gift from my grandmother Clara Stone's Waterbury friend Florence Miriam. My mother blushed when she became aware of her gaffe.

Every week my mother baked cakes. I got to choose from angel food, devil's food, and white cake with chocolate frosting. Although I liked the angel cake best, I more often chose the cakes with chocolate frostings because I knew I would be permitted to lick the beater and the mixing bowl once the cake had been frosted. I participated actively in the annual preparation of Christmas cookies. I rolled out the dough, cut stars and Santas, and sprinkled the red and green sugar decoration on these happy figures before they were slid into the oven. In mother's kitchen I learned that work life involved following a recipe, but that it was also a social event that could be informal and fun. I have always tried to create this kind of atmosphere in my house and in my laboratory. And I do believe my lab was a place where people liked to be as well as to bake the cakes and cookies that were our scientific papers and books.

In inadvertent ways, my mother helped my scientific brain to grow. Aside from her unqualified support of my curiosity and her playfulness, she exposed me to primitive animistic thought in the uneducated women she hired to help her with the laundry and the ironing. I can still see two of them clearly in my mind's eye. Silva was a "high yellow" black woman from the Azores. She thought my dissection of snakes was dangerous because their spirits lived on and might seek revenge by haunting me. She based this fear on the observation that the snakes never stopped moving—even if they were dead—until sundown. According to Silva, snakes' spirits left their bodies only under the cover of darkness. I found this explanation as dubious as the color of angels in Sunday School. By staying up late one night, I easily satisfied myself that the spontaneous movements of my cut-up snake segments persisted after dark. I thought then that this movement might reflect the intrinsic excitability of the snakes' muscles and not some separate agency like a snake soul.

I had more trouble interpreting the results of another experiment, suggested to me by Indiana, a very black Jamaican woman who was an amateur folk doctor as well as our laundry maid. She said I could cure the many warts on my hands by rubbing a toad on the warts, then killing the toad and burying it. Like a snake's death, the toad's burial had to occur at night. To my amazement, the toad cure worked. But my experiments clearly showed that it worked whether I buried the poor creatures at night or in the daytime. It worked even if I didn't bury them at all. This was my introduction to the power of suggestion and to hypnosis, the powerful process that is known to cure warts by some mechanism that still is poorly understood. Brain research will provide an explanation for hypnosis one of these days. When it does, it will probably have nothing to do with animal magnetism (unless Mesmer's term is taken as a metaphor for neuronal electricity).

I don't remember discussing any of these important experiments with my parents. In fact, most of my childhood investigations were private and discreet. This was true of my social life too, and I have often wondered what would have happened had we all been more open about these matters. I will never know. But I guess that most important discoveries are made alone or they risk not really being discoveries at all. Having seen the colossal failure of Soviet science, we know that in order to flourish science must be free, individual, and private. What the Manhattan Project did for J. Robert Oppenheimer, Richard Feynman, and other creative physicists was create an envelope for them to work in, not a hierarchy of authority to dictate priorities and procedures.

My personal inclinations to be curious, playful, and skeptical flourished in the protective envelope provided by my parents and were encouraged by the access to nature that our home's location offered. These inclinations have been enhanced as well as hindered by my ambition, my stinginess, and my anger. Never satisfied with myself, and constantly believing that there is a simpler and more direct way to overcome obstacles, I continue to look at nature, to doubt existing explanations, and to believing that science is the best way to learn more about ourselves and about our world.

That the brain should be a focus of its own curiosity is not surprising. What could be more fascinating to one curious brain than another curious brain? And what could be more obvious than the privileged view of the brain that is afforded by mental self-observation? Our brain-selves are capable of looking at themselves, of recording their formal operations, and of analyzing their contents. With the help of modern neuroscience, we are now in a position to define the brain as a subjective object, and to objectify that subjectivity. I am my brain and my brain is me. In part III, I will discuss how these ideas developed.

5 Marginal Modes of Being

Where does family life leave off and formal education begin? Naturally, parental influence is greatest in the early years; friends, mentors, and schools are increasingly important as time goes on. Since both my parents were educated in public high schools, and achieved what they did by dint of very hard work, it was assumed that my course would be the same: right up the middle. And to some extent it was, but in many important respects my course was deviant.

To the extent that I had the luxury to experiment with marginal modes of being and of thought, it was the very strong sense of independence that my parents had inspired that allowed me to follow more original and unconventional pathways. My ever-curious brain kept saying "Try this, and if it doesn't work, try that." All the while, the parental voices said "Persist." It was a balanced but highly diversified program.

Experimentation vs. Authority

Public school education in West Hartford was very good, and I excelled easily. However, my report cards always said that I could do better. And it was true. I could have done better. But the truth of the matter is that I was less intellectually challenged at school than I was at home. My father was a stickler for good grammar and could draw flags that really appeared to be waving in the breeze. My mother was a voracious reader who helped me finish 120 books in second grade by taking advantage of forced two-week quarantines for measles, chicken pox, and mumps. Our small but challenging family library included *Moby-Dick*, which I read from cover to cover when I had chicken pox at about age 7. I didn't understand the book as an exercise in depth psychology, but I loved the adventure of the chase, the catalog of whaling techniques, the exotic cast of characters, and Rockwell Kent's woodcut illustrations.

My skepticism did not endear me to teachers of science any more that it made me popular in Sunday School. In fifth grade, my teacher, Miss Melin, was demonstrating that salt water could conduct electricity by placing two bare wires in a coffee tin filled with saline. Watching the demonstration like a hawk, I could see that the battery-powered bell rang only when the wires touched the bottom of the tin, and not, as Miss Melin claimed, when they were just under the surface of the experimental sea water. I asked permission to repeat her experiment and was able to demonstrate to my classmates that contact with metal was necessary to complete the circuit. As I later learned, the sodium and chloride ions of salt were in part responsible for the electrical activity of the brain and for conduction of electrical signals along nerve fibers. Miss Melin didn't know that any more than she knew that the resistance of her salt-water solution was far too great for the power of her 1.5-volt battery to overcome.

Although I was obsessed with natural fact and truth, it was as much the challenge to authority, the anger at being duped, and the desire to show off that motivated this kind of intervention. I wanted to trust my teachers at least as much as I trusted my parents. It was never easy for me to ignore intellectual sham. I even caught my mother out once. Eager to induce me to eat my asparagus, she told me that the soft mushy spears she served me from a tin were the same California asparagus I had tried once and liked. Those stalks probably had been fresh. I knew, however, that asparagus tasted quite different when it came from a can. When I retrieved the empty tin from the trash basket, I read, with scolding pleasure, "Grown and canned in New Jersey." To her credit, my mother let off the pressure on green vegetables as quickly as she dropped her zealous churchgoing after my defection from Sunday School and Holy Communion. Now I love asparagus, whether is comes from California or anywhere else—but only fresh asparagus, preferably swimming in a fresh, made-from-scratch hollandaise sauce.

Tastes change with development. I wonder if infants and children are protected by their preference for bland foods. And I wonder if gastronomic sophistication is a brain function that underlies what we call acquired taste. As I grew older, I became an avid gourmet. I learned to cook, and to eat with pleasure, an astonishing array of foods. But my visceral rejection of cabbage-family vegetables—a strongly conditioned reflex—remains strong to this day.

Public School, or Private?

In junior high school I began to realize how much my father's punctilious attention to grammatical detail and my mother's love of reading had benefited me. School was so easy that I had plenty of time to play soccer, basketball, and baseball, and to lead an active social life with my many friends.

In eighth grade I had an enthusiastic teacher, Miss Moriarty, who drove her class favorites around in her Chevrolet Bel Air convertible. "Miss Mo" was like a mother to me. But she wasn't my mother.

"Miss Mo" was also fond of the two friends whom I loved above all others, Serena Valverde and Sebastian Bonanno. There were other friends in the eighth grade who mattered to me too because they were bright, played sports, and liked girls as much as I did. Among them were Dick de Patie, John Hastings, and Larry Barrows, all of whom had decided to compete for the tuition-free scholarships that were offered to day students at the Loomis School in Windsor. Loomis was an unusual private boarding school in being tuition free across the board and in having a charter mandate to educate local children as day students.

I was distressed by the thought that if all of my bright peers went to Loomis I would be left behind in public school. I told my father about the possibility of my attending Loomis. "Public school was good enough for me and it's good enough for you," he said curtly. I wasn't satisfied. Might I still have a chance of admission at Loomis? Knowing that I could pay the cost of a year's lunches ($180) with my newspaper-delivery earnings, I set out to investigate.

Larry Barrows told me that I could better evaluate my chances of admission to Loomis if I was tested by Page Sharp, a Hartford educational psychologist who provided remedial tutoring for slow readers, especially those with dyslexia. Sharp's mentor at Columbia University, Samuel Orton, had described dyslexia, which he attributed to miswiring of the brain. Dyslexics might, for example, spell the word 'cat' as 'tac'. I screwed up my courage and made an appointment to be tested by Sharp. A bus took me down Farmington Avenue to his office at 74 Forest Street. Sharp's office was just opposite the Harriet Beecher Stowe house and Mark Twain's Victorian mansion.

Sharp gave me the Wechsler Adult Intelligence Scale test and the Wechsler Bellevue Intelligence Scale test and said he would get in touch with me when the scores became available.

Within a few days, Page Sharp called and asked me if I had ever taken those tests before. I told him I hadn't. Sharp then repeated the tests to be sure the scores were reliable before assuring me that I'd have no trouble getting into Loomis. I relayed this news to my parents, who had decided not to stand in my way, especially when they heard that a Loomis education was tuition-free because of the school's endowment. But my family's lack of social standing and my obstreperousness in junior high school *did* stand in my way.

I had a cordial but cool interview with Hull Maynard, the director of admissions. After taking the entrance exams, which I found easy, I was surprised and disappointed to be denied a place at Loomis. Several other applicants, whom I knew to be less scholastically competent than I, were admitted. What was going on? I thought this was supposed to be an open, competitive process. So I called Page Sharp, who was about to leave for the summer at his Camp Waya-Awi in Rangeley, Maine. I told Mr. Sharp that either there was something wrong with his tests or there was something wrong at Loomis. "Come in at once," he said. "Take the tests again, and if you do well I'll call the school." My test scores were unchanged. In my presence, Page Sharp asked Hull Maynard for an explanation of my rejection. Maynard said that I had not been highly recommended by P. D. Graybiel, the principal of the Sedgwick Junior High School. That didn't surprise me, but I knew it was only an excuse. Some of the boys who *were* admitted were not only academically marginal but also even less model citizens than I was. Page Sharp believed in me and in my ability. In him I had an advocate, even a champion.

Intelligence tests such as the Binet and the Bellevue-Wechsler have been criticized because they are context dependent. But in the context in which I lived, they were the first objective measures of my brain's functional capacities. The tests helped me to believe in myself and helped Page Sharp to become my advocate and mentor.

The Loomis entrance process made me aware that life could be unfair. But it also taught me that persistence could overcome prejudice and favoritism. (Loomis not only favored descendents of the benefactor family; it also favored siblings of former students, friends of the faculty, and friends of friends.) My anger and my ambition made me want to prove just how unfair—and wrong—it was for Loomis to have denied me a place. A year later, as Page Sharp had predicted, I got in. After a sophomore year spent catching up, I was ranked first in my class in my junior year and second in my senior year.

The Life of the Mind at Loomis

As important as it was to me to win a social battle, Loomis exposed me to the life of the mind for the first time. I loved it. The strongest teachers were in the English Department, which nourished and deepened my love of literature and of writing. Norris Ely Orchard was the most charismatic teacher of Shakespeare imaginable. An amateur actor, he knew many of the great passages by heart and could teach the plays without a text. NEO, as we called him, was a seductive, mischievous person whom I found irresistibly charming. And Jim Henderson used Joseph Conrad's *Heart of Darkness* to open our eyes to allegory. Donald Lay was a great tennis player, and Al Wise had once been an architect. Both Lay and Wise loved literature, and they communicated their enthusiasm to us adolescents effectively because they were more than just teachers.

Today, I suspect that it is as much my wide range of interests as it is my scientific talent that inspires my students. I also spend more of my time editing the writings produced by my colleagues than I spend supervising day-to-day scientific activities. It is crucial to communicate observations in convincing detail, to think clearly about their significance, and to enliven scientific papers with a literary spirit that makes them readable. Many of my students cannot write or spell, even though they are not dyslexic.

My brain had gotten me to Loomis, and Page Sharp had convinced me that we needed to understand the brain better if we wanted to understand the mind. Thus, it was the brain that beckoned. At Loomis, as my independent research project, I dissected a cat's brain and labeled its structural features. As I struggled to recognize the frontal, parietal, and occipital cortices, I had no idea of the fabulous cellular architecture that lay beneath those wrinkled surfaces. Nor did I envisage the functional dependence of those structures on internal activation from the brainstem below (which I could have seen if I had turned the brain over). Even eight years later, in medical school, I was so preoccupied with identifying the twelve cranial nerves that sprung from the brainstem that its internal and functional neuronal anatomy were entirely lost on me.

When I teach students now, I begin at the cellular level and show how Freud and Sherrington were blocked by having only the reflex doctrine to guide them. Neither Freud nor Sherrington was aware of the brain's spontaneous activity or of its intrinsic capacity to organize itself as a series of conscious states. I had to learn those things for myself.

Clearly consciousness changes its character when we fall asleep and when we dream. Given this precept, it is possible to look for built-in determinants of mental content—at least at a formal level. Thus, whether we perceive the outside world clearly or hallucinate, whether we think veridically or are deluded, and whether we remember or forget are all determined by the automatic control system of the brain.

My native talent for mathematics and for physics found more satisfaction in the texts and in the homework assignments than in the classroom.

At Loomis I did not encounter teachers who communicated the excitement of experimental science. My own enthusiasm and momentum were strongly reinforced by my relationship with Page Sharp, whose friendship-mentorship was continuous and was acutely focused on the subject that would become my life's work: the human mind and its relationship to the brain. This friendship-mentorship was deeply personal and so important that I will treat it separately in the next chapter, but here I will note that my champion was a person who measured the mind and who fixed its errors by retraining the brain.

Page Sharp suggested that I go to Wesleyan University (his alma mater), and later to Harvard Medical School (which he also had attended). In 1955, having been accepted by Harvard Medical School, I answered my father's question as to why I wanted to go there by saying "I think it's the best school." My father replied, simply, "That's a good reason."

A Year at a British Public School

Before going to Wesleyan and Harvard, I had another parental obstacle to overcome. My beloved English teacher, Norris Orchard, urged me to apply for an English-Speaking Union student exchange fellowship for a year of study at a British Public School. My father was strongly opposed to that. He perceived this postgraduate year in England as a dangerous and costly detour from the straight-up-the-middle educational pathway that he envisaged for me.

At first mildly motivated, I gradually became more and more enthusiastic about the prospect of living and studying abroad for a year. Everyone who did not have a vested interest in my future encouraged me to go. Even those who were initially negative, including my father and Page Sharp, came around eventually. I applied and won a full scholarship, including tuition, room, and board, for a year at the Sutton Valence School in Kent.

As with the Loomis lunch bill, I told my father I would pay for the incidental and travel expenses of the year in England myself. "How?" he asked. "With my newspaper earnings," I replied. "But you can't spend that money," he objected. Then I nailed him: "You said I should save it for something valuable that I really wanted. This is it!"

In 1951–52, the total cost of round-trip steamship fare, 10,000 miles of automobile travel with two American friends, and all my outings from school was $840. Having budgeted $900, I came home with $60 in my pocket.

Because of my father's fear that if I were to spend a year abroad I might then have to spend an extra year in college, I consulted John Spaeth, the Academic Dean at Wesleyan. Dean Spaeth was convinced I would learn more in a year abroad than I would as a freshman at Wesleyan. According to Dean Spaeth, if I were to take all the lab courses needed for a pre-medical education I would only have to pass three Oxford-Cambridge School Exams in England to graduate from Wesleyan in three years. Spaeth said Wesleyan would give me credit for those three courses. The three that I passed turned out to be those in English, French, and biology. I flunked the chemistry exam because I had not taken chemistry at Loomis and because my teacher at Sutton Valence, Edward Craven, was a dedicated rugby fanatic but not a good chemistry teacher.

One of the reasons that I wanted to go abroad was that I had become a close friend of John Allen, the exchange student at Loomis from the Wellington School in England. Also applying for English-Speaking Union scholarships were Donald Brigham and Christopher Gates. Don and Chris became my fellow travelers in Europe. These wonderful friends made me feel that I would be safe and happy in the alien culture that soon enveloped us.

My fears about cultural engulfment were further relieved when I met Brian Aspinall, headmaster of Sutton Valence, who came to pick me up at the train station in Maidstone. We chatted amicably as we rode to the school in his stylish Alvis convertible. During World War II, Aspinall had been in the British Secret Service and had be sent to Washington, where he had acquired a familiarity with and an enthusiasm for America. On becoming headmaster at Sutton Valence, Aspinall had decided to participate in the English-Speaking Union's exchange program. I was his first American exchange student.

In 1951, most British Public Schools, including Sutton Valence, were still very Victorian in social structure and atmosphere. Every Sutton Valence student had a number, which expressed his rank. This rank determined where he sat in study hall and in the dining room, where he kept his shoes in the boot room, and where he slept in the open and very unprivate dormitories. Authority was arbitrary and absolute. Physical punishment was normal. House prefects beat miscreants with shoes. School prefects and masters beat them with canes. The ominous swishing of those canes was enough to make mischievous small boys quickly metamorphose into stiff-upper-lipped Englishmen.

"Fag!" was the cry of house prefects summoning their servants. The house prefects—the eight most senior boys in each house—had studies called "shows," each of which housed a desk, an armchair or two, and a gas ring for cooking tea and toast. The fags—the bottom eight in a house—did the cooking. They also shined shoes for the prefects and brushed dandruff off the shoulders of their black coats and blue blazers. As the ESU exchange student—and, at age 18, a very senior boy—I was made a house prefect without ever having to suffer the indignity of either fagdom or corporal punishment. Adaptation to this and other challenges to my democratic assumptions required considerable suppleness and guile.

It was at Sutton Valence that I first encountered the work of Sigmund Freud. My friend Michael Everest, who was also headed for medical school, had read Freud and Proust in his spare time. Not only had he read these two great authors, he wanted to know what I thought of their ideas. To respond to Michael's questions, I had to read them too.

Only artists (Proust, Joyce) and psychiatrists (Freud, Jung) had written about the mind as an objective subject. No scientist worthy of the name had done so. And scientists, in their wisdom, eschewed the study of the brain as a subjective object. The excessive speculations of nineteenth-century philosophers and physiologists had allowed positivism to rule subjectivity out of intellectual bounds.

Both Jung and Freud had been trained in medicine and imbued with the hope of understanding the relationship of mind to brain, a hope that was high in the last half of the nineteenth century. But neither could see how to relate his interest in the mind to the activity of the brain. There simply was not enough known about the brain. As psychoanalysis developed, any relationship to neurology or to neuroscience was actively denied, even forbidden. Hence, until about 1950 the gap between mind and brain was being widened, not narrowed.

Unbeknownst to me, at just the time that I was being educated, the prohibition against subject-object integration was beginning to weaken. In work published in 1949, Giuseppe Moruzzi and Horace Magoun had shown that the awake state had its own specific form of consciousness and was a function of intrinsic brain activation. This had set the stage for Eugene Aserinsky and Nathaniel Kleitman's 1953 discovery of REM sleep, which had its own quite different form of consciousness but was also caused by internal brain activation. These epochal studies, which set the course of my life's work, were not in the Oxford-Cambridge curriculum. They were not discussed at Wesleyan University (from which I graduated in 1955), nor were they mentioned at the Harvard Medical School (from which I graduated in 1959). Nevertheless, the work was already done and just

The Sutton Valence rugby team. When I went to school in England, I learned many new and important things: self-directed learning, independence from family and friends, and the shaping force of culture. Nowhere was the cultural theme more forcefully illustrated than on the playing field. The English played rugby to win, of course, but they played for fun and for fairness, too. Because I had been trained in American football, I was quite useful to a school team that was not used to winning nine of its twelve games. For the first time in my overly ambitious athletic life, I made a difference. That's me, seated second from right, in the second row.

waiting to be more fully appreciated and exploited as psychology struggled to become a true science.

Extracurricular Pleasures

There was lots of spare time at Sutton Valence, which was academically Class C just as John Allen had warned me. Sutton Valence was mainly concerned with educating its boys to the level of entry into business in London if they were not wealthy enough to live as country gentlemen in Kent. As an antidote to such parochialism, a great strength of the British

Public School System was the imposition of a curriculum and standards for its mastery by an external academic body, the Oxford-Cambridge Schools Examination Board. By reading the Oxford-Cambridge syllabus detailing the texts and subject matter on which the four exams I would be taking would be based, I was able to construct a study program on my own and to learn most of the material outside of classes. My friend and fellow student Michael Everest taught me how to do that. The life of the mind thus took on a new aspect. It could be individual, private, and self-paced. So it became, and so it has remained for me ever since.

Although Sutton Valence was Class C with respect to organized academics, it was Class A as a place to be, as a place to think, as a place to play, and as a jumping-off point for London and the Continent. When I told John Allen that I would be going to Sutton Valence, he told me that all he knew about the school was that Sidney Wooderson, the former world record holder for the mile run, had gone there. Wooderson's portrait, showing him wearing black steel-rimmed spectacles and crowned with laurel, still hangs in the school's hall.

Rugby was king of sports at Sutton Valence. I had been under-sized for and under-talented in American football, but I had been over-trained. I could put my head down and run, and I could tackle young men who were much bigger than I was. As a consequence, I was easily able to play on the rugby First Fifteen, and to help Sutton Valence compile a winning record for the first time in years. Despite being matched with much larger schools, such as Dover College, St. Lawrence School, and King's School Canterbury, we won nine matches and lost only three. One of our victories was a lop-sided (29–3) walloping of our school's alumni team, after which the Old Suttonians took us all out for beer and supper. I was amazed by the mix of competition and conviviality. When the English say "It's just a game," they mean it. Win or lose, the pubs beckoned. The village of Sutton Valence, with its 300 souls, had three pubs, all elegant and welcoming. (My favorite was The Swan.)

Wanderlust Indulged

In England, students left school for a month around Christmas, for another month around Easter, and for six weeks in the summer. The assumption was that they would pursue their own curricula while visiting their families or vacationing abroad. Having bought a 1937 Morris Shooting Break (a small station wagon), my Loomis classmates Chris Gates (who was attending Harrow) and Don Brigham (who was going to Brentwood) and

I were able to travel 10,000 miles in twelve countries, and we began to appreciate how wonderfully variegated Europe was. Through this experience I began to appreciate the power and beauty of geography, architecture, and culture.

I doubt that I would ever have gone to Michel Jouvet's sleep neurobiology lab in Lyon or to Giuseppe Moruzzi's Neurophysiology Institute in Pisa, or ventured into Jean-Didier Vincent's rich world of art and science in Bordeaux, had I not had such a positive European experience in my year as an English schoolboy. Having already found that English English was not just a different language from American English but a different way of thinking and a different way of being, I found that much the same was even more dramatically true of French.

The importance of language to thought is clearly illustrated by the evident dependence of social behavior, including science, on the brain's way of talking to itself and to others. Narrative and language, two of the major pillars of secondary consciousness, are highly situation dependent. Though we all learn to speak, to think, and to tell stories, we develop very different contents for these universal forms.

We tend to assume that science is science is science. But there are many variations on the theme of cultural coding that can change our way of seeing nature and thinking about it. As a Frenchman, Michel Jouvet was consciously aware of the difference between what he called the synthetic approach to science (which he espoused and attributed to Claude Bernard) and the analytic approach (which he saw me as embracing in the Anglo-Saxon tradition of Charles Sherrington). When a copy of John Eccles's 1957 book *The Physiology of Nerve Cells* arrived in the mail, Jouvet scornfully scaled it across the room, exclaiming "Anglo-Saxon heresy!" He probably did this as a provocation for my benefit. I was duly impressed.

At age 18, I was ready to discover Europe, at least on its surface. My friends and I skimmed Europe much in the way one skims a book knowing that it will require a more careful reading later. Besides seeing important museums and monuments in France, Switzerland, and Italy, we learned how to keep the car going and how to find food and lodging on our stringent budget of $3 each a day.

To save money, we carpentered a dismountable bed platform that could be assembled above our luggage (in the back) and the two bucket seats (in the front) of our little chariot. If it wasn't too cold, and if we were sufficiently tired, all three of us could sleep quite well on the narrow platform, scrunched into our sleeping bags. This experiment taught me that I could sleep anywhere when I had to. I slept well, even in the most unpromising

settings, with unselfconscious abandon. During those comatose and prolonged bouts of sleep, my brain was secreting gobs of hormones that were
making my body grow and changing me from a boy to a man. At the same
time, pruning was changing the synaptic structure of my brain.

Improvisation and Social Experimentation

Gates, Brigham, and I had a kerosene stove and a metal box full of tableware
from my "show" at Sutton Valence. In Paris, we smuggled that equipment
into our small room on the sixth floor of the Hotel de Passy so that we
could heat up a can of Prudence corned-beef hash for Christmas dinner.
We emulated Parisian café life by drinking wine and dining from tins at a
small round table we had swiped from a Paris bistro. We lashed it and three
wicker chairs we had also stolen to the top of our jalopy one morning before
leaving Paris for Switzerland, where we planned to ski and to celebrate New
Year's Eve. We used the furniture to attract attention and sympathy by
setting it up in two feet of snow in an evergreen forest outside the Swiss ski
village of Lenzerheide after finding that there was not a room available
there at any price. Lots of passersby stopped to talk with us. We were ultimately taken in by a group of Seventh-Day Adventists who said we could
sleep on the dining tables of the chalet they had rented. So we skied and
celebrated New Year's Eve with our religious and charitable friends.

On January 1, 1952, we crossed the Julier Pass in a blizzard. That is a
day we will always remember because of its great emotional salience. It is
etched—like a legend—in our brains. With heavy snow forecast, we set out
for the 2,300-meter-high pass early in the morning. A blizzard quickly
overcame our inadequate English windshield wipers and our clip-on tire
chains. Two of us had to get out and wipe the windshield manually while
pushing the little Morris up some of the steeper switchbacks. We knew
that if we stopped we might never get the car going again, so we didn't
stop.

As we came down on the Italian side of the Julier, the weather cleared
and the full moon shone through scudding clouds on the shimmering
surface of Lago Maggiore. In the Lombard fields north of Milano, farm
buildings are often arranged to create an atrium. These atrium courtyards
provide a workspace, a weather shelter, and a safe haven. At midnight, in
complete peace and quiet, exhausted by our ordeal in the Alps, we pulled
up along the outside walls of one such complex. We were in our sleeping
bags, dozing off, when shots rang out. I can still hear the whine of pellets
from the shotguns of the farmer and his sons. Those *contadinos* laughed

uproariously when they perceived our innocence and our terror. We were so scared that we could do no better than to beg for mercy—in French. No Frenchman could have understood our garbled words, but the Italian farmers immediately perceived our ridiculous situation. They assured us that we could spend the night huddled next to their walls. The near-disaster did not keep us from sleeping. Had my experience been truly traumatic, I might later have had flashback dreams, but as far as I know I never dreamed about it in any way. Since many of my dreams concern fearsome menaces, it seems odd that the experience was never replayed. Evidently that's just not the way my dream memory works.

In contrast to what I would expect if dreams simply replayed important life events, such as those that occurred on January 1, 1952, the following dream report represents some of the themes of my scientific life and its European aspects but also demonstrates the distinctively bizarre manner in which these themes are represented in dream consciousness. A sense of uncertainty and disorientation pervades this dream. Anxiety is the prominent emotion, and it is related to compulsive movement in a perilous landscape from which I seek rescue:

I am at a meeting in a strange city. It feels like an EEG group with which I am unfamiliar and I'm not sure why I am there. The day's sessions are ending and people are discussing where to have dinner (as is usual). I am ambivalent about this somewhat pointless discussion since I do not really connect with the group. It suddenly occurs to me that I should leave when I recognize that there remains only the half-day session on Saturday morning in which I have little interest. So I make a partial adieu by saying 'In case I don't see you again' which is purposefully vague. I emphasize that all of this cognitive shilly-shallying is taking place in a fully hallucinoid scene—modern, anonymous, hotel décor, with two-piece suited scientists mulling about. I have the idea—in the dream—that the hotel might be in Europe, and that I might therefore have to change my flight reservations in order to get away early.

With all of these logistical issues unresolved, I leave the hotel, alone, and cross a busy city street deciding to hitch-hike, but the destination is left vague and after one or two vehicles speed by me, I decide to walk/run along more tranquil side streets.

Immediately, I am deep in the country on a dirt road which is exceedingly steep and consists of barely worn vehicle tracks. A car approaches at high speed and, as I turn to make my gesture for a lift, it swerves toward me, forcing me into the bushes. When I recover my equilibrium, I see the car plunging downhill and continuing to turn to the right. It finally comes to a stop in an extension of the same row of shrubs and trees in which I have taken cover.

I run down the hill cursing 'you bastard!' and am amazed to perceive that the car has been traveling on a single track—really a footpath, impossible for a four-wheeled vehicle. My anger gives way to puzzlement but my quandary about the scene is left unresolved. On reaching the bottom of the hill, I look at the back of the car sticking out of the bushes. It is a small gray Renault and the driver is trying to open the left door but it is hampered by tree branches.

Without any reason, as if I were somehow just propelled, I continue on across a brook and encounter a complex set of fences which I must pass. There are fine green wires, perhaps electrified, of a kind that I have never seen and the maze of corner posts defies reason.

Having crossed the fences, I find myself in an exotic swamp-like setting which is at once a lush suburb (i.e., there are large ranch houses on large lots under large trees). I must walk (but then decide it is safer to crawl) across the tops of cut-off stumps which are 2–3 inches in diameter just under the surface of water which is about one foot deep. The whole scene is like a bayou but the trees are probably cedars, not cypresses, and yet they have side rootlets like orchid plants. My situation feels perilous and I am also aware that the homeowners might object to my trespass.

Indeed, an angry but not unattractive housewife emerges from the first house on the left and heads me off as I scurry along a now inexplicably normal sidewalk. Instead of the reprimand I anticipate, she says gently 'Now, I don't think that is exactly the way to do things, do you?' Relieved and impressed by her subtlety, I reply contritely 'Madam, I could not agree with you more.' This comment makes her guilty and even solicitous as she asks 'But, you look hungry, can I fix you something to eat?' I am agreeing when I wake up and arouse myself so as to remember the details of the dream.

The whole sequence would seem to have lasted 2–5 minutes, and was preceded by other dream action which my memory was not able to recover. This dream was recorded in my journal on the night of October 28, 2004. Besides the formal aspects of bizarreness and cognitive uncertainty, the dream demonstrates the constant movement of dreamers through dream spaces. My walking and running are Chaplinesque in their jittery frenzy. I suppose that such percepts are related to automatic activation of the brainstem's motor pattern generators, the same neuronal circuits that automate my walking and running in the awake state. The sensation of movement is convincing even though in REM sleep my spinal motoneurons are inhibited and thus I cannot really move.

Instead of accurately replaying any known experience I have had, this dream assembles a host of loosely connected travel themes from my life. I often feel a bit alien in some scientific sessions, but I never leave, and I usually end up making new friends and having a wonderful time. In real life I never encounter such wildly improbable events as the car that almost runs me down or the peculiar landscape that I must traverse in my dream. It is typical, however, for me to resolve even the most challenging displacements by finding someone to save me. All these themes are generically present in my Julier Pass experience, but my dream is more concerned with general issues of survival than with any specific one.

This dream is so typically wacky as to make us reconsider Freudian dream theory. According to it, my recollection recounts only the dream's manifest content. Its bizarreness conceals deeper latent meaning. Only Freud, or one of his disciples, could say what that meaning might be. As tempting as it is to suppose that such a theory might be true, I now prefer to think that I have already learned enough about how the brain works in sleep to ascribe the formal features of my dream to the distinctive pattern of brain activation in REM.

Latin Culture and Bucolic England

Our après-blizzard shotgun blitz was a fitting welcome to Italy, with its fabulous mix of violence, cynical humor, and art. Chris Gates's mother had told us that our visits to Florence and Rome would be the artistic high points of our year. They certainly were. But Mrs. Gates didn't warn us about the violence and the humor that make Italy so stimulating and so threatening. Now 77 years old, and married to a Sicilian, I am still learning about those themes.

Our later trips through the British Isles at Easter and through the Northern Continental countries in the summer were no less interesting than our trip to Italy, but they were more like confirmations and extensions of what we already knew than the blinding explosions of Latin spirit that we encountered in Paris and in Italy. After each of our continental trips, it was reassuring to get back to doughty old England. The English sense of fair play, of wit, and of reserved gentility constituted a welcome antidote to the perils of Latin passion. We three American schoolboys were at home in England because we spoke English and had been educated in schools that admired the English universities, English literature, English mathematics, and English science. At Sutton Valence, I even learned to admire the English tea tradition, to drink sherry and port, and to eat roast beef and roasted potatoes with gusto.

During our Easter holiday in 1952, the English-Speaking Union sent us from one genteel home to another. We stayed with no fewer than twenty families in the course of our thirty-day jaunt around England, Wales, and

Scotland. This domestic tour kept us away from galvanizing adventure and protected us from harm. The closest we came to trauma was the night we spent sleeping in our car in a low-ceiling garage in Wigan, then a dark, Satanic mill town if ever there was one. Wigan was black and we were homeless. We knew that England had a Labour government, and we had been harangued by our cabin steward on the *Queen Elizabeth* about the plight of the English working man, but the grit and grime of England's industrial midlands had to be seen to be believed. Despite our strong physiological drive, we did not sleep well in that dank Wigan garage.

After Wigan, we were relieved to discover the idyllic Lake District. This was the land of William Wordsworth, and these were the hills that inspired the Lyrical Ballads that were such a welcome item on my Oxford-Cambridge exam syllabus. I knew that Wordsworth's collaborator, Samuel Taylor Coleridge, had used drugs and was reputed to have written "Kubla Khan" after an opium binge—or was it a dream? I didn't learn until much later that Coleridge was also a friend and an early exponent of David Hartley, a founder of British Associationist psychology. It was Hartley who proposed that "we dream in order to forget," anticipating by 180 years the dream amnesia theory of Francis Crick. For Hartley, it was important for the brain-mind to have a way of loosening associations that would otherwise become fixed, leading, in Hartley's view, to insanity.

At age 18, I had never heard of David Hartley, and I had no idea that associationism implied that memory was plastic. All I knew was that if I was going to be entering Wesleyan as a sophomore the next fall I would have to pass those Oxford-Cambridge exams. I also knew, as Dean Spaeth had predicted, that I was learning things I would not encounter in school, in college, or even in medical school. I was learning to think for myself. I was learning psychology in an existential way. And through voluminous letter writing to my parents, I was learning to observe, to keep track of my observations, and to report on them. Most important, I was experimenting with pluralism and plasticity. There were many points of view, many ways of thinking, many ways of being, and many ways of communicating.

Science was one way of thinking, but I was still far from understanding how it worked. Poetry was another way of thinking, and its appeal to me was more direct than that of science. Romanticism was connected to poetry but extended into all corners of my life experience, including the positive emotional response to nature I had always felt. I came to see that every day, every person, and every experience was filled with observable novelty. I thus became a Romantic of subjective experience. I have no recollection and no written record of whether I had remembered dreams during those formative years. But as I interacted with people, I began to become interested in psychology. It was supposed to be a science of the mind, whether the conscious experience that I so enjoyed was recognized to be a part of it or not.

Psychology at Wesleyan

At Wesleyan, I discovered, to my dismay, that scientific psychology was pretty much restricted to investigating learning in rats. It was clear that rats might help us to understand learning, but I wanted to understand memory. Rats can learn, but they cannot report their memories if they have them. (Since rats don't have narrative, I now wonder if they have any memories at all.) After one semester of Psychology I-II, I dropped the course.

Clinical psychology had invaded both the humanities and the social sciences at Wesleyan. The university was a hotbed of Freudianism, with the classicist-turned-sociologist Norman O. Brown and the irresistibly charismatic professor of English Fred B. Millett providing much of the heat. Within the constraints imposed by my wish to complete my pre-medical laboratory requirements in three years, I took as many courses with Millett and Brown as I could. My honors thesis, which was on Freud and Dostoyevsky, allowed me to graduate with high distinction and to get into Harvard Medical School after only three years at Wesleyan.

I read all of Freud's and Dostoyevsky's major works during my junior and senior years at Wesleyan. In my thesis, I claimed that Freud's psychology flowed more directly from the romantic world view of writers like Dostoyevsky than from scientific observation. In order to develop my case, I got myself a carrel in the stacks of Olin Library. It was easy for me to ignore the grunts and groans of the players and the cheers and the boos of the crowds watching the varsity football and baseball teams that I had quit after a disheartening sophomore year spent rushing from the physics lab to the practice fields.

At that time, I was too young and too immature to be deeply critical of Freud's work. Not much of a dream watcher myself, I tended to take his theories on faith. But even then it had begun to dawn on me that psychoanalysis, however heady, was unbridled speculation and certainly was not experimental or even clinical science. Worse yet, psychoanalysis had nothing to do with the exquisite neurobiology that was being taught by the comparative anatomist Rudi Haffner and the cell physiologist Vincent Cochrane in the advanced biology courses of my Wesleyan pre-medical science program. From Haffner I learned that brains had evolved dramatically in the evolutionary transition from reptilian to mammalian species. From Cochrane I learned about Hodgkin and Huxley's model of the ionic basis of the action potential. But no one mentioned the EEG or how it changed in sleep. How strange, I thought, that psychology and the brain sciences were so separate! To me, they belonged together.

At Wesleyan there was some debate among faculty members about Freud's legitimacy, but critical scientists like Vince Cochrane were no verbal match for flamboyant humanists like Norman Brown, and I was seduced—as were many others in the 1950s and the 1960s—by the fundamentalism of Freud, which promised to remake the world in its own narcissistic and playful image. "Where ego was, there shall id be," declaimed Brown as he sailed a paper glider down from the balcony of the theatre where John Cage and David Tudor performed their "prepared piano" piece.

Adolescents often follow gurus thoughtlessly. Though I was enchanted by the rhetoric of Brown's Public Affairs 60 course on Freud and the Social

Eugene Aserinsky and family at a University of Chicago Physiology Department picnic in the early 1950s. Photo by Ralph Gerard.

Sciences, I was intuitively wary of his categorical pronouncements. When I bumped into him one spring day on High Street and proudly told him I would be going to Harvard Medical School, he scoffed at me: "What a waste!" At the time, I felt quite hurt and angry at this rejection of my chosen career path. Now I see how gullible and how intellectually short-sighted Brown was.

In 1953, budding behavioral biologists like me had no idea that Eugene Aserinsky, at the University of Chicago, was finding that young children had periods of brain activation and rapid eye movements in their sleep. And we blithely ignored the subsequent reports of William Dement suggesting that this REM sleep was the physiological substrate of intense dreaming. We didn't even notice that, in 1953, Crick and Watson had cracked the DNA code, setting the stage for the paradigm shift to molecular biology.

Fred Millett was much less doctrinaire and considerably more supportive of students like me than was Norman Brown. I chose him to be my thesis supervisor because I loved his courses, in which we read, among other great books, Tolstoy's *War and Peace* and *Anna Karenina*, Proust's *Swann's Way*, Joyce's *Ulysses*, and Dostoyevsky's *Crime and Punishment* and *The Brothers Karamazov*. Millett was inspiring to me because he was comfortable with and enthusiastic about these works and their authors. He seemed to like them as much as he liked us students. By reading those novels, I not only found the thesis project I needed to deepen my interest in systematic clinical psychology; I slowly began to appreciate that phenomenology was the study of conscious experience.

Later, living in Boston, I enjoyed reading all eight volumes of Proust's *Remembrance of Things Past* at the leisurely rate of ten pages a night before going to sleep. I was becoming aware that the mores of the Bostonians I knew were changing constantly and gradually, as had those of Proust's Parisian friends in the novel. I needed about ten years to notice the change. Between 1964, when I returned from Jouvet's lab in Lyon, and 1973, when I went to visit Jean-Didier Vincent in Bordeaux, I read all of Proust, not just once, but twice. By using the vicissitudes of his own states of consciousness as the subject matter of his novel, Proust had created a psychobiography of quasi-scientific quality. At the same time, he had observed the participants in his small corner of Parisian society keenly, noting their idiosyncrasies and their foibles with the clarity and love of a great clinician. I was inspired by him. During my clinical training at the Massachusetts

Mental Health Center and at the National Institute of Mental Health, I wrote detailed summaries of my patients' life experiences without ever matching Proust's acumen.

To follow the consciousness and the behavior of one person closely over a 24-hour period, as Joyce did in *Ulysses*, was a tour de force that I found appealing. But the novel itself was less than compelling, because it was so freighted with literary claptrap that it was difficult to read with unselfconscious pleasure. I now recognize that Joyce's focus on his hero's day was a forerunner of the paradigm that Bob Stickgold and I later came to call the Grand Mentation Project. Stickgold and I set out to record, measure, and analyze the brain-mind in action over a series of 24-hour periods by looking at the reports of conscious experience of sixteen subjects over fourteen successive days and nights. Joyce certainly captured the situation dependency of consciousness. But it seems to me that Joyce missed one fundamental point. Consciousness is state dependent. Dreaming, the state of greatest state dependency, eluded Joyce altogether.

What has remained of Proust's inspiration is my personal journal, in which more than 600 dream reports are recorded. I began this project at the age of 40, when I began to travel more widely, to live more wildly, and to think more ambitiously. As I have already mentioned, the journal now runs to 150 volumes. Besides dream reports, it includes notes of scientific meetings, first drafts of papers, feeble attempts at poetry and drawing, and thousands of photographs, some of which are artistically pleasing. In keeping the journal I was also consciously emulating Anaïs Nin and Henry Miller, who influenced me strongly during my early medical and scientific career.

6 Experimental Social Structures

Almost all of my friends were my lovers in one way or another. Affection was what I craved, and touching was the most natural expression of affection. Like a naturalist, I was always watching my own life as my brain's desires played themselves out before my eyes. My love life was certainly experimental. Opportunism and lust combined with external factors to help me explore new kinds of intimacy.

By 1939, when we moved to Asylum Avenue in Hartford, I had already learned to play "doctor" and had more or less decided to become a doctor when I grew up. The idea of being paid to indulge my curiosity about the body was as persuasive as the salary inducement that recruited me to the choir of St. John's Church. Both urges were instinctual. They came from my brain. I wanted to see, to probe, to sing, to entertain, and to experience pleasure because my brain was wired to do so. My brain and I could have been more powerfully conditioned *not* to indulge those impulses, but instead we were handsomely rewarded by the consequences of indulgence.

My companions in my early experimental days were two boys and two girls, all younger than me and all quite willing accomplices in the woodland adventures that I have already described. This part of my brain odyssey began when I was 6 years old and ended when I was 12. One of my most persistent interests was in the female sexual anatomy. "Show me" was the name of the game we played to indulge that interest. Though I looked and looked at female external genitalia, I didn't get the picture of what was going on inside until much later in life. One problem was that we were all immature in both mind and body; another was the absence of educational materials, especially diagrams. Until I was at least 10 years old, I had no idea how babies were born. I recall my disbelief when Jack Leonard told me that babies resulted from the deposition of fluid from the penis in the vagina. Jack's insistence on the accuracy of his model impressed me, and when it was later confirmed by our junior high school hygiene teacher, Don Wilson (also our basketball coach), I became convinced.

To say that I was sexually precocious is both an understatement and an error. My curiosity and my experimentalism were precocious, but my sexual activity was laggard. I began kissing girls, in class, in first grade, and I have kept on kissing them, though not in class, ever since. But I was confused by the stylized pin-ups and the centerfold nudes I saw in the magazines *Esquire* and *Coronet*: they showed neither pubic hair nor vaginas. My first exposure to pornography, which probably occurred when I was about 10, was to a set of photos of an Italian prostitute.

I remember my father's awkward offer to tell me about sex. One day, when we were driving to West Hartford Center for a haircut, Dad asked me if I needed his instruction in the "facts of life." "I already know all that," I replied, even though it wasn't true. I didn't have a clue.

My adolescence was as painful as it was exciting. I flirted with delinquency as much as with girls. When my face broke out in pimples, I spent long hours in the bathroom, looking at myself in the mirror. Out in the world I imagined that everyone was looking at me, noting my inadequacies, and rejecting me out of hand.

Unbeknownst to me then, the organ behind my eyes, my brain, was pumping hormones into my bloodstream as I slept. Out of my hypothalamus and my pituitary gland came huge pulses of the growth and prolactin hormones that were responsible for my painful bodily metamorphosis. As I mentioned in chapter 5, this happened each time I slept deeply. I was in the grips of an internal brain mechanism over which I had no control and of which I was completely ignorant. And yet the self, which I and others regarded as a mind function, was required to take full responsibility for this alien abduction. After all, wasn't it "I" who had suddenly sprouted pubic and armpit hair? It was certainly I who was reprimanded for popping those pimples and spotting the bathroom mirror. During the four difficult years that transformed me from a boy into a young man, my brain and its sleep were going through a genetically programmed process that "I" was expected to welcome, to master, and even to celebrate. I had lots of help with this, but I needed much more than I got.

I must have been 12 or 13 when I first succeeded in masturbating. Tommy Wilson, who was a year older, showed me and his younger brother how he did it. We masturbated together, but we were not lovers.

My first love affair was with Sebastian Bonanno. At age 14, he was short, muscular, and very passionate. When Sebastian made it clear that he wanted to be friends with me, I was flattered. All through eighth grade, we spent hours alone together, either in the attic of the house on Meadowbrook Road where he lived with his immigrant mother or in my bedroom on Asylum Avenue (which my mother never entered if the door was closed).

Sebastian knew all the Italo-Americans in West Hartford center. The barber, the shoemaker, and the podiatrist were all my friends if I was Sebastian's friend. Those Italians had made a warm village out of the socially chilly New England town that was West Hartford. And Sebastian knew how to love with gusto as well as to insist, with operatic intensity, on amorous fidelity.

At the end of eighth grade, the balance of sexual power changed with the politics of education. Having failed to get into the Loomis School on my first try, I went back to Sedgwick Junior High. Sebastian went on to Hall High School. I went to baseball games and cheered when Sebastian hit a home run. Then Page Sharp entered the picture. All these factors made it difficult for Sebastian and me to continue our relationship. But Sebastian would not give up until I had wrestled him free of the jackknife that he had unfolded, threatening to kill himself. Operatically, I threw Sebastian's jackknife into Trout Brook and, like Pinkerton in *Madame Butterfly*, walked away from my wounded friend.

I traded Sebastian Bonanno in for Page Sharp, nicknamed Cupie, who had put his hand in my pants during one of my first testing sessions in his office. Maybe the fact that it felt good helped me accept his explanation that an examination of my private parts was clinically necessary. Every time I went to his office we enjoyed some sort of physical intimacy. My relationship with Page Sharp lasted until the end of my junior year at Loomis, when I decided to break it off myself. Frightened at the possible emotional consequences, I consulted my father, who was neither surprised nor shocked but simply said "Cupie is a nice man who will understand if you tell him gently." In the current climate of concern about sexual abuse, this story will probably excite the same discomfort in many readers as it did in many 1950s parents. As Proust points out, love takes many forms, and times change. I will not try to convince anyone about the rightness or wrongness of my love affair with Page Sharp, nor will I deny that it contributed to the sexual corner-cutting in my post-1960s life. What I will try to do is show how this relationship nourished me and how it shaped my life's work by tying my passion and my intellect together.

I have never regretted my love for Cupie. Through him, I was introduced to neuropsychology, to European mores, and to the enjoyment of good food and wine as natural pleasures. Cupie himself was a sexually inhibited product of Anglo-Saxon Victorianism whose experiences in Europe had changed him into something of a sexual maverick. I was happy to follow in his footsteps.

Introduction to Neuropsychology

Page Sharp's testing me for eligibility at Loomis was an indication of his faith in quantitative measures of brain activity. He used the Wechsler Adult Intelligence Scale (WAIS) and the Wechsler Bellevue Intelligence Scale to establish his clients' levels of intellectual ability. But Sharp's clinical interests were more sharply focused than that. He wanted to understand, to diagnose, and to treat dyslexia. One reason for Sharp's interest in me was that I had the pattern of mixed cerebral dominance that was a risk factor for dyslexia. I was left-handed (and left-footed). That's not as unusual as was then supposed. But I was right-eyed. That explained, said Sharp, why I threw the baseball with my left hand but batted right-handed—a fact that had always puzzled me. But why, as a "mixed dominant," didn't I have trouble with reading or writing? Why, moreover, was I so good at just those skills that might have been impaired? Sharp said that these were questions that could be answered only by brain research.

Brain research was a goal that Page Sharp himself never reached. Would I, at age 15, be willing to complete his life plan? Sharp told me that if I really wanted to make progress in neuropsychology, I would have to go to medical school. This was not strictly true. I could have gotten a Ph.D. and still done brain research. But then I could not have become a psychiatrist, treated patients, or prescribed medication. And Sharp had an even more specific goal for me: to complete the course at Harvard Medical School, which he had left in 1915, after his freshman year, to join the French Medical Corps.

So here we have a man in his early fifties and a boy of 15 who needed each other to become something neither of them could become alone. I was thrilled to become Page Sharp's psychology trainee and lover. It felt right to me. And my parents were amazed and pleased when, under Cupie's demanding influence, I stopped getting "could do better" comments on my report cards. Cupie said there was no excuse for anything less than excellence. My motivation was palpable. Suddenly I loved school because I could see where it might lead. And, as Sharp had predicted, I was a very good student at a very good school. From there my brain odyssey could lead almost anywhere.

In the summers of 1949 and 1950, while the scientific world was struggling to deal with Moruzzi and Magoun's concept of the reticular formation, I worked at Page Sharp's Camp Waya-Awi in Rangeley. There were 50 faculty members and 100 students. Each student got at least two hours of individual instruction every day. Sharp ran the camp with enormous energy, humor, and enthusiasm.

My official job at Camp Waya-Awi was to wash dishes and be a cook's helper in the kitchen, which was under the direct supervision of Laura Sharp, Page's wife. Laura was as tough as she was lovely. "More ammonia!" she would call, pouring half a bottle into the sink while I gagged as I washed the grease-caked cooking pans. Maybe she was getting even with me for being her husband's lover. In any case, washing dishes was my day job. My night job, which interested me more, was to be Page Sharp's office assistant and confidant.

To quantify the effects of eight weeks of one-on-one tutoring, Sharp and I gave all 180 students at the camp a battery of learning tests at the beginning of the summer and repeated the same battery of tests at the end. I scored the tests and I entered the data on graph paper so that the skill profiles of each student before and after tutoring could be directly visualized and compared. Using the data, Sharp compiled a detailed report for the school and the parents of each student.

The Work Ethic and the Sybaritic Lifestyle

On Saturday nights at Rangely, Page Sharp and I would fill a boat with steaks, lobsters, and other special foods that I had taken out of the large barrels that had been delivered to the camp kitchen by truck from Portland. These victuals had been carefully squirreled away by me in the kitchen's walk-in ice box. Sharp would invite three or four other boys to go with us to his cabin across the lake (called Ganderwood, a mildly suggestive play on the word 'goose') for a cookout, a sing-along, and a sleep-over. Sharp taught us how to grill steaks, how to drink martinis, and how to sing songs as he played the piano. Later, we slipped in and out of his bed for kisses, hugs, and mutual masturbation.

A European influence was strongly evident in the Sharps' house in Hartford. I had dinner there with the Sharps every Wednesday night during my three years at the Loomis School. When I would arrived, Cupie would talk about his day, his thoughts, and his memories. His years in France (1915–1918) had marked him deeply. His stories of what he saw, what he felt, and what he said to soldiers undergoing hand-saw amputations of shell-maimed limbs (without anesthesia) made me a more determined pacifist then my own deep fear of war had already done. The violence

Page and Laura Sharp sitting on a bench outside the Camp Waya-Awi office in Rangeley, Maine, in the summer of 1950. They are joined by their poodles, Tico and Rousseau, to whom Page Sharp spoke French (while the poodles only growled, in dog, in return). This is a clear example of the difference between secondary consciousness (the Sharps) and primary consciousness (their dogs). Sharp was trained by the dyslexia expert, Samuel Orton, in New York and consulted widely to private schools throughout New England. Photo by Deford Dechert.

that Cupie witnessed at the front in France was matched in intensity by the sex he experienced in French towns and cities when on leave.

I never got to see Cupie's World War I journals; he burned them in a fit of pique. But I did receive letters, mostly handwritten—occasionally short notes but more frequently epistles running to ten, fifteen, or even twenty pages. They were letters about life which focused on feelings. There was nothing cold or analytical about Cupie's philosophy. It was warm, vivid, and very much situated in the here and now. Cupie's model rolled mentor, parent, and lover into one and influenced my approach to family life, to my work with laboratory colleagues, and to my work with patients (although I was never indiscreet with a patient).

To the best of my recollection, Sigmund Freud was never mentioned once in any of my conversations with Cupie.

The Cult of Virginity

Page Sharp was married, had two children, boasted of sexual conquests of French women, and thus was at least perfunctorily heterosexual. Today he might be called bisexual. There was never any effort on his part to deflect my strong heterosexual yearnings. They proceeded full speed ahead but always hit the wall of the virginity culture that surrounded me. As in the British Public Schools, homosexuality was the only sexual outlet available to unmarried young men. I had heard about prostitutes, but I never saw one before I went to England and France at age 18. Meanwhile, everyone talked about "getting laid," and some even claimed they had done so, but it would probably be closer to the truth to say that almost no one who lived in the genteel suburbs of New England in the early 1950s had sexual intercourse before they were at least 18. I was 22 when I first did. That wasn't for lack of girlfriends, time spent dancing cheek to cheek, or groping in the dark in cars, on porches, and on parlor couches. We would lie for hours in a drunken semi-coma, feeling with our hands for all of those fascinating and still mysterious body parts that we were allowed neither to have seen or to have used for any natural act. Besides Daniella Davis, my most passionate partner, I enjoyed flurries of puppy love with Blannie Dew and with Serena Valverde (my ideal woman throughout my adolescence, and my mother's choice for my wife).

I might well have married Serena were it not for the psychological crisis that took her away from me at the very time that I was pressing hard for more intimacy with her. I was well into my Wesleyan thesis and my reading of *Freud's Collected Works* when Serena was carried out of her mother's house by her father and taken to New Jersey. He was rescuing her from the woman he had divorced, who Serena thought was trying to kill her. Suddenly, the young would-be psychoanalyst was put squarely face to face with a classical nineteenth-century neurosis. Serena's symptoms seemed distinctly psychogenic, hysterical, and Oedipal. Several months later, with my Random House edition of *Freud's Collected Works* in my knapsack, I hitch-hiked to the New Jersey town where Serena's father had secreted her. There I found my love lying in bed, hovered over by her father, who never left us alone for a minute.

How very Victorian! I felt myself a failed Robert Browning, because instead of rescuing my own Elizabeth Barrett, I abandoned her. Why did I flee? I felt that I was being pushed and pulled by forces that were more powerful, deeper, and more dangerous than I could manage. So I sadly left Serena in her sick bed in New Jersey. With a sense of cowardly guilt, I hitch-hiked back to Wesleyan, back to my thesis, and back to my career path, which was now set more firmly on course by these very personal evidences of psychopathology.

Marriage

I might have married Blannie. But when I went to England for my exchange year at Sutton Valence, Blannie fell in love with my friend John Maloney. She married him soon after I got back. I cried at the wedding. I didn't want my friendship with Blannie to end. Luckily for both of us, it didn't. Now a very competent psychotherapist, she is happily married to the psychiatrist Edward Swain. We still see one another often, always with great pleasure.

In the summer of 1953, after my first year at Wesleyan, I met the woman who would become my first wife, Joan Harlowe. My Dutch exchange student friend Frank Tysen insisted that I come to Martha's Vineyard for the long Fourth of July weekend. Frank and Joan were working at the Harbor View Hotel on North Water Street in Edgartown. Joan was lovely and well educated. On our first date I could see that she was a bit shy, but definitely available and, I thought, socially flexible. Despite the geographical and psychological distance between us (she was attending Colby College, way up north in Maine), our romance flourished.

When I first met Joan, she was a bit lost. But she was quick to respond to my soaring goals, to my high level of energy, and to my strong need for intimate companionship. We spent the whole summer of 1954 together, working at the Harbor View Hotel. We were able to get together easily at holiday times, because our families' homes (one in Hartford, one in Providence) were only a two-hour hitch-hike apart. We both loved good books, good beaches, and good parties. We were strongly attracted to each other.

But in our path was that virginity cult, of which Joan's mother was a particularly vociferous exponent. By 1956 we were ready to consummate our liaison, virginity cult or not. When Joan graduated from Colby and I had finished my first year at Harvard Medical School, Joan said we could not live together in Cambridge, as I had suggested, without being married. So we got married.

My marriage to Joan was unbalanced and ill-fated from the start. I naively thought—following the psychoanalytic theories then being strongly promoted—that Joan would come out of her shell, develop strong intellectual and career interests of her own, and evolve into the super woman

Joan and Ian Hobson in France. When I worked with Michel Jouvet in Lyon (1963–64), I made excursions into the local countryside. I took this photo during a visit to the Palais Ideale of the Facteur Cheval in the valley of the Drome. Cheval was a postman who filled his mailbag with stones as he made his rounds. When he returned home, he used the stones to construct his ideal palace. The art instinct is universal and springs from within us. Even humble humans like the Facteur Cheval are naturally creative. My first wife, Joan, and my oldest son, Ian, are both good sleepers and creative people.

that I needed as a life companion. That did not occur. Joan was a good wife, and she was a fine mother to our three children, Ian, Christopher, and Julia, but she remained shy and I was never satisfied with our relationship. So I constantly surrounded myself with other male and female friends.

I was so busy at medical school and so committed to my upwardly mobile social life that I missed the excitement that was then building in behavioral neurobiology. Joan shared my disdain for psychoanalysis, but neither of us could envisage the obvious alternative provided by the emerging cognitive neuroscience of mental states. I did not learn of Aserinsky and Kleitman's 1953 discovery of REM until 1960, when I met Irwin Kremen in the library of the Massachusetts Mental Health Center. Irwin was working with David Shapiro and Bernie Tursky in the psychophysiology lab, trying to replicate the Chicago findings.

It took a long time for the state paradigm to become clear, and chance had a lot to do with my later initiation into sleep and dream research. My skepticism, my moral indignation, and my refusal to accept received ideas played important parts, too. To her credit, Joan shared and supported these intellectual concerns, even when our series of relocations caused us great inconvenience.

Social Life in Boston

I decided, early in medical school, that I should develop a social network outside of the constricting professional context of medicine. This motive was strengthened when I decided to go into psychiatry because almost all of my colleagues were headed for psychoanalysis and practiced it on each other. In contrast with the camaraderie and the psychologically uninhibited atmosphere I sought in my time off, my pro-Freudian colleagues indulged in constant psychological gossip about themselves and about our teachers. I found it tiresome to be with such people.

I also wanted a social life that was mature and urbane, not a continuation of the fraternity-style drinking parties that I witnessed in Vanderbilt Hall, Harvard's residence for medical students.

At Wesleyan I had learned to play squash—a game that later would help me to meet many of my lifelong friends—through Roger Prouty, a displaced Bostonian who was eager to make me his sports and social companion. When I went to Harvard Medical School, Roger went to MIT to teach history in the expanding humanities program. Soon we were meeting to play squash at the Union Boat Club and spending weekends at his house on Nauset Beach on Cape Cod. I joined the boat club and became a Massachusetts squash champion. In the boat club's sauna, I met Peter Thomson. At the Tennis and Racquet Club, I met Louis Kane. Peter and Louis became the nucleus of my lifelong network of Bostonian friends.

The Sexual Revolution

In Boston in the late 1950s, the first rumblings of the sexual revolution could be heard. By 1960, this rumbling had become a tumultuous roar that even the sexually deaf could not ignore. Dinner parties on Beacon Hill— with dancing till 3 a.m.—soon assumed a more intimate character as extra-marital affairs grew so commonplace as to achieve statistical, if not moral, normality. I had been married for four years when I had my first fling. It was wonderful. At last, I thought, I could have a love life unencumbered by domestic squabbles, emotional quibbles, and post-Depression economics.

But how to manage the intense jealousy that I felt when my wife enjoyed her own newfound sexual privileges? Our notions of open marriage were overturned. "Don't ask and don't tell" became our policy. I followed it for 25 years. When children came and my work became all-absorbing, there was little time and space for dalliance. But I found what little time and space there was to be more than enough, especially when I discovered love in France. Love, as Cupie had told me, was wilder and easier in France than in the United States, even after 1960. The French, who had learned to wink at double standards, found an eager proselyte in me.

Between 1962, when I worked in Michel Jouvet's lab, and 1986, when my marriage fell apart, I had three French female companions. One of them is now dead, another has divorced and remarried, and the third is still married and still my friend. My tactic, during this long French period (1962–1986), was to extend a visit to Europe for a professional meeting in order to spend a few days with my girlfriends. In this way, vacation, travel, and the good vegetative life were integrated. Moreover, because my expenses were paid by my scientific hosts, the stingy part of me was tempered and the puritanical part that didn't want to cheat on my wife was at least financially assuaged.

"If you love France so much," French friends kept telling me, "you should go to Italy!" And I did go to Italy—more and more frequently after 1977, when my dream theory was first unfurled. Sometimes I went with French friends and sometimes I went alone. In 1984, I was taken to Sicily for the first time by the last of my French lady companions. Now I live there with my second family. Life in Italy is theatrical and it is passionate, though Italy is not as libertine as France.

Between 1973 and 1995, I was experiencing the change of sexual interest that is so common in men over 40. I was increasingly attracted to younger partners, often 10, 20, or even 24 years younger. The reasons are obvious. The disparity in the effects of age on male and female sexual behavior is related to fertility. With my several younger American lovers, I took advantage of that disparity without ever fathering a child or wanting to do so. This was admittedly inequitable. But I was completely honest about my interests, and those discreet relationships worked as well for most of my partners as they did for me.

Divorce

As Joan aged and struggled with her own career as an arts administrator, she grew less and less happy with me. We divorced in 1992, probably at least 10 years too late. But in 1982 our daughter Julia was only 10 years old, and I felt sure that I did not want to marry any of my friends. (Why spoil a wonderful romance?) I also felt deeply devoted to Joan, to our three children, and to the rich social life we had in Brookline and at our farm in Vermont. Many of the people who had been our compliant collaborators in the heady experimental days of the 1960s had become great friends. I thought a divorce would threaten that precious social network, so I opposed Joan's desire to divorce me even more vigorously than I had opposed her wish to be married in the first place. I thought that we had made our bed together and should lie in it.

Once she discovered the extent of my infidelity—in 1985, by surreptitiously going to my office and reading my journal—it became increasingly difficult, and finally impossible, for her to be intimate with me. This probably is another important difference between men and women. Even though she had the same freedom as me, once she had exercised that freedom she wanted to marry her lover. And so she did. I have never had that feeling.

Between 1980 and 1990 my affairs with younger American women were exciting accompaniments to the creative spirit that was flourishing in my art life as well as in my science life. The Dreamstage exhibition, conceived in 1975 when I was 42, was produced in 1977, when I was 44. Dreamstage continued to require major investments of my time and energy until 1985, when I was 51. It still interests me today.

Critics might attribute my adulterous behavior during the years 1960–1985 to a midlife crisis. It certainly was an effective antidote to the effects of age on my body and my brain. I found myself invigorated intellectually, scientifically, and even poetically by these relationships, and I do not regret

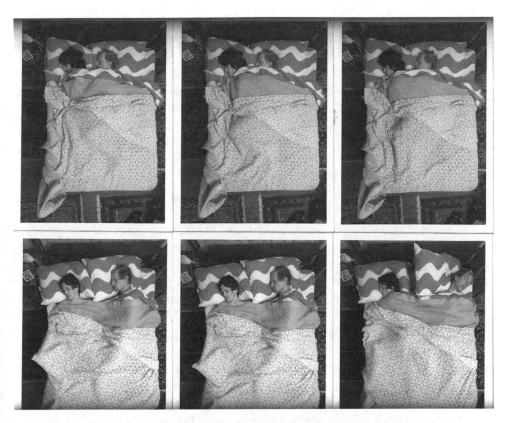

Sleep portrait of Joan and me, 1976. Theodore Spagna was the first photographer to document the posture shifts of normal sleep. Spagna's photographs of sleeping couples celebrate the elaborate synchrony of shared intimacy. When couples sleep in narrow beds like this one, they tend to synchronize their NREM-REM sleep cycles via the mutual stimulation of their movements. Sleep posture shifts can, in turn, be used to diagnose brain state and to give quantitative indices of sleep quality. This simple technique led us to invent the Nightcap, a two-channel event recorder.

them. I am sorry to have hurt anyone, especially Joan and my children. I never wanted to abandon any of my lovers. I just wanted them to be with me in ways that, for one reason or another, became impossible.

The Two Bobs

My two principal collaborators during my laboratory career (1968–2003) were Robert McCarley and Robert Stickgold, both nicknamed Bob. I always felt that I should work alone, and I never sought out collaborators. It is to the credit of the two Bobs that things worked out as well as they did.

McCarley and Stickgold were brilliant, quantitatively inclined, scientifically talented, personally pleasant men without whom my life and my
work would not have been the same.

I first met Bob McCarley in 1964 when I returned to Harvard from
Michel Jouvet's lab in Lyon. By then, I had decided to work on the brain
basis of REM sleep and dreaming, to focus on the brainstem, and to use
single-cell recording to try to get at the triggering mechanisms at that level.
As part of my residency work at the Massachusetts Mental Health Center
(which I finished by working half-time in the years 1964–1966), I decided
to offer a seminar for residents interested in research.

Bob McCarley was one of the few MMHC residents who stuck with that
seminar. He was certainly the brightest and the most highly motivated. He
presented an excellent overview of Edward Evart's work without knowing
that Ed had been one of my mentors at the National Institute of Mental
Health (NIMH) and without knowing that I was then trying hard to get
the Evarts-Hubel method for recording individual nerve cells working in
the Physiology Department at Harvard Medical School. McCarley understood, right away, how useful this approach might be. And he perceived,
far better than I did, that the data would require sophisticated quantitative
analysis.

When McCarley first asked if he could help me out in the lab, I demurred,
saying, quite honestly, that I wasn't far enough along to offer him anything in the way of mentorship. Despite my discouragement—or perhaps
because of it—McCarley was very persistent. He kept coming around to see
me in the small, dingy backroom of Elwood Henneman's lab in Building
C of the Harvard Medical School. By 1968 I had gotten my own first grant
and had moved to the Massachusetts Mental Health Center, in Boston's
Longwood Medical Area, to set up shop. McCarley was on board the
U-Haul truck we rented to move our equipment. We first got him a
National Institutes of Health Special Fellowship when I was finally able to
give up mine. By then I was receiving full-time salary support from the
Commonwealth of Massachusetts. Thereafter, McCarley and our early
work were supported by my NIH grant.

Bob McCarley and I were very different in our personalities, our skills,
and our lifestyles. For that reason our efforts were complimentary. I was
good at surgery, at tinkering with apparatus, and at generating optimism
and enthusiasm for experiments that most of my mentors and colleagues
thought were impossible, useless, or both. I was sure that I could find novel
and surprising evidence of the brainstem cellular and molecular mechanisms of state regulation.

I thought that the brain must be the seat of subjectivity. But how was subjectivity organized by the brain? I thought that understanding the brain basis of the differences in subjectivity that distinguished dreaming and waking might help us to answer this question.

I had the mistaken belief that this revelation would be qualitative. And in an ultimate sense the revolutionary revelation *was* qualitative. Our discovery of REM-off cells in the locus coeruleus was a completely unanticipated breakthrough from which everything that was original in our theories flowed. Before 1975, when we found those REM-off neurons, we had spent seven years working with the painstaking quantitative methods of data analysis that Bob McCarley championed, spearheaded, and mastered. In emphasizing this role division, I do not mean to suggest that Bob was not an idea man or that he didn't work well with his hands. He did both. But what was most remarkable about Bob was his capacity to focus on computational and mathematical details.

McCarley insisted that we get ourselves trained to operate the Department of Physiology's PDP-12 computer. For two weeks in the spring of 1969, we drove together each morning to the Digital Equipment Corporation's plant in Maynard to take a two-week course in machine-language programming. Soon we wanted a computer of our own. After a tense struggle with peers who didn't see things our way, we got one. We won the day when I said that doing extracellular unit recording in the late twentieth century without a computer was like farming without a tractor.

I was often frustrated and maddened by McCarley's immersion in statistics. Clouds of pipe smoke encircled his head as he twirled his hair whorl, read, and calculated. Bob McCarley was a bit like Young Edward Lorenz. When he was thinking, you couldn't get to him. But Bob was much more social than Lorenz, and lots more fun. When I organized the sixth annual meeting of the Sleep Research Society in Boston, in 1969, we suffered all the normal logistical snafus and professional prima donna assaults that make meeting organizers swear they will never do it again. I think it was my idea to offer a prize for the best pseudo-scientific abstract. Bob's entry, titled "Sleep '69," was a spoof of our own scientific efforts. Bob has a great sense of humor as well as a keen intelligence.

Separation

In 1984, when Bob McCarley moved to the Brockton facility of the V.A. Boston Healthcare System, we had worked closely together for 16 years. Bob was seeking scientific independence and a larger share of the recognition that our work received (which tended to be focused on me). But he was also seeking an academic promotion, and our Psychiatry Department's chairman, Miles Shore, said he did not think he could support two professors working on the same subject at the same hospital—especially if that subject was sleep.

Sleep research was not mainstream psychiatry. And sleep research was also the orphan child of physiology, so it tended to fall through the academic cracks, even in the mid 1980s. Now there are more than 100 people working full-time at Harvard on sleep, because it is a natural focus for multidisciplinary, integrative research on physiology and because it is directly relevant to a science of consciousness.

I regret the friction that administrative rifts caused in the lab at a time when our science was going so well. And I regret the fact that Harvard was not really there for us when we needed its backing. Miles Shore's breaking up the Hobson-McCarley collaboration was particularly difficult to accept because Shore's own avowed academic interest was in the collaborative work of "creative pairs." The NIMH was unstinting in its support, and Bob McCarley easily got his own grant and a career fellowship award to pay his salary. He even masterminded a training program to help him recruit students. By 1984 it probably was time for us to go our separate ways, but it would have been better for us to separate naturally rather than under a political gun. Separating from Bob was almost as painful as my divorce from Joan, but I handled it better.

Since his move to Brockton, Bob McCarley's career has blossomed in ways that could never have happened at the Massachusetts Mental Health Center. Our hospital and its research effort had been under severe stress from about 1980 until the hospital closed in 2003. In-patient care was abandoned, and the Commonwealth of Massachusetts turned its back on the basic science that is so crucial to understanding how the brain creates its normal and abnormal mental states. Knowing how dreaming is organized by the brain is a big step in the direction of understanding the pathologic conditions with which it shares formal features.

By now, you know that by formal features I mean those mental phenomena that beset our patients when they were awake: hallucinations, delusions, cognitive defects, emotional intensifications, and memory loss. Luckily for us normal people, we experience these difficulties only while asleep. And we don't usually remember them.

For me, the loss of Bob McCarley as co-worker and colleague was partially compensated by the energy, imagination, and support of Ralph Lydic and Helen Baghdoyan, who had begun working with both Bob and me as postdoctoral students in the mid 1980s. Ralph and Helen helped me to regain a temporary lapse in grant support and to move our program forward at a difficult time. The position paper that we wrote for the journal *Behavioral and Brain Sciences* in 1986 let the NIH and our colleagues know that we were still a force to be reckoned with. But when Ralph and Helen fell in love with each other and decided to go to the Penn State Medical School in Hershey in 1990, I felt abandoned.

Teaching at Harvard

Ever since the Dreamstage exhibition (1977), I had enjoyed contact with the art world at Harvard. I was often invited to events like the luncheon I attended one day in 1989 in honor of one of Ingmar Bergmann's actors. By chance, I was seated next to Dean Michael Shinagel of the Harvard Extension School, who recruited me—on the spot—to teach a course on sleep science.

When Mike Shinagel said "We pay well," I was hooked. I had never been paid to teach at Harvard. In fact, I had never been much encouraged to teach at all up to that point. Having by then written *The Dreaming Brain* (1988) and *Sleep* (1989), I had no difficulty constructing a thirty-lecture course, which I called "The Neuropsychology of Sleeping, Waking, and Dreaming." Beginning in 1991, the course was given in fifteen two-hour Monday evening sessions during the spring term at Harvard College.

That course, which completed its tenth year in 2000, was as popular and as rewarding as it was demanding. In 1990 it was taken by about forty students, including Robert Stickgold, Jane Merritt, David Kahn, and Cynthia Rittenhouse, all of whom would later become my collaborators in what might be called the third phase of my work. (The first phase, 1968–1975, was neurophysiological, the second, 1975–1990, neuropharmacological, and the third neuropsychological.)

Cognitive neuroscience is another name for what we did in the third phase (1990–2003). That name came from the other new activity that enriched my intellectual life: the John D. and Catherine T. MacArthur Foundation's Research Network on Mind-Body Interactions, which began in 1990 and lasted a decade.

Integration

The task of integrating dream psychology and sleep physiology, which had motivated me from the start, suddenly had an outlet via my course in the

Harvard Extension School and the supportive framework of the Research Network on Mind-Body Interactions. Both activities gave the psychology of dreaming a legitimacy and an appeal that it had previously lacked. Before 1990, I felt that Harvard and the NIMH were both more interested in basic neuroscience than in the applications of that science to psychology, psychiatry, and philosophy. But if it was called cognitive neuroscience, the study of sleep and dreaming could take its rightful place at the integrative table.

It was cognitive neuroscience that brought Bob Stickgold and me together and helped our collaboration to flourish. When Bob first came to me in the fall of 1990 wondering about a job, I had only my basic science grant and no position to offer him. Despite an excellent formal education in neurobiology and biochemistry, Bob had not worked in science for ten years. It seemed unlikely that we would find the means to work together. But we did. As in Bob McCarley's case, persistence, talent, and goodwill paid off. I told Stickgold "You can work as a volunteer for a year and we'll see how it goes." During that time, we needed to find a workable problem and a source of funding.

I had been studying dreaming in earnest since 1986 and had already had some success in quantifying mental-state phenomena to map onto the brain phenomena we had unearthed with our microelectrodes. But we needed an intermediate program. With support from the MacArthur Foundation, Bob Stickgold got a scientific handhold that enabled him to create an entirely new way of looking at the effects of sleep on the mind. Our intermediate program was a way of studying the mind entirely objectively. The behavioristic goal of experimental psychology had become the goal of cognitive science. Humans performed cognitive tasks, and from the reaction-time data that were generated the underlying brain mechanisms were deduced.

I was recruited into the Research Network on Mind-Body Interactions to help answer Murray Gell-Mann's challenge: Solve the mind-body problem! Murray said that since physicists had so easily solved the problem of sub-atomic structure then surely physiology-minded psychologists could find out how the mind really worked. Robert Rose (a psychiatrist at the University of Texas at Galveston) became our director. Ken Hugdahl (a psychophysiologist from Bergen, Norway), Arthur Kleinman (an anthropologist at the Harvard Medical School), and I were the founding members of the network.

Altered states of consciousness—sleep, dreaming, and hypnosis—were early and persistent themes of the group's deliberations. I myself was privately convinced that the mind-body problem was nonexistent or had already been solved. But I didn't reveal that I harbored such heretical thoughts, since I was at last being encouraged to do the work I had waited all my life to do.

In the early days of the Research Network on Mind-Body Interactions, we cast about for a handle with which to examine mind-brain integration. We came up with attention, the mental capacity that was most central to our shared interests. In addition to sleep, we considered hypnosis and trance to be states of altered consciousness that we thought might be pursued with the tools of attention research. We consulted with Mike Posner, who had done exemplary work on attention in St. Louis and in Oregon. Mike also shared our interest in sleep. He generously educated me about the classic tasks used to study attention, including semantic priming and perceptual cuing. Bob Stickgold and I set out to study the effects of sleep on those tasks.

Like his predecessor Bob McCarley, Bob Stickgold was a naturally talented computer analyst. In this case, the computer was used not just to crunch numbers from neurons but also to run experiments, to keep track of sleep as it happened, and to analyze and illustrate sleeps effects on attention. We were able to show that subjects awakened from REM sleep were not only likely to give reports of bizarre dreams but also likely to show hyperassociative cognition in tests of what is called semantic priming.

Semantic priming is the conditioning of brain networks to recognize words more rapidly if they have been associated with previous verbal stimuli. By means of this paradigm, we felt that we were indeed objectifying subjectivity. With the help of other students recruited from my extension school course at Harvard College and young psychiatrists from the MMHC residency, we were also able to greatly increase our attention to such details of dream consciousness as dream emotion (Jane Merritt, Roar Fosse), the orientational sequencing of dreams (Jeff Sutton), face recognition in dreams (David Kahn), and the memory sources of dreams (Ed Pace-Schott, Roar Fosse, Magdalena Fosse).

Ed Schott took my Harvard Extension School course in 1991 and came to be a staff member in the same way as Bob Stickgold. By resuscitating the laboratory seminar, Ed has played a major role in helping me and my other colleagues to communicate with each other and with the literature (which he carries on his back in his computer knapsack and shoulder bag full of reprints.) Ed has also collaborated effectively in our recent spate of monographs and reviews.

Within a year, Bob Stickgold and I had enough pilot results to ask the NIMH for a new grant in sleep cognition, and we were ultimately successful in funding that program. We focused on the functional implications of memory changes in sleep. Building on our growing interest and experience with cognitive science, Ed Schott and I then persuaded the National Institute on Drug Abuse to fund a study of sleep and cognition in cocaine addicts.

Until November of 2003, the laboratory was humming. We had programs in basic neuroscience, in cognitive neuroscience, and in sleep medicine. All well funded, they were well managed by a team of ten. The loop between education and professional life was as tightly closed as the loop between mind and brain. Both loops are integrated, self-reinforcing, and self-organizing.

III The Nature of My Experiments

7 Psychoanalysis as Thesis

My curiosity about the body and my strong need to investigate its workings drove me naturally to experimental medicine. In previous chapters, I have given accounts of the many ways that this drive to see and to understand human physiology emerged in my childhood play, in my adventures in the woods, and in my early education. By age 10, I was convinced that nature was both fascinating and understandable. By that time I had also come to see experimentation as the best defense against superstition and belief. Why, then, did I not proceed—like Young Edward Lorenz—to a career in pure science? And why, instead, was I so taken in by the pseudo-science of Sigmund Freud? In other words, why did it take me so long to find my career paths in the neurophysiology and the neuropsychology of sleep and dreaming?

One obvious answer is that I was nowhere near as bright as Edward Lorenz. And the corollary to this shortcoming is that I was much more extroverted and sociable than Young Edward and therefore more easily influenced by what other people thought, felt, and said. Another answer is that I was not exposed to compelling models of experimental science until I got to medical school. Yes, I did have encouragement: from my father, who helped me build a chemistry lab in our cellar at age 10; from my uncle, Harry Sanborn, who taught me and my cousin Jim to make gunpowder in his laboratory at the National Can Association in Washington when we were 12; and from Page Sharp, who told me when I was 15 that if I wanted to study the mind I needed to find out about the brain.

But none of these people was really an experimental scientist. Nor were the science teachers that I met in high school or even in college really scientists. I knew that Rudi Haffner, my professor of comparative anatomy at Wesleyan, was interested in bioluminescence and studied the light organs of deep-sea fishes. But that subject seemed so arcane to me that I never visited Rudi's lab. I can now see that Rudi's work was a kind of neurobiology, but that wasn't at all clear to me in college. I didn't have the faintest idea of what Vince Cochrane, my inspiring professor of cell biology, did in his lab (or if he even had a lab). Perhaps if I had spent four years at Wesleyan, instead of only three, I would have had more time to shop around for research projects of potential interest. And perhaps I would have recognized some exciting precursor of behavioral neurobiology. But I doubt it. I was simply too naïve, too brash, and too easily fooled to believe that a scientific career was more than an odd adaptation for social misfits! And those Wesleyan exponents of Freudianism, Fred Millett and Norman Brown, were so charming. They were humanists who loved Freud's ideas whether those ideas were scientifically valid or not.

In order to understand that science was essential for me, I needed to recognize that I had been fooled, how I had been fooled, and why I had been fooled. And I needed to recognize that neuroscience was an effective antidote to the excesses of psychological speculation. I am grateful to psychoanalysis for providing me with the opportunity to find this out.

At first I thought that psychoanalysis was scientifically valid. By the time I entered medical school, I suspected that psychoanalysis was playing games with people's minds. But not until much, much later did I began to be sure that psychoanalysis was a speculative philosophy, quite probably a pseudo-science, and even perhaps an intellectual and social deception.

A Citadel of Science: Harvard Medical School, 1955–1959

At Wesleyan I already had my doubts about Freud. How could he be so sure of his pronouncements? On what evidence were they based? Why did he always deride alternative explanations instead of taking them seriously? But I did not ask these questions often enough, and there was no one, except myself, to respond to them. My favorite humanities professors, Fred Millett and Norman Brown, were both scientophobes. The professors of basic sciences were so skeptical about psychoanalysis that they hadn't even read Freud's books! They had rejected Freud out of hand.

In psychology, the same sort of split played itself out in a slightly different way. The mainstream courses in psychology, when they were scientific, were dominated by conditioning paradigms. It was the age of Skinnerian behaviorism. B. F. Skinner regarded the brain as a black box and the mind as beyond the reach of science. Subjectivity and consciousness were not considered legitimate topics for scientific inquiry by psychologists. According to Skinner and his many psychologist followers, only behavior could be studied scientifically.

Sigmund Freud in London, on the balcony of his Hampstead apartment, with his two pet chows. By the time he left Vienna for London, Freud was recognized as a theoretical genius who had developed a highly specific theory of mental life in general and of dreaming in particular. His 1900 book *The Interpretation of Dreams* offered a clear and inviting target for my efforts at revision and replacement. For Freud, dreaming and waking were seen as antagonistic. I regard them as cooperative.

Why didn't those behaviorist psychologists study sleep behavior? Even in rats, that would have been useful. The reason for this oversight is that sleep behavior was assumed to be so monolithic and so inactive as to be uninformative. Sleep was considered to be the absence of behavior—a non-behavior. Not even the ethologists, those animal experimentalists who were interested in innate instinctual behavior, studied sleep.

I needed the impetus of sleep's association with dreaming to become motivated enough to devote my life to science. I knew I wanted to be a doctor. Thus, it was the clinical side of psychology that appealed to me most. But the clinical psychologists were, in one way or another, Freudian, and most of them were no more scientifically critical than the humanities professors. Instead, clinical psychology was swept up in the excitement of the thought that psychoanalysts could help them explain abnormal, normal, and social behavior in psychodynamic terms. In 1955, at age 22, I was trying too hard to learn psychodynamic theory and to apply it to my own life to entertain scientific doubts about these dogmas.

When I first went to Harvard Medical School, a variety of factors began to strengthen my innate skepticism. First and foremost, I was immediately aware that the only field in medicine without any visible foundation in biology was psychiatry. I was still gullible enough to believe the claim that psychoanalytic science was different from—or even superior to—biology because it transcended the corporal level and could thus be extended into all domains of human life.

In 1955, Harvard Medical School was a bastion of hard science and bold experimentation. It was full of brilliant professors and students. During my first year there I lived in Vanderbilt Hall. In the dining room of the dorm I met William Donellan, a young cardiac surgeon who had spent some time with Albert Schweizer in Lambarene. Bill was helping the pediatric surgeon Robert Gross to develop the heart-lung machine. Recruited by Donellan, I began working in Gross's lab nights and weekends. There I met another medical student, Judah Folkman, who was doing his own experiments on heart block while helping Gross with the heart-lung project. This was my first exposure to laboratory research, and I loved the excitement of it. I reveled in the opportunity to do surgery—real surgery—on living animals. But while working full-time in Gross's lab in the summer of 1956, I quickly found that I was not cut out to be either a surgeon or a clinical scientist.

Although I still enjoy doing surgery, I was quickly bored by repeating any procedure that I had learned to do. The minute I got good enough to do an operation, I wanted to do something else. This was not a good prognostic sign for a surgical career! Furthermore, I found the extreme pragmatism of the surgical research program unsatisfying. Our goal was to get that pump to work, not to understand why it didn't! To accomplish that goal, we kept changing experimental parameters, looking for success by trial and error. Ultimately, heart-lung pumps were made to work, and they revolutionized cardiac surgery. But by then I had gone off looking for a scientific opportunity in psychiatry.

By 1956, the year I married Joan Harlowe, I had been exposed to enough Freudianism—as taught and practiced by trained Freudian psychoanalysts (not English professors)—to see that there were severe intellectual, institutional, and moral problems associated with psychoanalysis. As first-year students we were required to take the introductory course in psychiatry taught mainly by Greta Bibring at Boston's Beth Israel Hospital. Professor Bibring, and most other analyst teachers I met as a medical student, seemed to have no doubt about the scientific solidity of their theories. This blind faith had prevented any of them from becoming even faintly experimental. I found Professor Bibring's lectures uncritical and unconvincing.

The arrogance of my psychoanalytic teachers was made worse by the implication that any question raised about the veracity of the assertions they put forth was a function of my neurosis rather than a scientific shortcoming of their theory. All substantive questions were answered by authoritarian dismissal rather than by shared skepticism. I felt like I was back in Sunday School, being asked to color angels that I couldn't see! Because most of my classmates just colored the angels, and because there wasn't the equivalent of a semi-professional choir to join as an alternative, I went respectfully along with the charade, at least for a while. Looking back, I think I should have bolted much earlier. But then I probably would not have gone into psychiatry at all. In order to be trained in a good psychiatric residency, one had to pay at least lip service to psychoanalysis.

By 1960, the psychiatry departments of nearly all of the leading American medical schools were chaired by individuals trained in psychoanalysis. All full professors, they had been appointed by medical school committees, and presumably they had been vetted as scientists—clinical scientists, at least. Who was I to doubt their intellectual authority? It all seems so silly now that I know so much better how things really work. But it is also shocking and astonishing that it took so long for me to notice that those Harvard professors were perpetuating an illusion. Now that psychiatry is scientifically discredited, it is unusual to have more than three or four Harvard students each year apply for a residency. But in my graduating year, 1959, there were 25 applicants, among them some of the brightest people in my class. I wasn't the only gullible victim of psychoanalysis.

The institutional problems of psychoanalysis were related to the administrative, financial and intellectual isolation of the psychoanalytic institutes. In our first year of medical school, many of the would-be psychiatrists in my class were already gravitating toward the very conservative Boston Psychoanalytic Society and Institute. Those fellow students of mine were just holding their breath to survive their immersion in medical science while awaiting elevation to the Olympian heights of human wisdom that psychoanalysis offered.

The more I heard about the rigidity of the Boston Psychoanalytic Institute, the more certain I became that I could never go there, owing to my deeply rebellious anti-authoritarianism. But I was nonetheless gulled and intimidated by the Institute. I held my tongue. I now regret both my intellectual weakness and my emotional fearfulness.

During my second year as a Harvard Medical student, when I was still looking for a scientific mentor, I sought out Daniel Funkenstein, who had interviewed me for medical school using his famous stress interview. Funkenstein—a neurosurgeon who had been converted to psychiatry by the Air Force during World War II—had a theory of personality that was based on physiological response patterns. This was my introduction to psychophysiology, the relatively weak but nonetheless scientific field in which sleep research first took root.

Working with Daniel Funkenstein was more than an introduction to psychophysiology; it was an introduction to clinical psychiatry. My job was to administer a battery of psychological tests—including the Minnesota Multiphasic Personality Inventory—to patients at the South Huntington Veterans Administration Hospital. This task provided a link to the psychometric work I had done with Page Sharp. I loved scoring the tests and plotting the results on graphs. Those Veterans Administration patients were afflicted with schizophrenic and major affective psychoses. They were being treated not by psychoanalysis but by electroshock and by insulin coma therapy. Neither of these radical physical interventions seemed to be well understood, and both seemed dangerously crude to me. I quickly recognized that psychiatry had its own organic theories and its own organic treatments, and that they were at least as ill-founded as its psychological ones! Little by little it dawned on me that both psychodynamic psychiatry and biological psychiatry needed a firmer base in neuroscience. In 1960, that neuroscience base simply wasn't there.

My moral indignation mounted sharply when I began to see psychoanalysts interacting with severely ill patients at the Massachusetts Mental

Health Center. Some of those analysts were downright hostile toward the patients; others blamed the patients (or the parents of the patients) for the states of severe mental disability that rendered them helpless. It seemed to me obvious that the patients suffered from the intellectual and emotional disorder of their tumultuous brains. When psychotic symptoms were interpreted as defenses against primitive sexual and aggressive instincts, most of these poor patients had no idea what the analysts were talking about. They were too confused and too poorly educated to use the abstract and scientifically dubious models that were being taught to young psychiatrists in Saturday seminars at the Boston Psychoanalytic Institute.

Not all the psychiatrists who followed psychoanalytic principles were mean to patients. As a third-year medical student, I met Lee Hasenbush, who supervised some of my inpatient work. Lee was as gentle and as genuinely concerned about the patients as many of his colleagues were indifferent. This probably is because he had been trained in the ecumenical and still white-coated department of psychiatry at the University of Rochester's school of medicine. Lee Hasenbush helped me to see and feel that the Hippocratic edict "First, do no harm" was as every bit as valid in psychological therapy as it was in physical medicine. Moreover, Lee's example made it clear that insight and support could both be achieved without recourse to complex psychoanalytic theory.

Inspired by Lee Hasenbush, I began to make my own approach to psychotherapy more commonsense, more direct, more supportive, and more transparent. If we had no science to go on, at least we had the relatively healthy parts of our selves to work with. If we couldn't cure severe mental illness, we could at least offer acceptance, understanding, and support. Having added the judicious use of medication to my naturalistic variety of psychotherapy, I achieved gratifying degrees of symptom reduction.

Looking for a Scientific Haven

In the late 1950s, Harvard's Department of Psychiatry was so deeply enthralled with psychoanalysis that we medical students were offered little else. There were no vociferous critics of psychoanalysis among the members of the Psychiatry faculty to whom we were exposed in our regular instruction. Fortunately, there were one or two outspoken critics who could be sought out. They were usually in departments other than Psychiatry. To me, the most appealing of them was Mark Altschule, who gave two lectures on anxiety in my second-year medical school course in pathophysiology. Mark was a brilliant cardiologist whose wife had been hospitalized for schizophrenia at McLean Hospital in Belmont, Massachusetts. To be closer to his wife and to defend her from the psychoanalysts, Mark became the internist-in-residence at McLean and set up a lab there to study organic determinants of mental illness.

Along with Dick Wurtmann, Bud Veach, and Donner Denckla, I worked in Mark Altschule's lab during my third and fourth years of medical school. All four of us were mavericks who hoped to replace psychoanalysis with biological science. We were inspired by Mark's experimentalism, his humorous skepticism, and his love of the history of psychiatry.

The science we did in Mark Altschule's lab was weak because Mark himself was enamored of the promise offered by such will-o'-the-wisp treatments for psychiatric patients as pineal extract. I felt that the direct injection of such crude material into the veins of psychotic patients was as foolish and at least as immoral as asking them to free associate. Informed consent was not formally required, internal review boards did not exist, and Mark Altschule—a good physician—was grasping at straws. He wanted his wife back.

Mark Altschule was scholarly, witty, and rambunctious. At Harvard, in the late 1950s, he was a voice crying in the wilderness. Without him, I wonder if I would have survived, even though I quickly became aware that I needed more than his independence of mind to make a serious contribution to psychiatric science. By his example, Mark helped me to give up surgery for internal medicine. In those days, one had to choose one or the other, because the best internships were structured along those two lines. Surgeons acted with dispatch (psychoanalytic critics would say they were impulse driven), while internists thought analytically (psychoanalytic critics called them obsessive-compulsive).

Mark Altschule helped me to see that I wasn't cut out for a career in biochemistry. The results of the project I worked on were published as my first scientific paper, titled "Glyoxyclic Acid and Mental Illness," in the then-prestigious Journal of Experimental and Clinical Investigation. I was pleased to be a published author, but soon I found that glyoxyclic acid was one of a large number of organic compounds that produced color spots on chromatograms of psychiatric patients' urine. The spot that glyoxyclate made was purple. My simple experiments showed that there were a lot of purple-spot-making molecules in the urine of schizophrenic patients. The problem was that these spots were produced not by the biochemistry of schizophrenia but rather by such non-specific factors as diet, psychoactive drugs, or cigarette smoking.

Metabolites of the then-popular antipsychotic drug chlorpromazine (better known as Thorazine) were known to produce purple spots.

Later studies revealed that many of the factors associated with chronic hospitalization could also cause abnormal body chemistry that had nothing directly to do with a patient's illness. Such false leads were daunting and disheartening. But I was also uncomfortable with the abstract nature of biochemical experimentation. For me, inferring disease from color spots in urine was like the arbitrary coloring of angels. I wanted to be able to see—with my own eyes—the processes of interest at they evolved in the living organism.

I was alarmed at my own intellectual shortcomings. If I could not do biochemistry, how could I be expected to develop a career in biological psychiatry? Humphrey Osmond and John Smythies were then theorizing that the metabolic breakdown products of brain chemicals were abnormal because of genetically caused enzymatic defects. Fifty years later, we still do not know whether that theory is correct. But the emphasis that was then placed on the importance of neuromodulators (such as serotonin) turned out to be prescient, as the sleep science that I later pursued has convincingly demonstrated.

Bellevue Hospital, Lewis Thomas, and Hans Lukas Teuber

Still unsure of my choice of psychiatry as a specialty, I did my best to secure a top-level internship in internal medicine. Everyone at Harvard Medical School wanted to stay in one of the Harvard programs in Boston. But nearly every one of us was matched elsewhere. A large number of my classmates went with me to Bellevue Hospital in New York. Among the other Bellevue interns were Jim Pritchard, Norm Robbins, and Stan Rapaport, all three of whom became productive neuroscientists.

I was assigned to the Medical Service of New York University, distinctly less prestigious than the Columbia or Cornell Internal Medicine divisions at Bellevue, but marked by two uniquely attractive features. One was the broad-minded and generous chief of service, Lewis Thomas, not yet famous as a writer but already conspicuously broad-minded and generous. The other was the responsibility the New York University medical service had for all the medical problems in the very large mental hospital affectionately known as "Bellevue Psycho."

Bellevue Psycho was even more deserving of that epithet than the Massachusetts Mental Health Center (called by some patients "the Psycho"). When opened, in 1912, the MMHC was more appropriately called the Boston Psychopathic Hospital. I spent five months of my twelve-month NYU medical internship taking care of patients with at least two diagnoses each. One diagnosis was psychiatric, usually schizophrenia. The other was medical; it could be almost anything that affected the brain—for example, tuberculosis, meningitis, or lupus erythematosis. It was at Bellevue Psycho that I learned that many organic brain diseases could produce the clinical picture of schizophrenia. That meant that you didn't need to have an abnormal molecule, or even abnormal genes, to be psychotic. All that was needed to produce craziness was a turbulent brain state.

In a typical Bellevue Psycho scenario, a Dutch sailor was picked up ranting and raving on a Manhattan street. He was shackled and brought for examination to Bellevue, where he was diagnosed as mentally ill and admitted. On the admission ward, a temperature reading of 106°F indicated that an infection might be causing the schizophrenia which the patient evinced outwardly. With two orderlies holding the patient down, my spinal tap needle entered the Dutchman's epidural sac. Cloudy spinal fluid gushed forth. I ducked as the pus-filled liquid shot by my ear. Three days later, after receiving massive doses of penicillin, that Dutch sailor was sane and walked out the same door that he had earlier entered in a strait-jacket. I was pleased to have cured schizophrenia so easily. But of course the Dutch sailor didn't really have schizophrenia. Instead, he had the organic mental syndrome known as delirium, which could have been caused by almost any kind of brain turbulence, including withdrawal from alcohol or amphetamine. Now we know that even normal sleep can produce the delirium of dreams.

Sleep Deprivation, Emotional Equilibrium, and Cognitive Function

Like my patients at Bellevue, I got little sleep. In 1960, we interns worked 36 out of every 48 hours, including every other weekend. From my own occupational sleep deprivation, I learned how important sleep was to cognitive and emotional functioning. I was irritable to the point of embarrassing rudeness toward patients whose reasonable demands on me seemed exorbitant. My need for sleep drove my brain to the point of life-threatening errors of judgment. For example, because I failed to warn my colleagues that one patient had a right-sided heart, the surgeons who responded to an emergency call when he had a cardiac arrest (and I was upstairs on another ward) cut through his heart wall when they opened his right chest cavity. He died within seconds.

One of my distinctly unofficial reactions to such discomforting inepti-tude was to recruit an NYU medical student to share the onerous night duty responsibilities with me. At NYU, as elsewhere, medical students were eager to be more involved in the hands-on care of patients. My young colleague Simon Stertzer was outstandingly bright and motivated. Si slept on the floor of my narrow bedroom in the Bellevue House Officers' Quarters. When the phone rang in our room, we got up together to answer the call to duty. Though both foggy, we were able to function better as a pair than alone. Our collaboration was as much emotional support as cognitive elaboration.

In spite of my chronic and debilitating sleep deprivation, I chose not to sleep at home because, in my 12 hours off, I wanted to make up for all that lost social time. It was amazing what my wife and I were able to do on my earnings of $125 a month (about 35 cents an hour). Joan's modest stipend as a junior high school teacher helped. Among other things, we heard Leonard Bernstein play the complete Mahler symphony cycle at Carnegie Hall, and we saw many of Fellini's and Bergman's films at the Thalia Theater on the Upper West Side. (I slept through much of the Mahler but never nodded off at the Thalia.) And we dined at fancy New York restaurants. One of our favorite haunts was the Czardas.

Bellevue was overburdened. It was also understaffed and underfinanced. Many of Bellevue's patients were poorly paid, poorly housed, and poorly fed. This was especially true if they had chronic alcoholism and lived on the Bowery, which was in our district. As an inexperienced intern, I was asked to care for the neediest people with the most complex diseases imaginable. To say that we lacked adequate supervision is a gross understatement.

In one night of heroic efforts, five of my Bellevue patients expired. The nurses and attendants on the medical-psychiatric ward, Q4, thought I was foolish even to try to save these very sick people and only reluctantly offered me very perfunctory aid. The assistant resident who was my immediate supervisor was sound asleep. I remember vividly that one nurse's aide sat in the nurse's station reading the Daily News as I struggled to save lives. I also remember going home at 6 o'clock that morning to seek solace from my wife. Joan and I lived in a fourth-floor walkup at 489 First Avenue, across from Bellevue. I hadn't slept a wink, and my white uniform was blood-spotted from my botched attempts to use a gastric balloon to stanch the hemorrhaging from esophageal varices of a patient with end-stage cirrhosis of the liver.

Besides making a political liberal of me, I learned that there are many medical conditions that can affect the brain in such a way as to simulate the so-called functional psychoses. Bellevue thus taught me to take brain research much more seriously than I had before. I was inspired by the no-nonsense bedside teaching of the neurologist Morris Bender and by the neuropsychology laboratory of Hans Lukas Teuber, which was just outside wards P&Q3 where I worked. I was also awed by the Olympian intellectual grandeur of my service chief, Lewis Thomas. Although I think I was a good intern and hence desirable as a resident, Thomas could see in a minute that my heart was in psychiatry. He encouraged me to follow that interest, suggesting that the absence of a strong science base might even be advantageous to my career. "You can build one," he told me.

During that Bellevue internship year, the results of my tuberculosis skin tests changed from negative to positive. This was, no doubt, due to my exposure to Bowery denizens, many of whom had open cavitary tuberculosis. In Boston, I had been taught to stain smears of sputum but had never seen a tubercle bacillus. At Bellevue, those red bugs were dancing on nearly every slide. I was relieved to be told that my final chest x-ray was negative, which meant that I had not contracted the disease while I was acquiring immunity to it.

In the early morning hours of July 1, 1960, I drove up the Merritt Parkway, through Hartford, and on to Boston in the blue Ford sedan that Bill Donellan had given to Joan and me as a wedding present. The sun was breaking, the birds were singing, and the trees were a garden green. I was ecstatic to have survived Bellevue. Five of the twelve interns in my group had acquired active tuberculosis. And I was still young and naïve enough to believe that my residency in psychiatry at the Massachusetts Mental Health Center would finally reveal to me the power of psychoanalysis.

The Light That Failed: Psychoanalysis at Boston Psycho

In the early 1960s, residencies at the Massachusetts Mental Health Center were highly coveted, drawing applicants from all across the United States. My residency class included people who would later become leaders of academic psychiatry, many via brain research. On my service were Paul Wender (who would do groundbreaking work on the pharmacology of attention-deficit disorder), Judy Rapoport (who would become a distinguished clinical scientist working with children), and Eric Kandel (who would receive a Nobel Prize in Medicine and Physiology for work on learning in the sea snail aplysia).

Why was the Psycho so attractive and so powerful? In the early 1960s, the promise of psychoanalysis and unmitigated gall made it possible for Harry Solomon (an old-school organicist) to trade jobs with Massachusetts' Commissioner of Mental Health, Jack Ewalt (a swashbuckling Texan psychoanalyst). In 1960 the leadership model was medical and the scientific model was psychoanalytic.

In 1960, Boston Psycho was not only geographically and politically well placed; the time was also right for it to flourish. When John F. Kennedy was elected president, in 1960, Action for Mental Health—a national scheme cooked up by Jack Ewalt and his cronies—went on the front burner, and federal dollars poured into the MMHC and other university centers. Trainees like me were sure that we would win the war on poverty via psychoanalytic enlightenment. It is not an exaggeration to say that this sense of mission had the force of a crusade. The Psycho was a temple for the priest-acolytes who would transfer the new psychoanalytic faith to the masses.

Unfortunately, many of the wonderful minds that went from the MMHC to the Boston Psychoanalytic Institute were caught in a web of superstitious intellectualism and financial obligation that led them to treat only upper-middle-class patients and one another. Even my scientifically sophisticated peers were convinced that psychoanalysis was intellectually solid. In this atmosphere of religious idolatry, I knew that I wouldn't get beyond the first year of the BPI if I even got through the door. It was a worse prospect than being asked to color the angels in Sunday School. Panic stricken to find myself cut off from physiology and medicine and sure that I had fallen into the abyss of still another low-minded creed, I had the same impulse to flee that got me out of Sunday School and into the choir. I made straight for the National Institute of Mental Health, hoping to find a scientific anchor and a compass to guide me over the treacherous seas of mind-body interaction.

I have written at length about my experience with a catatonic schizophrenic patient that was assigned to me when I arrived at Mass Mental on July 1, 1960. Bertal's story is detailed in my book *The Chemistry of Conscious States* (later republished by the MIT Press under the title *Dreaming as Delirium*). To help the reader understand me and the domination of MMHC psychiatry by psychoanalysis, I emphasize here the position taken by my service chief, who was a psychoanalyst:

• Bertal's schizophrenia was caused by his mother's hysterically seductive and rejecting behavior. She was a typical schizophrenogenic mother.

• Bertal's acute catatonic psychosis that July was caused by the departure of his resident therapist. The moral implications of using patients like Bertal as guinea pigs for us trainees was overlooked by our supervisors, but we felt it.

• Bertal's schizophrenia could and should be treated with psychoanalytic psychotherapy alone. We were advised to read Freud's Psycho-Analytic

Notes on an Autobiographical Account of a Case of Paranoia, in which Freud attributed Judge Schreber's delusions to repressed homosexuality.
• Giving Bertal drugs (among them Thorazine) to control his hallucinations and delusions was contra-indicated because it would interfere with the transference essential to his care by psychotherapy.

You will wonder, as I do now, how anyone could have been so foolish as to believe any of these absurd allegations. Please understand, however, that my own doubts were quashed by many older, authoritative voices. After all, this was Harvard, where all the top professors were psychoanalysts. I kept my skepticism to myself and tried to treat Bertal by the Freudian book. The pathetic comedy of this effort included the following scenes:

• I tried to coax Bertal into my office while he was in a state of catatonic excitement.
• When I asked what was on his mind, Bertal warned me about the swooping dive bombers from which he ducked to protect himself.
• When Bertal ran out of the hospital in what my supervisor said was homosexual panic, I followed him. (If the interpretation was at all correct, my behavior doesn't make much sense, does it?)
• When Bertal rolled under a car parked on Fenwood Road, I lay down on the sidewalk next to him and tried to conduct psychoanalytic psychotherapy while both of us were prone.

I told my chief all these details and was reassured that I was doing the right thing. I kept suggesting medication, but was scolded and told that this would dilute the transference that was developing. I was told to be patient, as I was on the verge of a therapeutic breakthrough. The breakthrough would occur when Bertal would perceive that his psychosis was a defense against his homosexual longings for me. Indeed, Bertal did talk, in a confused way, about sexual identity. So I kept waiting for the dawn of insight and the change in Bertal's mental state. Forty years later the Bertals of the world and I are still waiting for any such epiphany of understanding.

As it turned out, Bertal got put on Thorazine and his psychosis cleared dramatically. What caused this reversal of policy?

• Bertal was so out of control that the ward nurses insisted on putting him in a seclusion room.
• My psychoanalysis service chief made evening rounds and went into the seclusion room to talk with Bertal.
• Bertal attacked my chief aggressively, giving him a black eye with a point-scoring punch.

• My chief ordered intramuscular Thorazine to protect Bertal from his aggressive impulses.

The scales fell from my eyes. Psychoanalysts could be as arbitrary, as retaliatory, and as self-contradictory as any other set of ignorant believers. This episode and others like it prompted me to talk with my fellow residents, about half of whom were as disaffected as I was after encountering psychoanalytic psychotherapy. Encouraged by Eric Kandel, who had already spent three years at the NIH working with Alden Spencer on the neurophysiology of the hippocampus, I began to plan my own escape from Bedlam. In truth, I got more support and more solid teaching in psychiatry from my fellow residents at the Psycho than from the illustrious Harvard faculty. The only teacher who really encouraged critical thinking was Mark Altschule.

If you were to ask me today "What was really wrong with Bertal?" I would hazard the guess that he suffered from a functional brain disease. His genetic predisposition made him unable to control his conscious states. Hallucinations, delusions, and anxiety, and anger could no longer be restricted to his REM-sleep dreams, as they are in most of us. Instead those brain-initiated events expressed themselves in the awake state. I will later explain the clear differences between this concept and the psychoanalytic notion of the dynamically repressed unconscious.

When Bertal hallucinated dive bombers, he really saw them (just as I have seen hostile aircraft in my dreams). In such a fragile state, he was psychologically dependent on, and fearful of, his doctors. One wrong move and Bertal attacked. No amount of any kind of talk was powerful enough to combat these forces, any more than decades of study help me to recognize that I am dreaming when I am dreaming. When he was eventually given Thorazine, and his D2 dopamine receptors were blocked, Bertal's psychosis subsided. This symptomatic treatment was successful because of a monumental shift in the neuromodulatory balance of Bertal's brain. Such a monumental shift in neuromodulatory balance also occurs when I wake up and recognize that I have just been asleep and dreaming.

Sentimentally on Target

Elvin Semrad, the son of a family doctor in Nebraska, had distilled folk wisdom and decanted it into bottles labeled "vintage psychoanalysis." Semrad's ability to establish emotional contact with psychotic patients was justifiably legendary, and his case conferences had the conversion power of prayer meetings. In retrospect, Semrad was right on target. But his Midwest folk-wisdom charisma could not be imitated by us East Coast

WASPs and Jews. This was because the country boy in Semrad could focus on emotional salience in a remarkably forceful and non-threatening way.

Semrad counseled against our going to the library to read the psychiatric literature. He said that there was nothing in books that could teach us as much as a live patient. We should immerse ourselves in the experience of the patient in order to understand psychosis and to begin to reduce its pain. Healing would come via empathy. It might take a long time, perhaps even a *very* long time. For that reason, these patients were our responsibility—for life. Our great guru was so steadfastly anti-intellectual that we became furtive in our efforts to get the external perspective we needed to balance the vertiginous pull of Semradism into the existential pit of life-long dedication to our crazy patients.

Beyond testimony and witness, what was the evidence for Semrad's radical and idealistic claims? The encounter with Elvin Semrad threw me back to Wesleyan, to my thesis, to Dostoyevsky, and to *The Brothers Karamazov*. Semrad was the head monk, Father Zossima, and I was Alyosha, his gullible young acolyte. This metaphorical perspective helped me to rebel.

In defiance of Semrad's warnings, I read and read. I immersed myself in the already voluminous literature of psychotherapy research. Nowhere could I find evidence that psychotherapy worked better than placebo for psychotic patients. Freud himself had warned against this expectation. My fellow resident Lester Grinspoon and our boss Jack Ewalt were about to show that even the best analysts were as impotent as the greenest residents in influencing psychoses with psychotherapy.

Speaking Out for Science

Before leaving the Massachusetts Mental Health Center for the National Institute of Mental Health, I had two experiences with Jack Ewalt that showed him to be free of cant and to be able to act in the interest of his students even when he disagreed with them. First-year residents were expected to choose a topic in the history of psychology, philosophy, or psychiatry and report on it to Ewalt and their 24 peers at a weekly meeting in his office. As my topic, I chose the American pragmatists John Dewey and William James. Dewey and James appealed to me because of their practicality. My presentation focused on their position in terms of what I perceived to be the scientific plight of psychiatry: a plethora of theory, no data base, and no evidence of therapeutic efficacy.

Ewalt heard me out and then asked if I really believed that scientific progress was possible. Without hesitation I snapped back: "Of course it is possible. Look at what has already been achieved in psychopharmacology." Sensing my irritation, Ewalt played the psychoanalytic ad hominem trump card: "You sound like you are talking to your father." I had heard quite a lot of this transference trash talk and was therefore primed to respond quickly and pointedly: "Oh no, my father would never make a silly remark like you just did." The group shuddered, but I never had any difficulty with Jack Ewalt again. Instead, he became my ally.

When I told him I was going to the NIMH to work on the biology of schizophrenia with Seymour Kety, Jack Ewalt seemed quite pleased even though my departure would deprive him or a resident. I said I needed scientific training and a cutting-edge line of research work to sustain me in psychiatry. "When you are ready to come back," Jack replied, "just give me a call." This was his way of saying goodbye and of keeping his door open to a student whose independence of mind made him a prospective professor.

8 Brain Science as Antithesis

When I got to the National Institute of Mental Health, I was dismayed to find that the chief of its Clinical Science Lab, Seymour Kety, had gone to Johns Hopkins University to be head of the Department of Psychiatry there. My job at the NIMH, supervised by Philippe Cardin, was to manage the medical care of the fourteen patients on Ward 2 East. Those patients had been selected by Kety for his standard-bearing experiments on the biological genesis of schizophrenia. Most of Kety's studies used rigorous controls to correct the errors of others, such as my discovery of color spots in the urine of schizophrenic patients that were caused by medication rather than by disease.

Mine was not an onerous job. I made rounds every morning and tended to the patients' medical needs. I took advantage of the relative leisure to read, to reflect, and to reconnoiter the various research opportunities that presented themselves at the NIMH. After six years of dogged work in medical school and postgraduate clinical training, it was the first time that I had the chance to slow down and think about what I really wanted to do and how I should direct my experimental nature. My brain was ready to work, but on what problem and with what methods?

Sleep Research with Fred Snyder

I knew I didn't want to do biochemistry. That ruled out working with the Nobel laureate Julius Axelrod, who wisely brushed me off when I approached him about working in his lab. I thought I didn't know enough to do neurophysiology. That ruled out Edward Evarts, who was working on the effects of LSD on the visual system and had taken Kety's place as Acting Chief of the Lab of Clinical Science to which I was assigned. My brain needed a clinical connection to move ahead scientifically. While dabbling in psychophysiology with the visiting Swedish scientist

Ingmar Durmann, I met Fred Snyder, a research psychiatrist whose office and lab were on Ward 2 East, where my patients too were housed. When Fred told me that he could tell when people were dreaming by looking at their brain and eye movement potentials, I was incredulous. "It's not possible!" I exclaimed. My skepticism derived in part from my earlier encounter with Irwin Kremen at the Massachusetts Mental Health Center.

"Come in tonight and see for yourself," said Snyder, who needed the technical assistant that I was fast becoming. That night I saw for myself the periodic brain activation and the flurries of rapid eye movements that gave REM sleep its name. I also heard the subject give a detailed dream report when Snyder roused her from REM sleep by calling her name over

While I was learning sleep science from Fred Snyder at the NIMH, I continued to enjoy the intellectual stimulation of young psychiatrist peers in Boston. Under the tutelage of Mark Altschule (seated at center in this photo), we wrote and read papers on topics of interest. On Altschule's left in the photo is Anton Kris; on his right is Paul Wender. Standing (left to right) are Eric Kandel, Stanley Palumbo, George Vaillant, Ernest Hartman, John Merrifield, and me. My essays were titled "Serendipsomania, Disorder of Research" and "Diagnosis: Art or Artefact?"

an intercom. I immediately understood that the relationship of brain physiology to mental activity in sleep and the awake state deserved multidisciplinary study.

Why did Fred Snyder need my assistance? Because, in addition to his daytime clinical research responsibilities at the NIMH, he was not only engaged in a personal training analysis with the famous Washington psychoanalyst Harold Searles but was also treating patients as "control cases" to satisfy the requirements of certification by the Washington Psychoanalytic Institute. This meant that every night spent in the sleep lab added to Snyder's mounting sleep debt. Snyder paid this debt back by falling asleep each evening in his chair behind the control patients' couch in his NIMH office. He was so tired that he also fell asleep as soon as he lay down on Harold Searles's couch early the next morning.

Harold Searles was famous because he dared to treat schizophrenic patients using only psychotherapy. I had already seen him in action—with a patient—on the stage of the huge MMHC gym before a large and enraptured group of young psychiatrists. Like Elvin Semrad, Searles had a nose for emotional salience. He was also something of a bully, and he used psychoanalytic concepts to shape his aggressive clinical interventions. This made him more dramatic than the low-key Semrad. But it also made him more dangerous to the patients and students who were in his thrall. Searles used strong interpersonal moves in theatrical ways to demonstrate that contact with psychotically regressed patients was possible. That such contact, like Semrad's gentler interventions, yielded emotionally salient communications with those hard-to-reach patients had an immediate impact on us trainees. That impact was so strong that it wiped out our doubts, made us uncritical, and swept us along as if it were somehow proof of the truth of psychoanalysis. (Turning up the volume and clarifying the message is a good way of getting anyone's attention in an advertising campaign.)

With me as his eager and energetic lab assistant, Fred Snyder became even more sleep deprived. That made him more and more prone to dozing off when he hit Searles's couch in the early morning. What were practical, commonsense men like Frederick Snyder doing in psychoanalysis? Why did it take them so long to realize that they weren't getting anywhere while either lying on their own backs or sitting behind their patients while they dozed off to sleep? Having heard stories of dozing off from people who were not doing sleep research, I know that sleep deprivation was not a necessary trigger. The boredom of this once-a-day couch ritual sufficed to induce sleep, especially in the early morning or the early afternoon.

The surprising fact of the matter is that in 1962 the NIMH was willing to pay for the training or the personal psychoanalysis of its scientists. Orthodox analysts might say: "No wonder Snyder couldn't be analyzed. He wasn't paying for it himself." It was then thought that payment of a fee was an essential ingredient to successful psychotherapy. But you don't have to pay for the penicillin that cures you of strep throat, and almost no one can afford a year of Clozaril, the drug that is now so effective in relieving some treatment-resistant schizophrenics.

I offer this story of financial obligation as further evidence of the grip that psychoanalysis held in the highest academic circles in the early 1960s. But please do not miss the practical point. The federal government was subsidizing psychoanalysis on the ground that it would improve the cognitive acumen of its scientists by clearing away emotional cobwebs. We are talking about four or five sessions a week at $75–$100 a session for three to five years. That comes to a minimum of $15,000 a year ($45,000 in 1960 dollars) for three years of analysis. This is very hard to believe today, when third parties—including Welfare and Medicaid—are loath to reimburse patients or physicians for more than 5 or 10 minutes of talk. Today's financial reticence toward physician-patient communication is as arbitrary and unwarranted as yesterday's munificence toward psychoanalytic free association.

The manifest absurdity of psychoanalysis, as it was practiced in the United States in 1960, helped Fred Snyder and me to throw off the career-crippling restraints that held so many of my bright friends in its thrall. It saved me from Saturday mornings spent in Institute seminars, self-doubting sessions with training analysts, and hours of waiting in vain for patients to recall a childhood trauma that would—via catharsis—release them from the stranglehold of their neuroses.

In more than 40 years of clinical practice, I have never seen a patient do well because he or she achieved insight through free association. Many patients got better without free association, and some failed to improve—or got worse—with it. Insight, self-understanding, self-acceptance, and self-realization can be achieved in much simpler and more straightforward ways.

The Golden Age of Sleep Science

By 1960, it was time for psychiatry to embrace science in earnest. Young psychiatrist-scientists had almost limitless support. The federal government had decided to fund sleep research unstintingly. Even though this policy meant that much shoddy work was financed, it was a wise decision. It was wiser, in my opinion, than underwriting psychoanalysis.

It was a wise decision because sleep research raised and answered questions about the state in which we spent one-third of our lives. More strategically, sleep research opened a window on the psychosis-promoting mechanisms of the normal brain. The formal approach specifies the following properties as definitive of dreaming:

1. Hallucinations, especially of vision and movement but also hallucinations involving other sensory systems. Without any sensory input, we see things clearly that are not there.
2. Delusions. When we dream, we harbor the conviction that we are awake. We are also prone to uncritical belief in physically impossible and/ or improbable dream scenarios. During dreams, we almost never correct these errors of judgment.
3. Cognitive abnormalities. These include loss of declarative memory (amnesia within the dream), loss of orientational stability (the discontinuity and incongruity of dream bizarreness), and marked reductions of declarative memory of the dream upon awakening (amnesia). Thus, when dreaming we are as cognitively impaired as we are perceptually enhanced. This is exactly true of patients with so-called mental illness.
4. Emotional intensifications. Dream elation, anger, and anxiety are three emotions which are often perturbed in schizophrenia, in major affective disorders, and in neurotic conditions.

REM sleep can thus be viewed as a normal condition of the brain—a condition that serves as the substrate of the cardinal features of psychosis that characterize many of the most severe forms of mental illness. The fact that we are all capable of dreaming means that we are all capable of a completely normal and natural form of madness. Dreaming also proves that madness can be functional as well as structural. We need not have abnormal genes, biased neuronal receptors, or traumatic life events to become quite floridly psychotic. All we need is the normal change in brain state from the awake state to REM sleep.

This is not to say that dreaming is abnormal or that awake-state psychosis is normal. Neither is the case. But the fact that the two conditions share formal properties means that understanding how (and why) the brain dreams during sleep will provide a useful scaffold for the more ambitious task of finding our how and why it becomes psychotic in the awake state.

I saw immediately that understanding sleep was the scientific challenge I had been looking for. REM sleep was so global, so visible, and so physiological as to satisfy my need for concrete observation while simultaneously promising understanding of the causation of dreams. (By 'global' I mean all-enveloping. REM-sleep dreams are nearly always totally absorbing. Consciousness is entirely taken over by them.) I now believe that the paradigm of studying the brain and dream psychology together is a strong one. It has already yielded a rich harvest, it continues to offer new scientific data, and it promises even more in the future.

How I Became a Lucid Dreamer

Sleep deprivation played a major role in liberating my mentor Fred Snyder from psychoanalysis. Sleep deprivation also cemented my interest in sleep research by making me a lucid dreamer. When I was working five nights a week in Snyder's sleep lab and providing medical care to Seymour Kety's schizophrenic subjects of on Ward 2 East, I was lucky to get home to my bed in Washington by 11 a.m. I was very tired, so I fell asleep easily. I got up in the late afternoon because I didn't want to miss out on my social life. I had met Alice Denney and had became a part of a wild art scene. So I often got up at 5 p.m. and went to a cocktail party or a dinner party before returning to the sleep lab. At one of Alice's parties I met Albert and Jennifer Hamilton, who later invited me for dinner at their house in Cleveland Park. During our conversation, Jennifer told me that she was a relative of Mary Arnold-Forster, who had experimented with lucid dreaming and had written a book called *Experiments in Dreams* (1920). Jennifer even lent me her copy of that landmark publication.

"If you want to become more aware of your dreams," Mary Arnold-Forster wrote, "you need only pay attention to them. To help you do this, you must give yourself the pre-sleep order to notice that strange (or bizarre) events signal dream consciousness. Having noticed these dream signs, you can then simply watch the plots unfold, or influence their development in any direction that interests you." Mary Arnold-Forster had learned to fly up and down the stairs of her large house, and, like most dream aviators, she loved flying.

Since I was then chronically sleep deprived, I was able to sleep deeply in broad daylight with the curtains open. I often awakened spontaneously with vivid dream recall. Although I wasn't yet keeping a journal, I remember my own experiments in lucid dreaming clearly. By following Mary Arnold Forster's instructions, I was soon able to know that I was dreaming when I was dreaming, to influence the dream content voluntarily, and to wake myself up to ensure good recall. I could even go back to the same dream if I wanted to. This meant that I could gain insight into and control of a psychosis-like mental state simply by sensitizing my mind and my brain. To do so, no psychoanalysis was necessary.

I became a subject of my own scientific interest. It was my consciousness that was being altered by changes in my brain. Most of these changes were beyond my control. But my consciousness was capable of gaining access to its own normally hidden activation, of influencing my awareness of that activation, and of changing the direction of my dream experience. My consciousness was plastic and could be causal of its content, even in dreams. These revelations fueled my interest and motivated me to pursue more microscopic and more abstract aspects of neuroscience. I wanted to know more about how my brain-self worked.

The Need for an Animal Model

In 1961 it was already clear at the National Institute of Mental Health that recording human sleep and performing awakenings in the sleep lab were not enough to gain more than correlational data. Fred Snyder knew this. Fred also knew that an animal model of REM sleep had been discovered by Bill Dement in 1958 and was being exploited by Michel Jouvet in Lyon with brilliant success. When I read Jouvet's papers I knew I wanted to work with him. I arranged to have him invited to give a seminar at the NIMH.

I picked Michel Jouvet up when he arrived by train at Union Station and drove him out Wisconsin Avenue to Bethesda in my little Riley. En route, we negotiated the terms of my scientific training year in Lyon (1963–64). I agreed to find my own fellowship money and Jouvet agreed to speak nothing but French in the laboratory. I wanted to learn to speak French and knew that would be more difficult if my collaborators used me to perfect their English.

Having an animal model of a physiological state associated with dreaming is like having a mouse model of a genetic disease. It enables the biological scientist to move to the analytic level rather than settling for a merely descriptive and correlational study. By asking what will happen to REM sleep if we make experimental interventions in our animal model, we might learn about the deep mechanisms and functions of sleep. This was preferable to recording surface phenomena, as we were confined to do in the human sleep lab. Before 1953, when REM was discovered, psychiatric

William Dement (center) and Allan Rechtschaffen (right) with Michel Jouvet (left) in his Laboratory at the University of Lyon in the fall of 1962. Each of these three scientists contributed in a significant way to the rapid growth of sleep and dream science. Working with Nathanial Kleitman, Dement led the early investigation of the relationship of REM sleep and dreaming. Jouvet was the first to demonstrate the importance of the pontine brain stem to REM sleep generation through the use of surgical ablation, stimulation, and pharmacological manipulation of this system. Dement then attempted to test Jouvet's hypothesis regarding the role of serotonin in generating sleep. Together with Rechtschaffen and Christian Guilleminault, Dement also initiated sleep disorders medicine, a movement which he continues to lead. Rechtschaffen later demonstrated the importance of REM sleep in the maintenance of temperature control in mammals.

research had no such paradigm. Because sub-human animals have no mind to go out of, there is no good animal model for mental illness.

By means of radical animal experiments that utilized his neurosurgical skills, Michel Jouvet had been able to show that the pontine brainstem contained the neuronal circuits necessary to trigger the REM-sleep episodes of his cats. He later showed that those circuits operated via the very same chemicals thought to be deranged in mental illness. Not surprisingly, those chemicals were also the targets of the array of new drugs that since 1955 had helped to empty the mental hospitals. I am referring to the biogenic amines norepinephrine, serotonin, histamine, and dopamine, all of which have been shown to modulate perception and mood. But I am also referring to acetylcholine, which has been thought to facilitate memory.

Ed Evarts as Role Model

Once I knew that I would be able to go to Lyon to work with Michel Jouvet, I turned to the psychiatrist-neurophysiologist Edward Evarts, who had taken the place of Seymour Kety as chief of the Clinical Science Lab. "Help me learn to do sleep studies in cats," I asked Ed, who was already doing such experiments himself. He readily agreed to aid me. In Ed's lab, while still working day and night on human sleep and dreaming with Fred Snyder, I learned to do the implantation surgery, to record cat sleep, and to score the records. All these skills were necessary to success in my upcoming year with Jouvet. In Ed Evart's lab, I also saw how a great neurobiologist worked. It was a revelation to me.

When Edward Evarts focused his scientific attention—as, for example, when he was interested in finding out the relationship between the firing of motor cortex neurons and hand movement in the monkey—he planned his experiments in detail. Complex apparatus was carefully designed to hold the animal's head still while allowing free movement of the forearm. The programs for delivering stimulus cues and rewards to the monkey were prepared and tested. Most important, the approach to quantitative data analysis was worked out in advance. It would be almost a decade before my work on sleep even approached these criteria, but Ed's clear example was firmly fixed in my mind.

Ed Evarts's example also helped to carry me on through the thick and thin of the less elegant research protocols that I encountered in Lyon. The phenomena we studied there were robust. If Michel Jouvet was right in concluding that the pons contained a neural trigger and timer for REM, then those functions would reveal themselves in the firing patterns of pontine neurons. Evarts's example also helped me to persist in this quest when two of my respected contemporaries, Emilio Bizzi and Giovanni Berlucchi, both told me that I could not expect to learn much from recording pontine brainstem neurons in cats. I will never forget their discouraging comments in the parking lot of a motel where, in 1964, we had just heard Ed Evarts give an inspiring talk on the neuronal mediation of behavior.

Michel Jouvet, the Pontine Cat, and Anglo-Saxon Heresy

Before my stay in Lyon, I had seriously underestimated culture's effect on science. Since then, I have been amazed by that effect. Even though I now know it is powerful, I am still surprised to see just how powerful it can be.

In Lyon, culture played itself out in thought, in experimental practice, and—of course—in interpersonal relations.

To explain the effect of culture on science, I begin with the interpersonal level, because it is so easy to understand. I found my young French scientist peers to be so respectful of hierarchy and so fearful of official reprisal that no open or honest upstream discourse was ever possible. I had become used to the critical, dialectic climate that prevailed at extra-psychiatric Harvard and at the NIMH, where young people were encouraged to speak up and to speak out if they had questions or challenges to what they were taught. I could see, feel, and hear the shudders of dismay coming from my young French colleagues when I questioned Michel Jouvet about his concepts, procedures, and interpretations. Arbitrary authority was a feature of French science that was shared by psychoanalysis!

As Jouvet and I tried to find a *modus vivendi*, he suggested that his approach was synthetic (á la Claude Bernard) whereas mine was more analytic (á la Thomas Henry Huxley). This distinction made a certain amount of sense on the face of it. Jouvet certainly had strong preconceived ideas about how the brain worked and how the link from brain to behavior must be created. He therefore set out to prove his own ideas by selecting data that favored his concepts. This meant ignoring any data that were contradictory.

One example shows just how right and how wrong this approach can be. Because dreaming and the awake state were so different as mental experiences, Jouvet assumed that the brain activation pattern would be different in the two cases. More specifically, he believed that the limbic system would be activated in REM sleep to a greater degree than the neocortical system. Jouvet gave me this problem to solve by studying the effects of experimental damage to the brainstem on the REM-sleep EEG of the cat. Damage to the more ventral limbic midbrain circuit (first described by Walle Nauta) was predicted by Jouvet to have a more potent effect on the EEG activation of REM than damage to the more dorsal reticular activating system (first described by Giuseppe Moruzzi and Horace Magoun).

In a futile effort to demonstrate the expected difference, I did 25 different experiments. Without any systematic overall design, I made complete transections of the brainstem at several different levels and destroyed nerve cells by passing radio-frequency current through a wide variety of brain structures. Nothing worked. It should have been clear to Jouvet and to me that we had not tested his hypothesis adequately—the lesion method was so imprecise and created such horrendous side effects that the results were impossible to interpret with confidence.

We failed to note that the EEG might not be able to show a difference even if there was one because of the electrical conduction of activation from one part of the forebrain to another. And we did not consider the possibility that activation might decline in one part of the cortex (e.g., the frontal areas) and increase in others (e.g., the posterior regions). Jouvet's hypothesis could still have been correct even if both pathways were activated but to differing degrees. Because there were no observable or measurable differences between the EEG activation following dorsal lesions and following ventral lesions, I concluded that the hypothesis was invalid, whereas all I had done was fail to find evidence supporting it. This mistake did not reduce the tension in my relationship with Jouvet.

Time has since shown that Jouvet's intuitive hypothesis was correct. When PET scans are made in human subjects, there is selective activation of the limbic system in REM sleep, just as Jouvet had predicted on the basis of his own intensely emotional dream experiences. Furthermore, there is a reciprocal deactivation of the frontal cortex, which no one, including Jouvet, had anticipated. This example is so telling that it is worthy of further consideration. It shows that the causal arrows linking mind and brain formalism run in both directions (or that there are no arrows at all if we are looking at a unified system).

We knew that dreaming was highly emotional. As a consequence, we predicted selective activation of the limbic brain in REM. This was Jouvet's limbic-midbrain hypothesis. But we also knew that thinking was impoverished in dreams. This should have led us to predict selective deactivation of the frontal cortical centers of working memory and of directed thought. But we didn't take our formalist psychology far enough or seriously enough to make this now-obvious prediction. Even if we had, we might not yet have been in a position to test our hypothesis because our methods were not up to that task either. Certainly the EEG, when visually inspected, was too weak an indicator to detect the regional changes later revealed in the PET scans. Now we wonder if more focused, more quantitative EEG studies could do so. We have good reason to believe this may be so.

When I went to Lyon in 1963, I was already uneasy about the limitations of lesion and electrical stimulation methods. Once I had arrived and had begun to use those techniques, I rapidly became even more skeptical. Since I shared with Jouvet a passion for understanding how the brain activation of REM was actually engineered, I began to advocate single-cell recording of the sort I had seen in Ed Evarts's lab at the National Institutes of Health.

Jouvet inveighed strongly against this analytic approach. He felt it was just another example of what he called the "Anglo-Saxon heresy" of cellular neurobiologists such as John Eccles. I gradually became aware that underneath his internationalist bonhomie, Michel Jouvet was very, very French indeed. As the son of a town doctor in Lons-le-Saulnier in the Jura region, he felt alienated from his Parisian colleagues who used the analytic neurophysiology techniques that were imported from England. Indeed he was vehemently opposed to them. Jouvet's intellectual disdain was a superficial manifestation of much deeper historically based hatred of anything English by many French people. This animosity went back at least to Napoleon's loss at Waterloo, but it more clearly marked the events of World War II when, in Jouvet's words, "perfidious Albion" sank the French fleet at Toulon. According to Jouvet, this act sprang from anti-Gallic hatred and had not, as the English claimed, been done so that the French fleet could not be captured by the Germans.

Gallic swagger, already intense, grew greater after Charles de Gaulle's return to power. Michel Jouvet and many others felt that French culture should be advanced in the New World by promoting French Canadian interests in Quebec. The schismatic results of this policy are now frighteningly clear. At international scientific meetings, de Gaulle's injunctions against speaking English were mainly ignored; however, I remember fiery debates about this issue in our laboratory. Jouvet, who spoke better English that I did French, advocated the francophone policy.

The puffy arrogance of the French coxcomb was also seen clearly in Jouvet's relationships with women. He was not discreet about his affairs. This alienated his wife, Daniele Mounier, who was also a fellow scientist in the laboratory. Jouvet's scientific nonchalance also offended some of his closest co-workers, but most of them kept quiet and waited until jobs elsewhere took them out of the lab. I was young and foolish enough to want to challenge these behaviors, and so I did. Sometimes I was open and sometimes I was more discreet in my rebellion.

In any case, my skill at speaking French improved exponentially because I was not only able to speak it every day in the lab but also to use it in a wide variety of social settings. One of the most satisfying friendships that I made was with Luce Michel, then the wife of my lifelong friend Francois Michel, co-discover with Jouvet of the muscle tone inhibition of REM. Another was with Jouvet's wife, Daniele. Both Francois and Daniele left the lab soon after I went back to Boston. They needed independence and recognition but never really got much of either.

Experimental Animals Include Humans

Before I met Luce Michel, it had never occurred to me that animal research was considered morally unacceptable by many people. It later became clear that animal-rights activists had strong feelings about this and that a few were willing to invade and destroy laboratories to express their views. Luce Michel was an artist and fantasist whose witty and sophisticated renderings of the brain were much appreciated. She also had an uncanny way of sizing people up and cutting to the quick of their weakness.

At a fancy banquet in the Grand Parc de Lyon on the occasion of the 1963 International Congress of Sleep Research, Luce Michel regaled the scientists at our table with a story of a visit to a house in which animals, mostly cats, performed experiments on the brains of humans. Her story was so detailed, so carefully constructed, and so vividly compelling that it seemed as real as any dream report. The scientists, who were as taken in by her story as they were by their own dreams, didn't known what to do or say.

Ten years later, the Brazilian artist Jonas dos Santos performed an improvisational theater piece called "Dog's Dreams" in my Brookline living room. In Jonas's imaginative play, two dogs captured and conducted brain experiments on a hunter-experimentalist (reluctantly played by me at Jonas's insistence). As with Luce's imaginary cat doctors, I wasn't sure that these dogs wouldn't cut my flesh. This was a clear signal that I myself was an experimental animal and a warning that if I deserved respect as a subject, so did my animal co-workers.

Despite such clever and penetrating remonstrances, I remain comfortable with using animals, including myself, as subjects of scientific inquiry. I share with Luce, with Jonas, and with animal-rights advocates a commitment to the most humane possible treatment of both human and subhuman experimental animals. But I do not accept the judgment that invasive procedures are wrong when they are designed to further understanding of the brain. My conviction goes all the way back to medical school when I attended a hearing in the Massachusetts State House in which animal research was under attack. The pediatric pathologist Sydney Farber won the day by showing slides of children who were hideously disfigured by disabling diseases. To his rhetorical question "Do you really want to find out what causes such horror in your children?" nearly all the legislators answered Yes.

For many people, and I am one of them, the need to better diagnose and treat the multitudes of severely handicapped mentally ill people is the equivalent of Farber's empathy with sick children. There is simply no alternative to animal experimentation if we wish to gain the knowledge that we need to help our fellow humans relieve the pain and disability of chronic mental illness. This point must be made even more forcefully now that the brain is so frequently an object of scientific interest and scrutiny. It is true that we have non-invasive PET and MRI methods of imaging regional differences in brain activation. But what do these measures mean at the level of cells and molecules? Without conducting basic research in animals we will never know. And we must know if we are to give psychiatry the strong scientific base it needs and deserves.

Back to MMHC, Harvard, and Cellular Neurophysiology

As much as I liked France and the French people, I believed that my scientific learning curve was flattening out just as my cultural sensitivity trajectory was increasing exponentially. For both of these reasons, I decided to leave Lyon after only nine months. I feared that if I stayed much longer I would become French and stay there forever. From Michel Jouvet I had learned the robustness of the pontine localization theory of REM sleep and one way of studying it.

From watching Jouvet at work, I had also learned ways of not doing things. One bad habit was his tendency to reset the sensitivity of a kymograph when it failed to register the muscle atonia that was used as a proxy for REM in those experiments. The result was an exaggerated regularity of pontine cats' REM periods. Despite these misgivings, the REM generator problem became the narrow focus of my scientific work. Jouvet deserves full credit for framing this problem clearly.

Within the larger context of the relationship of brain physiology to dreaming, I reasoned that if the specifics of REM generation could be worked out at the cellular and molecular level in the pons, it might be possible to deduce the difference between awake-state and REM-sleep patterns of brain activation. My own work was clearly a dreamlike hybrid of Edward Evarts's and Michel Jouvet's approaches. The Anglo-Saxon heretic and the Gallic maverick were thus happily married in my work on the cellular analysis of pontine brainstem activation in REM sleep.

I had Jack Ewalt's promise of a soft landing when I went back to finish my residency at the Massachusetts Mental Health Center. But I needed more than that. I needed to know that I could continue my science, and that I could do science while completing my residency requirements in psychiatry. From Lyon I wrote to Eric Kandel, who had by then set up his own neurophysiology lab at the MMHC. Eric had given up the lab space at Harvard Medical School that he had borrowed from Elwood Henneman. That little back room in Henneman's lab had a low ceiling, no windows, and was painted a hideous soft acid green. It had been electrically shielded by Hallowell Davis, who in the late 1930s had done the first EEG recording in the United States. Davis had had help from Albert Grass, who had built the first American EEG machine. One of Davis's first subjects had been B. F. Skinner, who later gave me the original tracing of his own brain waves made in that very room.

Kandel suggested that I approach Elwood Henneman to see if I could help advance the studies of sleep that he, John Pappenheimer, and Manfred Karnovsky had proposed to the National Institutes of Health. Their proposal was boldly functional. They thought that sleep must play some critical role in recovery from fatigue. If sleep were prevented, then sleep-promoting chemical substances might accumulate, as the French scientist Henri Pieron had reasoned earlier. Since none of the three senior Harvard grantees had ever recorded sleep, I was a welcome recruit to their project and was offered the "Davis green room" to pursue my own physiological studies of sleep on a half-time basis. Jack Ewalt readily agreed to let me finish the required second year of my psychiatric residency in the other half of my time if I worked for two years. This was a feasible arrangement. Since it was outpatient psychiatry that I needed, I could schedule my clinical appointments in half-day blocks. I also knew that I would be free to go to the lab for long periods of time on weekdays as well as in the evening and on weekend days.

My long-range plan was to develop a single-cell recording approach to determine the pontine neuronal mechanisms of REM-sleep generation. Starting from scratch, this was a tall order. At first, I worked with the Henneman sleep research team to find a simpler animal model for sleep than the cat or the rat. I tried to record the EEGs of fish, salamanders, and frogs. I succeeded only with the frogs. None of these lowly creatures had either the behavioral or the EEG signs of sleep that were necessary to establish them as valid models for what happened in the brains of sleeping mammals. They all had quiescent rest phases, probably evolutionary antecedents of sleep. But without thalamus and without cerebral cortex, they couldn't really be expected to qualify as models for mammalian sleep, much for less dreaming as we humans know it.

Eric Kandel, who had switched from the cat's hippocampus to the aplysia's abdominal ganglion in his efforts to understand learning and memory, was very encouraging of the development of a simpler animal model for sleep. It is likely that the basics of sleep, especially the circadian rest phase on which all sleep is built, can be studied in lower animals, perhaps even in the fruit flies that are the darlings of behavioral geneticists. But I was interested in mental states that those lower animals could not possibly possess. Although Eric's snails can learn, it seems very unlikely that they have memory in the Proustian sense of the word.

Although I got more reprint requests for my three frog papers than for any of the papers I later wrote on cat sleep, I devoted more and more attention to my own experimental goals. That meant using a mammalian model. Elwood Henneman, a spinal cord physiologist of the Sherringtonian era, was extremely supportive of these efforts. Both he and his former co-worker Vernon Mountcastle were enamored of sleep and eager to see someone else walk the scientific plank that they had so wisely eschewed. Since I wanted to use the chronic moveable microelectrode technique, it was logical to turn to David Hubel and Torsten Wiesel, who were about to be awarded the Nobel Prize for their neurophysiological discoveries of how the cat visual system encodes the visual world.

It is a little-known fact that David Hubel developed his sophisticated vision cell recording technique in order to study sleep. He and his mentor, Herbert Jasper, had expected to find that most brain cells shut off in sleep, as Sir Charles Sherrington had predicted. When they found instead that many neurons fired more in sleep (and especially in REM sleep) than in the awake state, Hubel decided to abandon his sleep project in favor of vision, which lent itself more easily to experimental analysis using the Sherringtonian reflex paradigm.

Hubel told me that sleep was much too complicated to be understood at the cellular level. He also declared that none of his many home-made micromanipulators would be available to me, because if he were to lend me one he would be depriving me of the chance to learn the engineering involved in apparatus construction. Making that fussy piston-in-cylinder system work so that microelectrodes could be lowered to targets in the brainstem was difficult enough to make a fully trained mechanical engineer cry. But it made me fume to spend so much time on an activity that was not very useful. Two years later, with help from Ed Evarts, I got a micromanipulator working. But I learned very little engineering in the process.

Neither Hubel nor his psychiatric co-worker Torsten Wiesel was very encouraging, even after I got my system working. Both were skeptical that anything useful would come of it. They shared concerns about the identification of brainstem neurons and hence about knowing what kind of cell was being recorded with Ed Evarts, Emilio Bizzi, and Giovanni Berlucchi. In their experiments, Hubel and Wiesel identified the cells that they recorded in terms of their response properties to light stimuli. Identifying neurons in the cerebral cortex certainly was problematic for us. We didn't know what kind of cell was being analyzed, and this limited our interpretation of our cortical unit recording experiment severely. But, fortunately for us, many of the most interesting neurons that were encountered in the brainstem identified themselves in ways that no one could anticipate. I will tell that story in the next chapter.

Two basic concepts were made clear by my dialog with my reluctant mentors. One was that, whereas the reflex paradigm was necessary and sufficient for studying the sensory inputs to and motor outputs from the brain, it was useless for studying what was done by the brain between the input and output stages. To study that seemingly hopelessly complex process, we needed some other paradigm. After struggling to define criteria for state control mechanisms, we came to call our new model the conscious state paradigm, which implies that the brain has something to do with consciousness—a point to which I will return.

In 1963 it seemed to me that no matter what shape that paradigm would ultimately take, consciousness must be our subjective awareness of an activation state of brain neurons. This conclusion followed inevitably from the obvious fact that visual perception was nothing more or less than activation states of certain brain cells. Light edges, bars, and shadows do not pass beyond the retina. From the end organ on in—and out again to the movements of our body—it is all nothing more or less than neural information that is processed. Of course we need to know more about how complex images are built up from the bits and pieces of visual code. We need to know more about how such images are perceived and then tied to memories, to feelings, and to thoughts as we respond to real objects or create inner visions. And we need to know how these brain processes are translated into motor action. But once we recognize the radical reality of neural representation, the mind-brain problem vanishes. It is a false problem. The mind is an activation state of the brain.

9 Cognitive Neuroscience as Synthesis

If psychoanalysis was the central thesis of psychiatry, and if psychoanalysis depended on the validity of its dream theory, then the challenge to that theory by the antithetical results of sleep science demanded resolution and the articulation of a new theory. In this chapter, I will describe how cellular and molecular neurobiology provided the details necessary to the creation of a new model of the brain-mind, and how the development of that model changed my understanding of myself.

The Activation-Synthesis Model was designed to account for dreaming as the psychological manifestation of a fundamental brain function, REM sleep. It did so at the very same cellular level of analysis at which Freud had originally tried to work. More than that, the cellular work has fostered a comprehensive model of brain-mind state that addresses a wide range of normal and pathological alterations of consciousness. Thus, the Activation-Synthesis Model of dreaming is a prime example of the integrative discipline called cognitive neuroscience. As I changed my own mind, by viewing REM-sleep dreaming as a state of my brain, I hope also to change yours and to give you a more accurate sense of your freedoms and constraints than the one you may currently have.

In 1968, when the time came for me to leave the Department of Physiology at Harvard Medical School, Jack Ewalt was more than permissively encouraging. I had consulted with him about the possibility of setting up a neurophysiology lab at the Massachusetts Mental Health Center. He had already helped Ed Sacher, Eric Kandel, Norm Weiner, and Joe Schildkraut set up basic biology research labs there. Many of those laboratories used animals in experiments. By the mid 1960s, there were snails, rats, and cats living in the basement of the MMHC and serving as proxies for the human patients upstairs. As the chairman of Harvard's Psychiatry Department, Ewalt wanted to be a patron of good science. He strongly urged his protégés to cut clinical work to a minimum, to dodge committee service whenever possible, and even to eschew teaching obligations if they compromised the science. This was unusual behavior for a psychoanalyst who had never done bench science himself. Mental hospitals were not then, and are not now, hotbeds of basic science. In fact, most of them have been closed.

Since about 1980, the Commonwealth of Massachusetts had become more and more explicitly hostile to basic science in its psychiatric institutes. This was a short-sighted mistake, as history will soon show. All levels of public finance must share the burden of training and research on mental illness. Cities and states have as high a stake in this unified effort as does the federal government. This is because those local public agencies must provide the infrastructure for the most humane and technically advanced care of the mentally ill. Since psychiatrists have a particular way of doing basic science that is some times uniquely useful, it behooves cities and states to provide at least the physical settings for both clinical and basic psychiatric research.

The Laboratory of Neurophysiology (1968–2003)

One factor made my entry into a scientific career much easier in the early 1960s that it would be today. Because the National Institute of Mental Health then recognized the scientific weakness of psychiatry, it decided to make training grants and research grants available to motivated young people like me. Without my NIMH special fellowship, I could not have gone to France to work with Michel Jouvet, I could not have spent three years in Elwood Henneman's lab at Harvard Medical School, and I could not have competed for grant support of my own independent work.

Even with a grant of my own, I didn't have a salary, a lab, or the equipment I needed to do my work. Jack Ewalt came to my rescue. Because he was a Massachusetts State Hospital Superintendent as well as the chairman of the Harvard Department of Psychiatry, Jack could give me a salary and assign to me already partially renovated research space. He told me that thanks to a general research support fund—again from the NIMH—I could buy the equipment necessary for my work.

To establish the cost of equipping my lab, Ewalt called Steve Kuffler, then the chairman of neurobiology, while I sat in his office. I can still see Ewalt, sitting back in his swivel chair, his hair slicked down on both sides of his thin forehead, saying, with characteristic gruffness, "Hey, Steve, how much does a neurophysiology lab cost?" Ewalt hung up, looked at me, and said to me: "Steve says it will cost about $50,000. You have $50,000. Just tell Catherine Hurley how you want to spend it." I cannot imagine such a thing happening today. Department chairmen no longer have such largesse. Even it they are as scientifically motivated as Ewalt was, there is little they can do to buck the public-sector and private-sector pressures to cut psychiatry staff. They must also force such personnel as can be retained into highly efficient, highly reimbursable encounters with patients. This bottom-line economic model serves neither the young physician nor the patients well. Furthermore, the research enterprise founders. This is especially sad because brain research is now in its heyday.

One can certainly ask why psychiatrists, of all people, should be doing basic research. Why take such highly trained clinicians away from patient care? Why not simply rely on Ph.D. neuroscientists, who are better trained technically and who are not distracted by clinical responsibilities? One answer to these good questions is that research psychiatrists—thanks to their clinical training—are sensitive to psychology and how it can be analyzed and measured so that it can be integrated with neurophysiological data. Psychiatrists also know what questions to explore using neurobiological tools because they have their eyes open to integration.

I hope it is not too immodest to claim that my laboratory has been successful both scientifically and economically. Our science has achieved national and international recognition. It has contributed to a revolution in thinking about the mind. And it has more than paid for itself, as federal and foundation grants have brought in much more money than the Commonwealth of Massachusetts invested. The Commonwealth should be jumping for joy at such an outcome. Instead, the MMHC and its research labs were closed in 2003.

The Harvard Medical School did little to oppose the short-sightedness of the Commonwealth in its decision to close the MMHC. There were some good reasons for this passivity. The MMHC had become an expensive embarrassment both physically and intellectually. Better to let it go than prop it up, it may well have been argued. But the policy of Harvard Medical School Dean Joseph Martin to resorb psychiatry into neurology is questionable. Though it is true that psychiatry has roots in neurology, psychiatry is not reducible to neurology any more than mind is reducible to brain. Any solid science of psychology must take account of advances in brain research, but that psychology will be worthless if it does not offer to neurology as much as it takes from that field. When the MMHC was closed, in 2003, scientific psychology was dealt a crippling blow.

From the minute we unpacked the rental truck that moved my scientific equipment from Harvard Medical School to the MMHC, the sense of adventure and the exciting prospect of discovery was palpable. The many young people who worked with me felt my excitement. There we were, in the back room of a state mental hospital, deciding how to investigate the brain mechanisms of dreaming. Upstairs were patients who dreamed with their eyes open.

Was I scared? Yes, but only a little. It seemed obvious that if I simply observed the neuronal activity of the brainstem carefully I would have to succeed in some significant way. After all, no one else had ever explored that important brain structure in unanesthetized animals. Even if we were in a cerebral no-man's-land, we would learn something. As it turned out, we stumbled into the brain's command center.

In the beginning, the group consisted of me, my student-collaborator Bob McCarley, and one employee: Lynn Cozza, who did our office work and all the brain histology. I wanted to record from individual nerve cells in the pontine brainstem of unanesthetized cats. I wanted to study the brain activity of cats that could wake and sleep naturally while I tuned in on their neurons signaling to one another.

Robert McCarley (right) and me in our recording room in the Laboratory of Neurophysiology at the Massachusetts Mental Health Center. We worked productively and happily for 16 years and became something of a household word in dream research (at least in households of psychoanalysts). When this photo was taken, in 1978, by Theodore Spagna, we had just published two articles about our dream theory in the *American Journal of Psychiatry* (1977), following our back-to-back articles in *Science* (1975) on the REM-off cells in the locus coeruleus and the reciprocal interaction model.

I had gotten the Evarts-Hubel single-cell recording system to work in the cerebral cortex before leaving Harvard Medical School, but in the MMHC lab it took Bob McCarley and me two years to get any useful data out of the brainstem. Success came from constructing a box that served as a confining bedroom for the cats. By keeping the cats awake at night, we taught them to sleep by day in the box with their heads immobilized.

Living by My Wits

In 1965 I had been married for nine years, was the father of two sons, and hankered for a home of my own. Too poor to buy property in Boston, I didn't want to move to the suburbs, and I needed to live near enough to the lab to go back and forth at any hour of the day or night. So I decided to stay in my apartment at 308 Commonwealth Avenue and buy my second home first. To my parents' deep chagrin, I plunked my entire life savings of $3,000 down on an abandoned dairy farm in East Burke, Vermont. The place needed work, lots of it. I thought I would ski at Burke Mountain, and I did, but as time went on I spent more and more time fixing up the farm.

While doing science in Boston, I learned carpentry, wiring, and plumbing from my friendly neighbors in Vermont. Those skills proved useful in the lab, and also in the house in Brookline that I bought in 1970. Everything started to go better for me about then. Nearly 40 years old and still just beginning my career, I was paid $18,000 a year, which I supplemented by consulting for the Massachusetts Rehabilitation Commission and by seeing private patients at night for $15 an hour. I worked 60–80 hours a week.

As I have already noted, Bob McCarley contributed significantly to progress in those early years by taking major responsibility for data analysis, including computerized calculation of data on neuronal firing. Because we could not (at first) record from the brainstem, we worked on the cerebral and cerebellar cortices, where neurons could be found, held, and studied with relative ease in free-moving behaving animals. We tried to anticipate what we might find in the brainstem and how we would quantify our data in relation to our ideas about the neurophysiological mechanisms underlying dreaming. We got some things right. But because we were also fishing in uncharted waters, we were able to make some surprising catches that we never anticipated and to land other treasures of the deep that had been thrown back by our more law-abiding colleagues.

The 1970s were our glory years. We first reported on the selective firing of pontine reticular giant cells during REM sleep in *Science* in 1971. Our

Laboratory of Neurophysiology colleagues, circa 1977. Gathered around the oak desk of our administrator Eve Melnechuk (smiling under plant in center of photo) is a group of co-workers with varied motivations and backgrounds. To Eve Melnechuk's right, I grin proudly while Robert McCarley (to Eve's left) looks more reservedly pleased. Ennio Vivaldi, a post-doctoral student from Chile, is gesturing with his hands in a typically Latin way. The photographer, Ted Spagna, points to his own head as if to say "That's crazy." Also present (right to left next to me) are Chantal Rode (my household manager), Siham Rashed, a visiting psychiatrist from Cairo, and Andy Stratham, a Harvard mathematical doctoral student. My daughter, Julia Hobson, then age 5, grins in the foreground.

three papers describing their discharge rates, patterns, and changes over the REM sleep cycle were published in the *Journal of Neurophysiology* between 1973 and 1975. This evidence of a state-specific change in neuronal excitability was the main thing we were looking for. We understandably overemphasized the importance and significance of this discovery.

The big surprise was our unanticipated discovery of selective deactivation during REM sleep of neurons in two of Michel Jouvet's favorite brainstem nuclei: the locus coeruleus (which Jouvet thought generated REM) and the raphé nuclei (which he thought generated non-REM sleep). According to Jouvet's theory, the neurons should have turned on during sleep. Instead, they turned off! Besides disproving both of Jouvet's hypotheses about how these aminergic systems really work, the behavior of those REM-off cells provided us with the physical basis of a model for the brainstem clock that timed and triggered REM.

We had been using the term "neuronal oscillator" to describe this mechanism long before we had the evidence needed to say what kind of oscillator it might be. The discovery of the reciprocal behavior of the REM-on cells (which we hypothesized to be cholinergic) and the REM-off cells (which we thought to be aminergic) led us to propose that waking occurred when the aminergic system was dominant and that REM sleep occurred when the cholinergic system was dominant. NREM sleep was an intermediate state of this simple push-pull neuronal system.

My Chemical Brain Self

What I take to be myself—the me who wakes and dreams—is, at a deep level, a brain whose billions of neurons have been activated by internal stimulation of spontaneous origin. Whether that brain-self is awake or dreaming is determined by chemical signals, also of internal origin. If these signals are predominantly aminergic (that is, mediated by the chemical molecules histamine, norepinephrine, and serotonin), then my brain self is awake. Without those chemicals, but with my brain reciprocally activated by acetylcholine, my brain-self dreams. I then say I am awake, but I am mistaken. It is only after I wake up that my brain can correct this error. In other words, my brain depends on its own internal chemistry when assessing its own state. Now I say that my state of consciousness has been chemically altered and realize that dreaming is an elaborate illusion created by my own brain.

Model Building (1975–1977)

Bob McCarley recognized that a system with the synaptic connectivity and excitatory-inhibitory features of our hypothetical REM-on/REM-off brain cell oscillator in the pontine brainstem might obey the mathematical rules set out by Volterra and Lotka to describe the interactions of prey and predator populations in field biology. Thus, the reciprocal interaction that we proposed as governing the dialog between the aminergic REM-off and cholinergic REM-on cells of the pons could be described synaptically (leading to a pharmacological hypothesis-testing program for our lab) and mathematically (giving the NREM-REM sleep cycle its first set of lawful governing principles).

It was immediately apparent to us that the brain-mind was constantly shifting its neuromodulatory balance. As psychiatrists, we had already been exposed to the idea of chemical imbalance, though we had never been able to specify it. The poles of the oscillation that we were looking at were not mental health and mental illness. Instead they were waking (which is aminergically driven) and dreaming (which is cholinergically driven). Waking was characterized by sensory exteroception and by active motor behavior; dreaming was characterized by sensory interoception and fictive motor behavior.

After the 1975 publication in *Science* of our two papers describing the firing properties of the REM-off cells and our sketch of Reciprocal Interaction Model, we published two papers—one on Freud's neurobiology, one on our Activation-Synthesis dream theory—in the *American Journal of Psychiatry*. In those two papers, published in 1977, we argued that Freud had been right to insist on the study of neurons as a step to a model of the mind and wrong to abandon that idea in favor of a speculative psychological dream theory.

By 1980, we had conceived a new research program and had begun to execute it. This program had two separate but integrated goals. One was to test the neurobiological assumptions of the Reciprocal Interaction Model. The other was to develop an entirely new approach to the psychology of dreams that would enable us to map back and forth between the domains of brain and mind.

We came out of hiding at about this time. At ages 39 and 44, Bob McCarley and I were two unknown psychiatrists who had retreated to an infrequently visited suite of rooms in the back of a dingy state mental hospital. As our work became more widely known, we were suddenly propelled into the national and international limelight because we claimed that we had the scientific data to propose an entirely novel dream theory that specifically regarded its psychoanalytic predecessor as ill-founded and incorrect.

We called the new dream theory Activation-Synthesis to capture the idea that dreaming occurred when the brain was activated in sleep. Next we proposed that the unique psychological qualities of dreaming were the brain's peculiar synthesis of its own internal activation signals. By 'activation' we meant spontaneous, automatic, physiologically determined increases in the level of firing by most brain cells; by 'synthesis' we meant the creation of a conscious experience with a scenario-like structure that integrated bizarre percepts (peculiar cognitions) and strong emotion. We said that dreams are as they are because during REM sleep "the brain makes the best of a bad job." In view of the isolation of the brain during REM sleep, that "best" is not bad at all.

At first we didn't notice how important our discoveries were. Nor did we appreciate how much attention we had attracted. We were still so deeply immersed in solving the day-to-day problems of EEG monitoring, single-cell recording, computer analysis of data, and histological reconstruction of the electrode tracks in the brain that we hardly looked up. Because no one wanted to work with us until the mid 1970s, we did all the experimental work ourselves. As we sat at our desks in that back room of the Massachusetts Mental Health Center, we began to think that if the human neurophysiology was similar to what we had observed in cats (as it probably was) then the implications for dream theory in particular, and for psychiatry in general, were profound. Even today, I estimate those implications to be greater than we or our peers yet recognize. I have been surprised by the reticence of some of our colleagues and astonished by the active resistance of others to what seems to me to be an essentially sound and irresistible paradigm shift. Dreaming is no longer mysterious. It is a natural phenomenon whose significance must be quite different from what we had been led by Freud to suppose.

It was when McCarley and I were working on our two 1977 *American Journal of Psychiatry* papers that our own minds began to change radically. Remember that, although we were somewhat skeptical mavericks, we were thoroughly immersed in psychoanalytic doctrine and were working in one of the world's leading citadels of that doctrine. If we were going to challenge Freud's Dream Theory, we were going to challenge all psychoanalytic assumptions about how the mind works, because that theory was foundational to psychoanalysis. Even the Freudian concept of the unconscious mind as a dynamically repressed cognitive function was called into question.

Whether a certain idea, emotion, fantasy, or dream scenario entered consciousness was, for us, not so much a question of freeing these psychic forms from repression as it was the result of a specific and selective sort of brain activation. Activation states differed most importantly according to the chemistry of the brain, not a shifting balance between such mental functions as superego, ego, and id. For Morton Reiser and some other psychoanalytic critics of our work, the neurophysiological mechanisms we had uncovered only confirmed Freud's theory. Reiser said that the subcortical brain that was activated during REM was the id and the inactivated cortex was the superego. This Freudianization of physiology is understandable, but it does not deal with our main point. That point was our ability to explain the bizarreness of dreams without resorting to the Disguise-Censorship Model of psychoanalysis. For us, dreams were intrinsically bizarre, not bowdlerized translations of forbidden wishes.

As soon as we came up with the name Activation-Synthesis, McCarley and I knew we had formulated a model that was the antithesis of Freud's Disguise-Censorship Model. For Freud, there was activation too, but it was an unconscious wish that was activated because of a lapse in vigilance by the censor, an ego structure that normally protected consciousness from unacceptable id impulses. Enter disguise, the transformation of the latent dream content into the innocuous and seemingly jumbled manifest dream content. For us, the activation was physiological and selective: the limbic lobe and the posterolateral cortex were turned on, which led to automatic generation of emotions and associated imagery. The dream story was a synthesis of these disparate activations. That dream story was bizarre and confusing because the dorsolateral prefrontal cortex was deactivated and the entire forebrain was deprived of norepinephrine and serotonin, so that the forebrain was playing cards without a full deck. We later guessed that there must be some advantage to playing the game of life this way. But at the time we knew nothing of the importance of REM to temperature control, and we only dimly perceived the function of REM as a virtual-reality generator for consciousness.

Instead of leaping ahead to novel functional theories, McCarley and I decided to go back to Freud's original texts to be sure we understood what he had said. We carefully reread *Project for a Scientific Psychology*, the 1895 work that immediately preceded *The Interpretation of Dreams*. It was in the course of writing about Freud's Project, his Disguise-Censorship Model, and his Dream Theory that it occurred to us that we should pay attention to the *form* of dreams. We needed, first and foremost, to describe and measure the kind of conscious experience that dreaming represented. We had to resist the natural temptation to interpret dream content until we had taken this essential first step.

Underlying this important and radical change in approach to dream psychology was the idea of brain-mind isomorphism, which McCarley and I used in our attempt to map from mind to brain and back from brain to mind. The principle of isomorphism states that, since all mental events are subjective experiences of brain events, there must be, at some level, a demonstrable similarity of form linking the two domains of discourse. Our concept of isomorphism became more radical when it further asserted that the two domains of discourse differed only at the relatively superficial level of language description. At a deeper level, brain activation *was* mind activation. In other words, our theory aspired to a fundamental monism. There is only one system, and it is fully integrated. I call it the Brain-Mind.

Three simple statements should suffice to clarify the points just made:

1. Dream vision is our subjective awareness of visual brain activation.
2. Dream emotion is our subjective awareness of emotional brain activation.
3. The poverty of dream thought is our subjective awareness of deactivation of the higher brain functions involved in directed thought.

Instead of resorting to complex psychological theories to explain dream vision, dream emotion, and dream thought impoverishment, McCarley and I decided to take a look at what the brain was actually doing during REM sleep, the state in which the most intense dreaming takes place. We found that dream form had nothing to do with what happened to us yesterday, with what happened in our childhood, or with what might happen to us in the future. Those are all specific and individual content issues. Rather, dream form has to do with what all brain-minds do whenever anyone, at any time and in any place, activates his or her brain during REM sleep.

What we were after was universality, the big game of the neuropsychological hunt. Once we had bagged and tagged the universals, we could look with new eyes at particulars. By focusing on defining, identifying, and measuring the formal aspects of dreams, we have been able to suggest how percepts, emotions, and thoughts may interact to make dreaming so different from the awake state as to constitute two distinct states of conscious experience. Those differences are based on radically different forms of brain activation. I know that many people, including some of my peers, do not yet accept this principle, but I am increasingly confident that our approach is both scientifically sound and ontologically robust.

McCarley and I have had inordinate difficulty convincing our co-workers and our sponsors of the necessity and the power of the formal approach to dreaming. It is important to clarify what we mean by "brain-mind isomorphism," which appears to be quite difficult to grasp. The isomorphism principle has somehow gotten lost in the shuffle of excitement about what sleep neurophysiology could or could not do for dream psychology. We said it could do quite a lot. Some of our peers said it could do nothing at all. Our adversaries based their pessimistic argument on the claim that dreaming and REM sleep are completely dissociable. We fear that many of our adversaries are reluctant to give up the snug comfort of Freudian psychology. We are the first to admit that it is chilling not to have a comprehensive psychodynamic theory of the mind.

The resistance to the replacement of Freud's Disguise-Censorship Model of dreaming with our Activation-Synthesis hypothesis is deep and widespread. This was clear from the defeat of my motion, made at the 2006 Toward a Science of Consciousness conference, that "Freud's Dream Theory is obsolete." My argument was opposed by Mark Solms, and two-thirds of an audience of our peers at the aforementioned conference voted me down. Fortunately, debates do not settle truths, but I nonetheless found the count disconcerting. We still have a long way to go!

In 1975, McCarley and I began to pursue dream psychology in earnest, even if we were neither paid nor praised for it. Our 1983 discovery that dream bizarreness could be reduced to orientational instability led us to the Dreaming as Delirium concept. Delirium is the pathological state that many of my patients at Bellevue had evinced. Delirium consists of visual hallucinations, disorientation to time and place, recent memory loss, and confabulation. Dreaming, which is normal, shows all four of these signs of and is thus delirium by definition. In REM sleep, we all became delirious, because the brain changes its own chemistry as radically as it ever does under the influence of the drugs or alcohol that cause pathological delirium.

My Dreaming Brain-Self

When I dream, my brain wrongly diagnoses its own state as awake. Why? Although the dream state has its own distinctive labels—such as the bizarreness in which times, places, and persons are confused, interchangeable, and internally inconsistent—my dreaming brain-self usually doesn't recognize its state accurately.

We now know that one reason for this egregious error is weakening of memory and thought as a result of loss of aminergic modulation of the brain and persistent inactivation of the dorsolateral prefrontal cortex. The brain-self (the I who dreams) is missing that important function that tells itself what state it is in. My self has thus lost the awareness of awareness that helps me correctly assess my state as awake. Because it seems likely that awareness of awareness—a critical aspect of secondary consciousness—may be mediated by the frontal cortex, it is natural to hypothesize that the loss of self-reflective awareness that is typical of dreaming is related to persistent deactivation of the frontal cortex.

In terms of protoconsciousness theory, it is remarkable how very much like waking consciousness is dream consciousness. Our comparative work naturally emphasized differences, and we found some significant ones that we were able to explain, tentatively, via neurophysiology. But this approach overlooks or minimizes similarities, which the functional theory celebrates. The idea that dreaming simulates the awake state and provides the brain with a virtual reality is every bit as important as the emphasis on differences, and perhaps even more so. I will return to this point in chapters 17 and 18.

Testing and Promoting the Models (1975–1977)

Because my wife Joan and I were friends of Kathy and Louis Kane, we were deeply involved in the planning of the "Boston 200" celebration of the American bicentennial. Planning for "Boston 200" began as early as 1972, the year our daughter Julia was born. When I heard of the new brain exhibit initiative at the Museum of Science, I felt sure that sleep and dream research could excite the public if it were presented as a process (experience) rather than a product (knowledge). If I could get the public to look at sleep and appreciate its internal dynamics, I could share with them the excitement of observation. The result was an exhibit called "Dreamstage," which opened at the Carpenter Center in 1977. The media storm it set off helped make REM sleep and the Activation-Synthesis theory of dreams better known.

I recall waking up on the beach at Ogunquit, Maine on the Fourth of July weekend of 1977 and seeing people sitting in the sand reading the cover story about our work in the *New York Times Magazine*. The article, titled "Watching the Brain Dream," was illustrated with images from the Dreamstage catalog. I was about to take my family to Tuscany, where we had rented a house in the village of Riolo. Riolo was situated on a mule-track road high above Bagni di Lucca, the spa that had attracted Byron and Shelley in the nineteenth century. There I began work on my first book, *The Dreaming Brain*, finally published by Basic Books in 1988. Riolo's only telephone was in the post office above a cow stable. It rang quite frequently that summer as requests for permission to reproduce the Dreamstage illustrations poured in from around the world.

The recognition that came as a result of the Dreamstage publicity made work in the lab and life at home more difficult for me. I don't really think the failure of my marriage was due to the modest scientific success of the Reciprocal Interaction and Activation-Synthesis models or to the waves of publicity that followed Dreamstage. These events nonetheless conspired with my deep love of adventure, travel, and intimacy to make the years

1977–1986 tumultuous for me. I was 44 in 1977 and 53 in 1986. Between those years, I very much enjoyed what others might have called a mid-life crisis.

Refining and Testing the New Theories (1977–1986)

A paradigm with which to organize thought or to dictate experiments is a great luxury in science. It is especially exciting if it is boundary-breaking. The Reciprocal Interaction Model of REM-sleep control provided the neuro-biological foundation of the Activation-Synthesis dream theory. McCarley and I set out to test each theory at its own level. It was a period of explosive ferment in the lab. As table 9.1 shows, many people participated and a wide variety of projects were developed. It was a heady, problematic time, the most exciting and stimulating decade of my life. But there were casualties. The most severe was my marriage, which was dissolved after 27 years.

Table 9.1
Some projects and people in the Laboratory of Neurophysiology, 1977–2000.

Microelectrode Studies of Brainstem Neurons and PGO Waves
Jack Nelson, M.D., PGO Burst Cells in the Peribrachial Pons
David Mann, M.D., DA Neurons in the Substantia Nigra
Ralph Lydic, Ph.D., 5HT Neurons Recorded over the Long Term

Neuro-Anatomy of REM Sleep Generator Network
Jim Quattrochi, Ph.D. staff associate, project director
Adam Mamelak, Medical School student, neural nets and Nightcap
Takao Hensch, Harvard College undergraduate, computer analysis
Oscar Hsu, Harvard College undergraduate, computer analysis

Pharmacology of Cholinergic REM Sleep Enhancement
Ennio Vivaldi, M.D., postdoctoral fellow
Tom McKenna, predoctoral student
Tom Amatruda, predoctoral student
Ed Silverman, Ph.D., psychiatry resident
Helen Baghdoyan, Ph.D., postdoctoral student
Margo Rodrigo, M.D., visiting scientist
José Calvo, M.D., visiting scientist
Subimal Datta, Ph.D., postdoctoral fellow

Formal Psychology of Dreaming
Edward Pace-Schott, M.S., co-investigator
Bob Stickgold, Ph.D., co-investigator
Jeff Sutton, M.D., Ph.D., psychiatry resident
Steven Hoffman, M.D., psychiatry resident
Jane Merritt, master's degree candidate, Harvard Extension School
Cindi Rittenhouse, master's degree candidate, Harvard Extension School

But I also lost Bob McCarley, who left for the Brockton V.A. Hospital after 16 years of collaboration. The survival of my career and the lab were functions of the establishment of new findings in the brain and new ways of thinking about the mind.

The paradigm shift that McCarley and I proposed was not only intellectual but also personal, social, and behavioral. Within five years, the Laboratory of Neurophysiology had switched from being a small work unit largely unknown to the world to a still small but larger and more diverse group of scientists whose ideas and data became well known internationally, even outside scientific circles. One reason for our notoriety was our direct challenge to Sigmund Freud, who had dominated thinking about dreams for 75 years. We threw down the gauntlet to the Freudians in our two 1977 papers in the *American Journal of Psychiatry*. According to the editor in chief, John Nemiah, those two papers stimulated more letters than any ever published in the journal. Most of those letters were critical, negative, or even downright hostile.

The debate with the Freudians continues to this day. Mark Solms is the most recent advocate of what we consider to be outmoded psychoanalytic views. Solms has even persuaded some prominent neuroscientists, including my old fellow-at-arms Eric Kandel, that Freudian psychoanalysis should be preserved.

The high points of the discourse between 1977 and 1986 were Dreamstage (1977–1982) and the 1975 debate at the American Psychiatric Association's meeting in New Orleans. In the debate, Bob McCarley and I were opposed by Morton Reiser of Yale University and Gerald Vogel of Emory University. A show of hands indicated that Bob and I had convinced at least two-thirds of the audience that Freud's Dream Theory needed major revision if not the complete replacement that we advocated. A spate of articles in the lay press promulgated our viewpoint. Chief among these was Edward Dolnick's cover story in *The Atlantic*, titled "Was Freud Wrong?"

While all the external hubbub was going on, the lab was humming. Some tensions over priority, credit, and leadership arose because Bob McCarley, only five years my junior, needed to spread his own wings and fly. We were told by our chairman, Miles Shore, that it was unlikely that Bob could be promoted to Harvard professional rank at the MMHC because both he and I had worked on the same projects and no department could afford two sleep and dream specialists. This was disappointing, to say the least.

With my strong encouragement, Bob got his own NIH grant to study the synaptic mechanisms of REM-sleep generation using intracellular recording. That meant that, instead of getting a metal microelectrode as close as one could to the outside of a neuron, the glass recording electrode would penetrate the cell membrane and measure the voltage difference across it. To my mounting distress, this methodological refinement split the lab down the middle. When I resisted dividing the space and the personnel into two separate laboratories, Bob began looking elsewhere. He was soon appointed Professor at the Brockton V.A. Hospital, where he has been very successful as a lab chief and where he now heads the Department of Psychiatry. I admire what Bob has been able to do on his own. I miss him, especially his wry sense of humor.

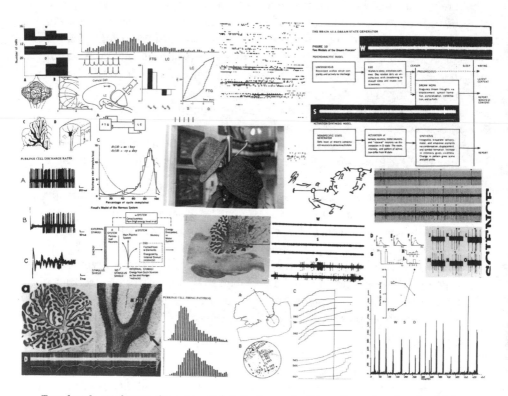

Two heads are better than one. Ralph Lydic made this collage showing the Irish tweed hats of Robert McCarley and me hanging on the clothes stand just inside the Laboratory of Neurophysiology at MMHC. Some of the scientific highlights of the first decade of our collaboration (1968–1978) are shown, including our work on cerebellar Purkinje cells and our studies of pontine tegmentum giant cells that revealed activity of the motor system in sleep and led to the model of reciprocal interaction between REM-on (cholinergic) and REM-off (aminergic) neurones. Dreaming was conceived by us as the subjective experience of brain activation and the synthesis of internally generated information in sleep.

The most important new achievement of these years was the establishment of cholinergic induction of REM sleep as a robust and physiologically meaningful experimental technique. At last we were testing hypotheses. At last we were real scientists. Instead of simply watching brain states unfold and inferring the mechanisms of that unfolding from the spontaneous activation patterns of neurons, we were intervening actively to evaluate the hypothesis that our acetylcholine-enhancing chemical probes would tip the balance of the brainstem in the direction of REM. It did.

We reasoned that if neurons that generate REM sleep were naturally activated by acetylcholine, then microinjection into the brainstem of chemical compounds that activated acetylcholine receptors would enhance REM. After microinjection of carbachol, bethanechol, and dioxylane, we did indeed observe immediate, prolonged, and intense enhancement of REM sleep. That this effect was truly cholinergic was evidenced by the equally robust REM enhancement seen after neostigmine installation. Neostigmine does not activate the acetylcholine receptor as do the cholinergic agonists mentioned above. Rather, it ties up the enzyme anticholinesterase that breaks down spontaneously released acetylcholine. The result is that endogenous acetylcholine can build up enough molecular strength to trigger and sustain REM sleep.

Many people worked on the studies that eventually led to universal acceptance of these findings. (Again, see table 9.1.) The pharmacological data, important in their own right, also helped to establish the underlying physiological model as valid. This important achievement gave indirect support to the Reciprocal Interaction model and the Activation-Synthesis model, both of which were creating firestorms of controversy. We were soon involved in a rear-guard action with our neurobiological peers over the validity of the REM sleep generator hypothesis, as well as in an ongoing debate with psychoanalysts over dream theory.

My Scientific Brain-Self

As the theoretical light dawned in my brain, I became a more complete scientist. Nature had revealed to me the mechanisms by which my brain changes its state. My view of myself as a subject changed. My view of myself as an object also changed. I was not an immaterial soul, floating in some unconnected way above my brain. These facts are still hard for me to accept. It is easier for me to understand how my brain-self came to regard its own conscious states as informative and worthy of scientific scrutiny. My brain-self discovered that it could look at itself and make intelligent inferences about its own workings.

I began to think of my brain as a subjective object and my brain states as objective subjects. Putting these ideas to the test became my goal.

The Growth and Development of the Reciprocal Interaction Model (1986–2003)

Skepticism about the models and questions about our scientific integrity resulted in the temporary suspension of our NIMH grant support in 1985. To counter our critics, we wrote a paper that was published in *Behavioral and Brain Sciences* in 1986 under the title "Evolving Concepts of Sleep Cycle Control." Ralph Lydic and Helen Baghdoyan were important allies in that project. They later married and left the lab for the greener pastures of Hershey, Pennsylvania; they are now professors at the University of Michigan.

Ralph Lydic and Helen Baghdoyan. When we were attending an international sleep congress in France in 1982, these able and loyal students met me for lunch at a small restaurant in the hills above Cannes, where I took this picture. During their time in the lab, Lydic documented the repetitive arrest in REM of raphé nucleus neuronal firing and Baghdoyan systematically studied short-term REM enhancement by carbachol. Together, we wrote the 1986 *Brain and Behavioral Sciences* monograph titled "Evolving concepts of REM sleep generation," which helped to establish the validity of the reciprocal-interaction model of sleep-cycle control.

Ralph, Helen, and I knew that simply rewriting our NIMH grant proposal was not enough, because our critics could continue to take pot-shots at us from behind the bushes of anonymous peer review. We needed to flush them out of the critical bushes by saying: "This is what we think. What do you think? Please stand up and be counted."

Behavioral and Brain Sciences features open peer review. We wrote what is called a target article. The editors then invited about 100 other scientists to shoot at it. Many of our peers took up our challenge and criticized us in writing. Even if we could not persuade them, we could at least rebut them. Some of our best-known opponents remained silent, however. Time will tell whether they were political foxes or intellectual cowards.

Within a year, our grant was not only funded again but elevated to MERIT status. The promotion gave our lab much-needed financial stability as it expanded its scope to include the cognitive dimension. A MERIT award is for ten years instead of the usual three to five. I will be forever grateful for that vote of confidence from the NIMH.

The upshot of our scientific experimentation and discussions from 1990 to the present is that the Reciprocal Interaction Model is the only theory that deals effectively with the surprising REM-off behavior of the aminergic neuronal systems of the pons. It has recently been incorporated into the flip-flop model of Cliff Saper. Furthermore, there is now overwhelmingly strong evidence for our hypothesized cholinergic excitation of the REM-on neurons. In 2002 we published a second *Behavioral and Brain Sciences* target article, which updated the evidence and modified the neurobiological model. We titled that paper "Dreaming and the Brain" because it also reviewed the psychological side of our story and synthesized it with the neurobiology. The paper's neurobiological portion evoked little dissent, which may mean either that our model is now widely accepted or that no one cares very much about it anymore. In 2002, it was our broader integrative agenda that came under attack.

The Scientific Study of Dreaming (1986–Present)

As soon as the Reciprocal Interaction Model was in place, Bob McCarley and I erected the Activation-Synthesis theory of dreaming on its base. We felt that the psychological side of the story was in need of more work than the neurobiology. But how could we study dreams directly? Dream theories based on content analysis were either questionably speculative or frankly superstitious. Though we were used to criticism, we felt that we could afford neither of these adjectives. Our answer was to take a formal approach rather than a content-analytic one. We asked: Is dreaming formally distinctive from the awake state? If it is, can the formal differences be mapped onto the differences that distinguish the neurobiology of REM sleep from that of the awake state? Our bias was to answer Yes to both questions, but getting the evidence turned out to be much harder than we anticipated.

Before Bob McCarley left the lab in 1984, we had begun a line of work that has continued to this day. Before discussing some stunning details of these results, I want to say that, for once, the NIMH let us down. Never, ever, did it offer the least bit of encouragement for our work on dreams. Why not? Because the deep conviction of most of our peers was that subjective experience is not amenable to scientific study. Whenever we submitted a grant proposal, we were told to stick to the neurobiology, or to do cognitive science and forget about studying dreaming itself.

We hope our work will now convince skeptics that dreaming is a subjective state of the brain that can be precisely defined, quantitatively measured, and scientifically analyzed. Although we probably would have done this work anyway, it is a pleasure to note that the MacArthur Foundation's Research Network on Mind-Body Interactions supported our efforts in dream psychology generously and enthusiastically during more than ten years of collaboration with that wonderful group (1990–2000).

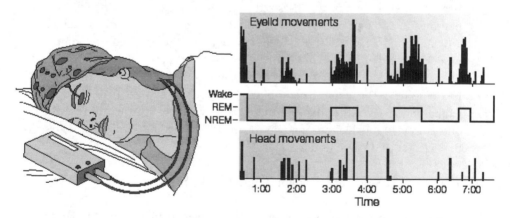

Bob Stickgold's daughter, Emma, recorded her home sleep for an eighth-grade science project using the two-channel recorder that we invented. Her photograph was used to create the drawing. Only two channels of data are needed to diagnose wake, NREM, and REM with 90% agreement with polysomnography, as the plots at right show. The Nightcap records major posture shifts from a forehead accelerometer and eyelid movement signals are derived from an eyelid sensor. A computer then performs an algorithmic estimate of brain states (1,1 = wake; 0,0 = NREM; 0,1 = REM). The device is useful as a screen for sleep pathology and for the home-based studies of dreaming.

What Is Dream Form?

By dream form we meant to identify and measure such universal qualities of dreaming as the following:

1. Sensory modality. The nature and intensity of internal percepts that are generated—e.g., dreams are visually vivid and the scenes are always beheld by the dreamer, who perceives himself to be moving through a vividly perceived dream space.
2. Cognitive features. Dreams are often bizarre, but this is neither noticed nor explained when we are dreaming—probably because other cognitive functions, including narrative memory, self-reflective awareness, and analytic thought, are also impaired.
3. Emotional features. Elation, anxiety, and anger appear to be common in dreams, but such awake-state emotions as shame, guilt, and sadness are not.

We thought that these course-grained formal features of dreaming would be found in all the REM-sleep dreams of all our subjects, whatever the content of individual subject matter might be. This hypothesis proved valid. More than that, such universals as dream bizarreness turned out to be not only measurable but scientifically reducible to those orientational processes known to be affected by the organic state of the brain. This insight led to our Dreaming as Delirium idea.

Our struggle to rigorously define, reliably identify, and precisely measure cognitive bizarreness is ongoing, but we have already achieved some success, and several unexpected insights have arisen from our efforts. For example, "dream bizarreness" does not usually refer to physically impossible monsters or those out-of-bounds dream features that the word 'bizarreness' first suggests. Instead, it grows out of a simple, robust discontinuity and/or incongruity of the structural details of dreams' plots. Children may often dream of monsters, but adults rarely do. Instead, in adults' dreams, character A suddenly disappears or turns into character B or a hybrid of A and B; or one room in one sort of building becomes connected to another kind of room in another sort of building, and the action suddenly changes from one of eager approach to one of anxious flight. We can now declare, without fear of contradiction, that times, places, and persons often change without notice in dreams.

Two of the dream reports reproduced earlier in this book offer abundant examples of the disoriented nature of dream bizarreness. In the report reproduced in chapter 4, I am in an unidentified hotel, then in an unspecified Greek temple, and finally on a hillside in Vermont. In the report reproduced in chapter 5, I am likewise engaged in three quite discontinuous activities: the EEG meeting scene gives way to walking and running in a city that suddenly becomes rural. In neither dream do I ever know exactly where I am, who is with me, or why I am there. In the awake state, such disorientation would be disconcerting to say the least. Awake, it would be upsetting to me unless I had advanced Alzheimer's disease and didn't know that I didn't know these basic facts of life.

To summarize this quality called dream bizarreness, we say that in dreams we experience *orientational instability*. This means that the Aristotelian unities that characterize awake-state mental life are constantly violated in dreams. It is just another way of saying "disorientation," which is one of the major symptoms of the organic mental dysfunction known as delirium. As I have already noted, delirium is commonly caused by the administration or withdrawal of drugs that affect the neuromodulatory control systems of the brainstem. It took us five years to recognize this fact of dream life. Now it seems obvious. But centuries of content analysis had almost entirely overlooked it. Freud thought dream bizarreness represented

José Calvo, Ennio Vivaldi, and Subimal Datta. The discovery by Vivaldi that the neurons in the peribrachial region of the pons fired in bursts prior to ipsiversive eye movements in REM sleep led to the documentation of long-term REM enhancement. Calvo and Datta were able to trigger ipsilateral eye movements and PGO waves by microinjecting carbachol into the peribrachial region of the pontine tegmentum. This effect was followed by a week-long enhancement of REM sleep, an effect which we called long-term REM enhancement. This experiment shows the complexity of REM sleep regulation by the brain and supports the theory that REM sleep (and its dreams) are the expressions of an intrinsic system designed to simulate waking behavior in sleep.

an active effort to disguise unconscious motives, but he never looked closely for the psychological essence of this trait. Without being able to disprove Freud's Disguise-Censorship idea, we now regard dream bizarreness as a function of the brain's own change in chemical state. The hypothesis that dreaming is a natural and normal kind of delirium, rather than a model of neurosis, is strengthened by the presence of all four formal aspects of delirium: visual hallucinations, disorientation, defective recent memory, and confabulation. A more sophisticated idea is that the brain benefits from its orientational instability in that it can change its orientation, if it needs to, in a hurry.

In rejecting the idea that dream bizarreness was the psychodynamic product of disguised unconscious wishes, I was not arguing that dreams have no meaning. On the contrary, I was arguing that strong emotions (including positive emotions such as elation, joy, and desire and negative ones such as fear and anger) play a strong role in shaping dream plots. Dream plots are therefore highly salient and highly informative about how we contextualize our emotional states. I hold that dreams, rather than disguising our emotions, reveal our affective repertoires emphatically and graphically. As such, dreams are unique psychological products that deserve our close attention. Pace Freud, through dreams we can see ourselves in a glass clearly. And by their close study, we also stand to learn the general rules of brain-mind function. Thanks to Freud, we are all now cognizant of the importance of feelings in shaping awake-state thought. Why not dreaming too?

My Psychologist Brain-Self

An important part of my life's work has been to become a psychologist who could help understand the mind in relation to the brain. From the time I first elected and then dropped the introductory psychology course at Wesleyan (1953) through the time I flirted with but rejected psychoanalysis at Harvard (1961) through the time I veered toward and then away from sleep and dream psychophysiology (1964), I wondered what kind of psychologist I should be.

The idea of studying the formal aspects of conscious states grew naturally out of the physiological revelations of our experimental work on the brain. Between 1964, when I gave up on the sleep lab psychophysiology paradigm, until 1984, when I decided to study conscious states assiduously, I was not really any kind of psychologist. I was, however, a psychiatrist, and my experience with the mental-status exam was significant in shaping the kind of psychologist I became.

Ever since my internship at Bellevue (1959–60), I had been aware that a formal approach to mental contact was an important clinical technique, and that it complemented the history-taking approach that by 1960 had become the all-but-exclusive instrument of the psychiatrist.

I knew from experience that history taking alone—like the heavy reliance on dream content reports—could miss important symptoms and signs, including disorientation, memory loss, and even visual hallucinations. If I wanted to rule out organic factors, I had to ask and to test patients about these important phenomena. Patients do not tell you about these symptoms any more than normal people mention these aspects of their dreams. When my mother had Alzheimer's disease, she could get through a dinner party without any of the other guests' being aware that she had no idea where she was, what day it was, or who the genial guests on her left and on her right were.

The Grand Mentation Project

Other novel discoveries we made through our formal analysis of dreaming include the ubiquity of movement, the diminution of self-reflective awareness and volition, the impoverishment of analytic thought, and the experience of elation, anger, and anxiety as the three leading dream emotions. We studied all these formal features intensively in a unique data set made possible by combining daytime beeper prompts to sample awake-state subjective experience with the Nightcap, our portable home-based sleep recording system. Using this technology, we obtained more than 3,000 reports of mental activity in five states: active wake, quiet wake, sleep onset, NREM, and REM.

We are indebted to Mihaly Csikszentmihalyi and Russell Hurlburt, who pioneered the "experience sampling" approach to awake-state consciousness. In experience sampling studies, subjects wear a pager-beeper and are instructed to recall and record whatever was in their mind when they were beeped. To combine this approach with a sleep-stage-specific awakening program is an obvious step. In the 50-year history of the laboratory study of sleep and dreams, the only awake-state reports that were elicited occurred in the laboratory just before or just after asleep. Not once were subjects sampled in the daytime, and not once in the field. We wanted a more naturalistic approach to these two questions: What kind of consciousness usually characterizes active and quiet waking? How does it change sleep onset in NREM sleep and in REM sleep?

The "Grand Mentation Project" conceived by me and Bob Stickgold has been moved forward by Roar Fosse. One of Roar's discoveries is that the capacity for thought declines as the capacity to generate internal imagery rises across the five states that we sampled. Thus, thought and internally generated visuomotor imagery are mutually incompatible. The implications for a general theory of mental illness are obvious. Anything that tips the brain's modulatory systems in the direction of REM is likely to increase internal perception (hallucination) and to decrease critical thinking (and thereby to increase false belief and delusion). Our hypothesis is that this may be a general rule that could apply not only to normal mentation but also to psychotic mentation. Roar Fosse also demonstrated that, although the tendency to dream increased during NREM sleep across the night, it was always significantly greater during REM no matter at what time awakenings occurred.

A Cognitive Approach to Dreaming, Memory, and Learning

So deep is the scientific suspicion of subjective data that most investigators who call themselves cognitive scientists rely exclusively on behavioral measures such as reaction time. They design tasks that subjects can perform while being precisely monitored by a computer program that presents stimuli and records the time it takes for them to respond. How could such an approach help us understand sleep and dreams? Obviously not by direct measurements of sleep and dream states, because subjects cannot perform those tasks while sleeping and/or dreaming. Their sensory and motor systems are off line in these states, especially during REM.

But subjects can perform such tasks just before they go to sleep, and just after they awaken from sleep (when their sensory and motor gates open again). This indirect approach is not a substitute for studies of subjectivity. There is no substitute. But it *is* complimentary, because it allows us to ask and answer questions about what gets accomplished in sleep. What does sleep do for us? More specifically, what does sleep do for our cognitive abilities? Sleep is so highly prominent in mammalian species that we scientists do not accept the popular idea that sleep is a waste of time. On the contrary, the active state of the brain during REM and the very distinctive changes in our memory function suggest that REM helps to reorganize memory.

This switch from hypotheses about mechanisms to hypotheses about function is both timely and fulfilling. No psychobiological theory of sleep and dreaming can be considered complete if it cannot say for what purpose these elaborate brain-mind processes have evolved. Beyond organizing memory, I have recently considered the possibility that REM sleep prepares the brain for waking consciousness and acts throughout waking as a virtual-reality generator. When dreaming, we experience this creative process in all its glory.

As with our studies of dream subjectivity, the Research Network on Mind-Body Interactions was catalytic in the initiation of a major change in our scientific direction. And it was the determination and ingenuity of Bob Stickgold that made the new approach work. Bob was one of several students I recruited from my Harvard University Extension School course, Psychology E-1450, in 1990, at about the time that my MacArthur-sponsored work began. Initially focused on attention and associative processes, this line or research had moved us to consider the effects on visual discrimination learning (and vice versa) and to track the incorporation of pre-sleep stimuli in sleep mentation.

Bob noticed an early report in the journal *Science* that the retention of learning required REM sleep. That report was written by the Israeli scientists Avi Karni and Dev Sagi (developers of the visual discrimination task) and Jean Ashkenasy (who ran the sleep lab). To make a long story short (as the story keeps getting longer and longer), subjects retain their learning if and only if they have long, deep NREM sleep early in the night and long periods of intense REM sleep later in the night. If they get lots of both kinds of sleep, they even improve their newly learned skill.

This is "sleep learning" with a vengeance. It is as if the brain were practicing its newly acquired skills and improving on them. This joint function of the very different NREM and REM sleep phases led Bob Stickgold to consider a two-stage model which posited that the transfer of material learned in the awake state into the hippocampus occurred during NREM sleep and that its distribution and fixation in the cerebral cortex occurred during REM sleep. Information can be sampled as memory fragments during REM sleep, but the hippocampus is not able to provide the integration necessary to reproduce narrative memories as the stories that we tell about our lives in the awake state.

Do the subjects dream of performing the visual discrimination task? No, they do not. This means that dreaming, as a subjective experience, tells us nothing—directly—about the material that is being learned in sleep. The fact that dreaming reveals such a diversity of fictive behaviors suggests that our repertoire of motor and emotional acts is being activated, perhaps in the interest of incorporating newly learned skills into preexisting brain circuits. The subjective experience of dreaming depends on what each of those many circuits contains as potentially conscious material, but it says nothing about whether the memory status of that material is being advanced, disregarded, or discarded.

Since the learning of the Karni-Sagi task is unconscious, this new hypothesis makes some sense. But it leaves unanswered the question of whether sleep enhances other kinds of learning, especially narrative or biographical memory. In our studies of memory and dreaming, we have discovered that, although subjects can easily identify a few fragments of their daily experience in their own dream reports, they almost never incorporate whole experiential episodes in their dreams. I emphasize this partial or fragmentary incorporation of waking memory into dreams and suggest that it is emotional salience that holds these fragments together. In other words, dreaming does not replay whole memories. Instead, it knits pieces of them together in an emotionally salient way.

Using the video game Tetris and the skiing simulator Alpine Racer, Bob Stickgold had been able to show that recent experience of a purely sensorimotor kind can be consciously represented in dreams, but only in dreams that occur at sleep onset. When awakened after sleep onset, the Tetris subjects often report seeing the little squares falling down through dream space, but they do not report playing the game. The essence of the task has been extracted for replay by the brain, but the irrelevant context has been dropped. This conclusion is dramatically supported by the fact that patients with amnesia secondary to hippocampal damage see the falling Tetris squares in their sleep-onset dreams but have no conscious recall of playing Tetris even when they are awake.

The main point of this book is that dreaming is both like and unlike waking consciousness. Dreams manifest the subjective experience in sleep of our perceptual, motoric, and emotional brain when it is selectively activated and when our dorsolateral prefrontal cortex is deactivated.

Is this our "true" self, as many dream theorists might claim? Since our dream self is only one part of us, the answer to this question as posed may therefore be No, because it isn't likely that the part of our brain that is dreaming really runs the show in the awake state in the way that Freudians assume. Rather, it helps waking consciousness by providing an almost correct picture, which external reality need only fine tune to achieve an accurate representation. Dreaming may also reflect the brain activation (and inactivation) processes necessary to more fundamental housekeeping tasks, including thermoregulation, emotional equilibrium, and cognitive competence.

On this view, dreaming as conscious experience could even be epiphe-nomenal, in that it is the underlying brain processes that are critical. Whether one is even remotely aware of those brain processes may not matter. Maybe we tend to forget dreams because the dreams themselves are useless or even misleading. It might even be suggested that paying attention to dream content is counterproductive if that attention is directed by a theory that is false or misguided. We should be much more cautious about the value of dream recollection than either psychoanalysis or the many related "New Age" dream mystiques that have proliferated in recent years.

By the year 2000, my scientific life had reached a climactic point. I had formulated a cellular and molecular model of brain state control and a brain-based theory of dreaming. I was 67 years old, remarried, and the father of five-year-old twins. During the decade that followed, I was edu-cated about the vicissitudes of life by a series of what I call experiments of nature. In part IV, I turn to these highly instructive experiments. I leave for another time a discussion of the tumultuous and simultaneous impact of my wife's decision to return to Italy, the better to pursue her own career and to assume responsibility for her eight children after the death of her parents. That unwelcome move forced me to change my own lifestyle in useful ways. Teaching and lecturing in Europe helped me to formulate my new theory of dreaming as evidence of the existence, in our brains, of a predictive model of the world.

IV Experiments of Nature

I went to Lyon to work with Michel Jouvet in 1963. My wife, Joan, our one-year-old son, Ian, and I embarked on a steamship, taking with us our 1.5-liter Riley automobile.

Our quarters in Lyon were a stylish modern second-floor suite with parquet floors and a balcony overlooking the Rhône River. The Rhône, with its gray, silt-stained water, comes roiling out of the Alps and meets, in Lyon, the more pastoral and placid Saône. The Lyonnais referred to their two rivers affectionately as man (the Rhône) and woman (the Saône). Their meeting was thus symbolic of heterosexual love, which even the reserved and hyper-Catholic Lyonnais liked to celebrate.

For those of us who were outsiders, excluded from old Lyonnais society, the Rhône and the Saône were no less worthy as symbols. I remember sitting in the sun on our balcony every morning, trying to learn French by reading Le Monde. I looked up three new words a day, and within six months I was beginning to converse with my friends.

One sunny Saturday, in the fall, we decided to go to see a rugby match. In preparation, Joan and I drove along the Quai Aristide Briand, which runs beside the Rhône, to pick up a babysitter for Ian, who was asleep in our apartment. Wanting to get back as quickly as I could, I double-parked the Riley and waited, with the engine running, while Joan ran in to fetch the babysitter.

I remember (or so I think) seeing, in the Riley's rear-view mirror, a car careening along the Quai in my direction. Instead of moving out into the completely free passing lane, the car plowed into the Riley at a speed of about 30 miles per hour. As I was in a bucket seat, my body, including my brain, was suddenly catapulted backward and just as suddenly accelerated forward when the Riley stopped moving forward. The result was what is appropriately called a whiplash displacement of my head on my neck and trunk. There is no evidence that my head hit anything; it was simply accelerated and decelerated, simply but violently. As soon as I stepped out of the car, I was disoriented, could not make a new memory, and could not even speak French with my newly acquired skill. I could see the other car, which had crashed into a bridge abutment about 100 yards down the Quai, but I failed to connect that scene with the badly damaged rear end of my sweet little Riley. My wife, who had heard the crash, ran down the stairs and tried in vain to explain to the crowd of onlookers that I was out of my mind.

"This car looks like it has been in an accident," I declared to my incredulous wife. "It looks like our car," I added, clinching the case for acute organic mental syndrome. All the crowd could do was cluck-cluck at my foolishness for double-parking and at my assailant's drunken driving. They made it clear that we should call a *huissier de justice,* who would prepare an accident report. Meanwhile, I continued to mumble nonsensically about the car that appeared to be mine but was horribly damaged as if it had been in an accident.

After about 20 minutes, I collapsed on the sidewalk. I don't know whether I lost consciousness, but I remember hearing the "oogah-oogah" of the ambulance as it made its way along the Quai and over a bridge to the Grange-Blanche Hospital, located on the Avenue Roosevelt right across from Jouvet's lab. It didn't take the emergency room doctor long to decide that I should be admitted for observation and perhaps for treatment.

I was wheeled to a four-bed room. In each of the other three beds was a man who looked to me to be dying. Why was I in such a place, I wondered.

My thoughtful wife had written me a letter, which I read over and over:

Dear Allan,

You have been injured in an accident. The car was badly damaged but I am OK and Ian is OK. Get well soon.

Love,
Joan

"So I have been in an accident," I thought to myself. I then promptly forgot my thought and retreated to my amnesia world. My dark delirium-dementia lasted about six hours. As the lights came back on, I remembered that my cousin, George Chandler, was due to arrive the next day. Moreover, George—the son of my mother's favorite sister, Helen—had offered to take Joan and me to dinner at the Pyramide Restaurant in Vienne. The chef, Fernard Point, had recently died, but under his wife the restaurant continued to garner three Michelin stars. I wasn't going to miss that dinner for any reason, including amnesia.

Fortunately for me, the amnesia had completely cleared by morning. I tried to convince the doctors to let me go. They said I needed at least two weeks of observation. I said that I worked with Professor Jouvet, who could observe me as well as they could. They were skeptical. Then I played my trump card: "My cousin has invited me to dinner tomorrow night at La Pyramide. He's paying." "Then, of course, you should go," they said. And I did.

I can still remember that dinner. La Pyramide was elegant and charming, the lobby decked out with paintings given by admiring artist guests and the dining room adorned by long-stemmed red gladiolas. If my memory serves me well, we had a first course of quenelles with a Champagne sauce. It was accompanied by Condrieu, a locally made white wine that at the time was not exported. What a treat!

What had happened to me? My speculation is that my brainstem had been stretched by the whiplash and/or the tips of my temporal lobes had been smashed against my skull. In any case, I had suffered a functional brain lesion that could not be seen in the x-rays that I dutifully acquired later. My skull was intact.

The bucket seat of the Riley may have contributed to the injury. Because there was no headrest behind me, my noggin was free to snap back on impact as the car and I were accelerated. It then snapped forward as the car stopped moving. Because I had no abrasion of the face or the scalp, it seems unlikely that my head hit the steering wheel. My brain injury probably was similar to those sometimes sustained by football players and boxers.

What is most astonishing about this story (aside from its happy ending) is that while I was amnesic I wasn't able to speak French. That means that my amnesia, which was making it impossible for me to grasp what had just happened and was still happening (and is therefore called anterograde), also obliterated my memory of events that had happened as much as two months earlier (and is therefore called retrograde).

Memory, it would seem, is both fragile and dynamic. Mine was lost for six hours and then, miraculously, re-found as I lay in my hospital bed. Now it functions so well that I can visualize La Pyramide, taste the Condrieu, and recount the events of that day in 1963.

My point here is to prod you to think about your forgotten dreams. Where did they go? Do you think they are still somewhere in your head?

Or do you believe, as I do, that those conscious experiences were never committed to long-term memory and are lost forever?

Sleep and dream research indicates that I can have intense perceptual, motor, and emotional experiences that never make it even into short-term memory. There is a very short memory buffer that enables me to recall and recount a dream if awakened from it. But if I'm not awakened from a dream, I will forget it entirely. Stranger still is the surprise I feel when I read in my journal a detailed dream report written by me many years before. I can scarcely believe I ever had that dream.

To me, this set of facts raises questions about our assumption that dreaming, as a psychological experience, is, in and of itself, terribly important. From time to time, my correspondents object to this conclusion, citing horrific or splendid dreams that they still remember from long ago. I cannot gainsay their witness, but I remain skeptical about their counterclaim. I think the brain has accomplished its maintenance function—which may include the refurbishment of memory—and cannot do so without running its programs in such a way as to create the illusions of dreams. The dreams themselves are not only illusory but may be dispensable.

Inadvertently supporting my claim is the truly fabulous power of my awake-state memory. True, I have become increasingly forgetful as I have aged. But some experiences and some bits of information are so deeply engraved as to seem unforgettable. One such experience is my automobile accident and my concussion in Lyon; one such bit of information is my old telephone number (232-0043) in West Hartford, which I have not used in 50 years.

How do waking memory, dream memory, and concussion memory differ? In suggesting that my brainstem may have been stretched when my car was rapidly accelerated in Lyon, I want to leave open the possibility that the three kinds of memory share a common mechanism. That, of course, is the aminergic demodulation I described in chapter 9.

Norepinephrine, serotonin, and histamine are necessary for the brain to solder its conscious experience in preparation for remembering. The difference between the awake state (in which memory, despite occasional falsification, isn't bad) and the dream state (in which, despite occasional exceptions, memory is very poor) may be due to the presence (awake state) or absence (dreaming) of aminergic demodulation.

In acute head trauma, a dream-like state of dementia-delirium (such as I had after the car accident in Lyon) may render a person incapable of accessing recent memories, and even incapable of accessing remote memories. It now appears that repeated insults to the brain, such as those suffered by football players and boxers, may lead to devastating disability. Muhammad Ali is perhaps the most famous example. His Parkinsonian brain degeneration is a sequel to the battering his brain took during his boxing career. The effects of my concussion were dramatic but short-lived, and, as far as I know, my subsequent brain troubles were not related to them.

11 Brain Death

On Saturday, February 2, 2001, while in Monte Carlo with my second wife, Lia, I experienced a sudden onset of vertigo and sweating, which was particularly intense on the right side of my head. The sensation of the world spinning around me (from left to right and in a right-side-downward tilted orbit) could be partially relieved by resting my head on the table of the café in which we had just finished breakfast and by closing my eyes.

Incorrectly supposing that my symptoms might be due to the sleep deprivation I had incurred on the previous day's overnight flight from Boston to Paris to Nice, I waited for them to subside. With Lia's help, I walked back to the Hermitage Hotel. Upon reclining, I immediately felt better, slept for three hours, and enjoyed a snack supper in my room. Since that fateful day I have always felt better in the prone position than erect. That night, after watching television, I slept fitfully. The next morning, I enjoyed my room-service breakfast. But while I was returning the breakfast table to the hallway, I noticed a distinct ataxia which told me that my troubles were not over. In fact, they had just begun.

By noon the next day, 24 hours after the initial attack of vertigo, I had begun to experience great difficulty swallowing. This was compounded by the greatly increased volume of saliva that suddenly welled up in my throat. The combination of increased saliva production and a diminished capacity to clear it made me feel as if I was drowning in my own secretions. Together with the vertigo and the ataxia, these two signs clearly suggested that neurons in my right lateral medullary brainstem were dying for lack of oxygen.

The death of neurons is the basis of all strokes. My wife—a clinical neurologist—already suspected that I was having a stroke. She had put me on aspirin (a blood thinner) and nicergoline (a vasodilator) to prevent further clotting in the blood vessels of my brain.

Clinical History

Because I had devoted my professional life to the scientific study of sleep and dreaming (and especially to the link between neurophysiology and psychological phenomenology), I was motivated to document my stroke experience in detail. This documentation effort was greatly aided by the constant attendance and support of my wife, Dr. Lia Silvestri, who is not only a clinical neurologist but also an expert on sleep medicine. Lia recorded my comments and notes every day until I regained the ability to operate a hand-held tape recorder, after which I recorded my own copious and detailed descriptions of my experiences. I hope this account will inspire other people to record their subjective experiences as they undergo cruel experiments of nature.

In Princess Grace Hospital

In the emergency ward of Princess Grace Hospital, an electrocardiogram revealed atrial fibrillation, which suggested that an embolic thrombosis of my right vertebral artery, near its posterior inferior cerebellar branch, might be causing my brainstem neurons to die. In any case, the circulation to my right lateral brainstem and cerebellum had been suddenly impaired, either by a plaque arising in the wall of one of my cerebral blood vessels or by a small clot shot out from the wall of my fibrillating heart. If the former, it would be called a cerebral thrombosis. If the latter, it would be called a cerebral embolus. Together these events are called strokes (or cerebral vascular accidents, a term that is as euphemistic as it is understated). CVAs are disasters, because the brain is so important to us and because new neurons do not replace dead ones. When brain cells die, we lose whatever functions those neurons were responsible for. Today, almost ten years later, I remain ataxic, I salivate like Pavlov's dogs (but without the bell), and I have a variety of peculiar and unpleasant pains in my right face and left leg. (In Lyon, I recovered from my brain concussion in only six hours.)

Whether the atrial fibrillation (irregularity of my heart rhythm) was the cause of my stroke or an effect of it was not clear. Only six months earlier, my electrocardiogram had shown no such abnormality. But atrial fibrillation can develop spontaneously, and it is a risk factor for embolism because the incomplete and poorly synchronized contractions of the heart that result from chaotic electrical signals increase the chance that blood will clot on the heart wall. Such clots can then send small fragments into the

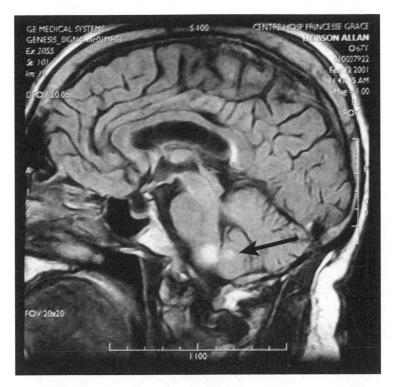

MRI taken in Princess Grace Hospital in Monaco on February 7, 2001. The medullary and cerebellar damage to my brain are seen as the white spots (arrow).

bloodstream. The small vessels of the brain are often clogged by these embolic fragments, because the great vessels of the head come off the aorta very near the heart.

At Princess Grace Hospital, a negative CAT scan ruled out intracerebral hemorrhage, but three subsequent MRIs showed a clear, discrete area of neuronal loss (called an infarct) of my right lateral medulla in the area of the distribution of the posterior inferior cerebellar artery. The damage was centered in the right restiform body, the adjacent medullary tegmentum, and the overlying cerebellum. Therefore, whether I had an embolus or a thrombus, my brain was deprived of oxygen, and many of my medullary and cerebellar neurons had begun to die. I say they were "my" neurons, but this is just a manner of speaking; as you know by now, my brain owned me as much as I owned it. A little bit of me died when I had that stroke.

On the third day after my admission to the hospital, and again on the tenth day, the neurological consultant declared, in French, that I was a

Table 11.1

Wallenberg's Syndrome

---

1. Motor coordination defects (called ataxia) due to damage of neurons in the cerebellum. This ataxia was (and still is) most severe in my right leg but also slightly affects my right arm. The ataxia is compounded by a loss of strength in those limbs. Fortunately, I am left-handed.

2. Impaired balance (called postural instability) and the feeling of falling, spinning, and speeding through space (called vertigo), which are due to neuronal death in the central balance circuits of my vestibular system (Cranial Nerve VIII–Vestibular Division).

3. Pupillary differences (called Horner's Syndrome) with dilation of the right pupil (relative to the left) due to the loss of parasympathetic (pupil closing) and/or irritability of sympathetic (pupil opening) neurons in the reticular formation of my brainstem. When she looks into my eyes, my neurologist wife still marvels at my pupillary asymmetry. I hope she still loves me.

4. Loss of normal sensation in the right side of my face (due to the loss of neurons in the Vth—or trigeminal—cranial nerve nucleus and the sensation of tingling, burning, or pain (called paraesthesias) in the same areas. These paraesthesias are presumably a function of imbalanced control of my surviving trigeminal neurons. Only I notice these unpleasant sensations.

5. A drooping of my upper right lip due to damage to the neurons of my right facial nucleus (Cranial Nerve VII) in the medulla. My lip drop is now gone.

6. Paralysis of the pharyngeal muscles in the right side of my throat, which was due to loss of neurons in the glossopharyngeal nucleus (Cranial Nerve IX). I still have trouble swallowing foods, especially soup and rice.

7. Paralysis of the right vocal cord, due to loss of neurons in the vagal nucleus (Cranial Nerve X) in my medulla. My hoarseness is mild but persistent.

8. Mildly decreased sensibility to pain and markedly decreased sensibility to temperature change on the left side of my body below the neck (due to interception of nerve tracts carrying pain and temperature messages from my spinal cord to my brain). I have to be very careful not to burn my left hand when cooking.

---

clear-cut case of Wallenberg's Syndrome. (See table 11.1.) "C'est classique," he announced proudly. As soon as he said it, I had a detailed memory of the page in Harrison's Principles of Internal Medicine on which this complicated syndrome was described. As a medical student interested in neurology as well as in psychiatry, I had struggled to remember and understand the many fascinating features of Wallenberg's Syndrome. Now I had only to pay attention to the changes in my body to know, too well, what Wallenberg's Syndrome really meant.

There was no clinical indication of damage to cranial nerve XI (the spinal accessory) or to cranial nerve XII (the hypoglossal), so I could still shrug my shoulders and wiggle my tongue. The residual ability to use my tongue ultimately allowed me to force fluids and food down my gullet, but I am in constant danger of inhaling food particles into my lungs because of the loss of swallowing-muscle propulsion in my throat.

The results of a surface electroencephalogram and of visual-field testing were normal, but I still see double when I look to the right. An ultrasound study of my cerebral vascular system revealed a blockage of the right vertebral artery and suggested that the clot might be due to a defect in the vessel wall.

Repeated electrocardiograms demonstrated persistent atrial fibrillation, but there was no evidence of a heart attack in the electrocardiogram recorded from my chest wall. Before concluding that there was no coronary heart disease, the French cardiologist wanted to check the electrical conduction in the back wall of my heart. However, his attempt to obtain an electrocardiogram from an electrode inserted into my esophagus on the eighth day of my hospitalization was unsuccessful, because the benzodiazepine the cardiologist had prescribed to calm me for the esophageal invasion caused a psychotic reaction. Convinced that I was being attacked by soldiers with medieval weapons, I forcefully repulsed both the physician and his probe. This vivid and fearfully convincing imagery was one of the early signs that my cognitive capacities had been compromised by my stroke. Later, at Brigham and Women's Hospital in Boston, a catheterization study showed that all my coronary arteries were wide open, ruling out any possibility that my brain problem was a consequence of a heart attack. This surprised me, because I have always liked rich foods and have always had high levels of cholesterol in my blood.

As a doctor, I knew and understood what the physicians who were treating me were thinking and saying about my illness and my treatment. But more importantly, because I was a research psychiatrist with specialized training and interest in how the brainstem controls consciousness, my curiosity was stimulated. I used my subjective experience as a source of data and of understanding, and as a way of coping with my disease. I recognized that after a lifetime of studying experimental animals—many of whom could not talk—I had become an experimental animal myself. The healthy part of me observed the sick part with intense interest.

The Dynamics of My Stroke and My Recovery

Acute Phase (Days 1–10)
Since there was no neurological service, I was placed in Princess Grace Hospital's acute coronary care unit. The internal medicine, the nursing,

and the ancillary clinical care were excellent. Because I spoke French flu-ently, I was very comfortable. My wife and I were confident that no defini-tive treatment was available anywhere in the world. For that reason, we decided to stay in Monaco until all the medical, logistical, and financial arrangements for my return to Boston were complete. When I asked about the prognosis, one of the attendants said "We are going to give you the best possible care and see what happens." This was not entirely encourag-ing, but I reconciled myself to being as patient a patient as a doctor can ever be. It helped me enormously to realize that I had been presented with a rare opportunity for self-observation, however unwelcome that opportu-nity may have been.

My care consisted of intravenous fluids, a nasogastric tube, and a bladder catheter. Medications that were directed at my heart failed to convert my atrial fibrillation to a normal sinus rhythm. Anticoagulants (heparin fol-lowed by coumadin) were used to decrease the risk of my heart's sending any more blood clots to my brain or other parts of my body. I was a very sick man, but my consciousness and my cognition were not as severely impaired as they would have been had my stroke killed neurons in my cerebral cortex. Because I had no aphasia and few cognitive defects, I could at least self-observe with a semblance of objectivity.

Recovery Phase (Days 10–40)
Once I had achieved cardiovascular stability, I was able to sit up and to get out of bed. I was then transferred from intensive care to a recovery ward. There Lia and I began to make specific plans to go back to Boston. I stayed in Monaco for three weeks and have nothing but gratitude for the loving care I received there.

I returned to the United States by Air Ambulance on February 22, 2001. I was then hospitalized in the stroke unit of Brigham and Women's Hos-pital in Boston, where I stayed for another three weeks. The most impor-tant therapeutic interventions that were made there were installation of a gastric tube on March 5, 2001, which improved delivery of foodstuffs to the stomach and stopped my precipitous weight loss, and electrical cardio-version on March 12, 2001, which reinstated a normal sinus rhythm. To maintain the reduced risk of recurrent emboli or thrombosis, I was con-tinued on coumadin/heparin anticoagulant therapy. Antibiotic treatment of a urinary-tract infection was effective, and further infection was averted by removal of the catheter.

Although my neurological progress was steady, the difficulty with swal-lowing and the excessive salivation persisted. Both resulted from the severe

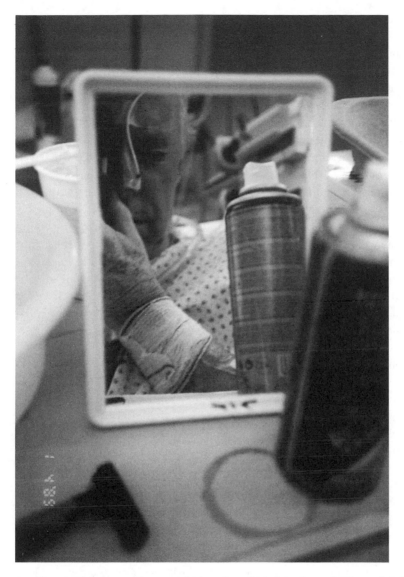

A self-portrait (taken with my right hand) as I tried to shave (with my left hand) six days after my lateral medullary stroke.

paralysis of my throat muscles and the automatic imbalance in the control of my salivary glands. And because of the damage to my cerebellum and my brainstem, I could not maintain an upright posture without feeling dizzy and falling to the right. These symptoms persisted well after March 15, when I was transferred to Spaulding Rehabilitation Hospital; in fact, they still persist today. Aspiration was a constant threat, and eventually I developed infectious consolidation in the lower lobe of my left lung. On two occasions, I had chills, headache, and photophobia, for which I received more antibiotic medication. This treatment prevented the development of even more severe pneumonia.

I was encouraged by the many neurologists, some quite famous, who told me I would recover completely. Unfortunately, they were completely wrong. Not only did I not recover completely, but in many ways my condition has worsened. No one knows why. My subjective experience must nonetheless be regarded as objective. When doctors can't explain a symptom or a sign, they succumb to the worst kind of dualism. The patient's symptoms are often called psychogenic, which implies that they are imaginary and can be ignored. I hereby apologize to any former patient of mine if I inadvertently doubted something that patient told me.

Rehabilitation Phase (Days 40–100)

At the Spaulding Rehabilitation Hospital, where I stayed from March 15 to April 15, 2001, I was taught to ambulate, first with a walker and then with a cane. By the time I went home, I could navigate (slowly) without external support. If I changed direction or level of ambulation, I had to be very careful to avoid the residual effects of my tendency to lurch to the right. Despite my caution, I toppled over twice, and in one of those falls I banged myself up quite badly on my stone garden stairway. I now live in constant terror of another fall.

Heroic efforts by Spaulding personnel to help me learn to swallow solid food were unsuccessful until about eight weeks after the stroke, the time at which most neurologists predict recovery. I called up my Harvard Medical School neurology teacher, C. Miller Fisher, and asked him why I was taking so long to recover my ability to ingest food. He said recovery was imminent. He was right. But my swallowing was not so much recovered as reconstructed. Even today, instead of swallowing as I once did, I now force food down through my pharynx by moving my tongue suddenly and vigorously backward. My deliberate effort usually clears the oropharynx of food and liquid, which otherwise tends to get stuck there, constantly threatening and sometimes occasioning inadvertent aspiration.

I then suffer spells of violent coughing as I try to clear my lungs. To avoid aspiration, I actively regurgitate the softened food and try again to bypass the still-paralytic spot in my throat musculature. By Monday, April 30, 2001, using the technique just described, I was gradually able to reduce the stomach-tube feedings, and the tube was removed.

Food and drink have always been near the top of my list of pleasures. For those inclined to believe in fate, being unable to swallow was thus a fitting punishment for my gluttony. But it was also a spur to my motivation. Some of my therapists had mistakenly come to doubt my determination because I couldn't even swallow ice cream in the several weeks after my stroke.

Within the first ten days at Princess Grace Hospital, I had nonetheless learned to get liquid down my gullet. One night I found that I could channel a mouthful of water to my left throat. It would then trickle down to my stomach with gravity's assistance. Even now it is hard for me to communicate what an important victory this seemed to me. By morning, I had polished off a liter of bottled French spring water. The feeling of triumph was so surprisingly strong that I imagined that I had vanquished death. On April 9, 2001, only two months after learning to "drink," I made this triumphant entry in my journal:

During the past week, my progress has been very impressive especially in the domain of eating. I now have a really full diet, which is transferable to the outside world. It consists of juice for breakfast. I can drink juice very easily if I lay at a forty-five degree angle. It goes right down. Probably because gravity helps it stay back. Then, I have an 8 ounce cup of vanilla yogurt with sugar, which is delicious. I then go to scrambled eggs, which I press with a fork so as to break up the lumps; the whole thing is held together with lashings of ketchup. It is really quite good. No coffee, no tea, no toast as yet. But they will come later.

My brain had partially recovered and, with practice, had relearned some of its lost skills. Because the stroke was localized to my lower brainstem, I have been spared the indignity of aphasia and other cognitive impairments of forebrain damage. I have also been alert, often too much so. And I have been able to communicate, by email, fax, and telephone, with a wide circle of well-wishers in all parts of the world. This support network has been of enormous psychological benefit.

Since the earliest days of my hospitalization in Monaco, and in spite of double vision, I have been able to edit monograph manuscripts, books, papers, and grant applications. Hearing the reaper's scythe swishing in the grass beside my head made me aware that my days were numbered. As soon as I could write again, I began contemplating my next major book project—this one. My motor difficulties were mainly dynamic and occurred only on assuming a standing posture. I functioned well while seated. I was able to drive my car to conferences with colleagues, to seminars, and to hospitals at which I was pursuing projects.

To an outside observer my recovery may appear complete, but I am afraid that I will never regain confident mobility, safe swallowing, and better control of salivation. No neurologist promises relief of the right facial pain or of the anesthesic and temperature sensation loss of the left side of my body below the neck. I am nonetheless happy to be alive. I am sleeping, dreaming, and engaging in other gratifying visceral behaviors, even if all of these functions are distinctly altered—perhaps permanently. As my loving twin sons put it: "Daddy has had a stroke. A part of his brain has died." I know that some part of "me" is lost and gone forever. But another part lives on—and tells this story.

Sleep and Dream Changes

Total Insomnia in the Acute Post-Stroke Period

Over the first ten days of my hospitalization in Monaco, I not only manifested most of the characteristic features of Wallenberg's Syndrome; I also suffered from total insomnia, a symptom not previously reported in the neurological literature.

My brain damage is precisely localized, and my sleep suppression resembles the insomnia I observed in cats with mediopontine transections in Lyon in the early 1960s. I will describe the subjective effects in detail. One of my goals is to inspire other stroke victims to document their subjective experience in the twin interests of humanistic communication and medical science; another is to attempt an explanation that could constitute a novel formulation in brain-mind science.

Here is a verbatim transcript of a note I dictated to my wife, Lia, on February 7, 2001, day 6 of my hospitalization:

Time is exquisitely attenuated in the hospital because there is nothing to do except try to keep from drowning in my own saliva or falling off the bed due to vertigo. So I lie for hours in my bed, flat on my back with my eyes closed. The worst time is the night because I am alone, usually from 7 p.m. to 7 a.m. and because I cannot sleep a wink. The usual side position does not help; I'm just awake, my mind working actively in the dark all night long. Attempts to watch TV are frustrated by the banal network programming and my own double vision. Toward morning, at first around 3 o'clock and subsequently as late as 7 a.m., I suddenly feel irresistibly sleepy but this is not normal sleepiness. Instead I am drawn into a hallucinatory visual world of great complexity which only occasionally bears a faint resemblance to healthy dreaming.

When I was acutely and severely insomniac, I recalled the dramatic arousal effects caused by mediopontine pretrigeminal transections of the brainstem of experimental cats I had done in Michel Jouvet's lab in Lyon in 1963 to test Giuseppe Moruzzi's hypothesis that there was an electro-encephalogram synchronizing mechanism in the medullary brainstem. Cats with such lesions remained fully alert with strongly activated electro-encephalograms for about ten days, roughly the duration of my own total insomnia. I remember feeling surprised and touched by their pained wakefulness. Now I was lying awake because of damage to my own medullary brainstem not unlike that which I had inflicted on those cats.

Whether or not my personal experiences bear on my previous experimental observations, they clearly indicate that major sleep disturbances can be precipitated by brainstem strokes. The insomnia that I shared with those cats also triggered recognition that now I was the experimental animal and that I should turn my own medical misfortune into scientific opportunity. I wanted to convey to everyone that, whether we have brain damage or not, we all have brains and we are all experimental animals in the sense that we can self-observe. I have long believed that careful self-observation is important to the emerging science of consciousness. Sleep and dream research is nothing more or less than a special case of consciousness science. In other words, we are all participating in an experiment of nature, whether we are sick or well. Our state of consciousness changes quite dramatically as our brains wake, sleep, and dream.

It seems reasonable to integrate the acute changes in my sleep with my neurological signs and to propose that it was damage to the pontomedullary brainstem that caused my insomnia. Among the relevant structures that were affected by the stroke were the trigeminal nucleus (V), which resulted in a persistent right facial hemianesthesia and paraesthesias; the oculomotor nucleus (VI) and pontine reticular formation pre-oculomotor neurons, which resulted in temporary double vision; the facial nucleus (VII), which resulted in temporary right mouth droop; the vestibular (VIII), which resulted in the persistent vertigo and lateropulsion; the glossopharyngeal nucleus (IX), which led to the persistent difficulty of swallowing; and the vagus nucleus (X), which led to paralysis of the right vocal cord and to hoarseness. Together with the damage to the nucleus ambiguus, the vagal nucleus damage probably contributed to the cluster of autonomic dysfunctions that I experienced: persistent excessive salivation, constipation, and arterial hypotension.

Dream Suppression and Visual Hallucinosis

It goes without saying that if sleep is almost totally suppressed, as it was in my case for ten days, normal dreaming cannot occur. My journal notes suggest that even three and a half months after the stroke I had not yet fully recovered the vivid dream life that I experienced before my stroke.

During the acute post-stroke period, I experienced abnormal visions between days 1 and 10. Immediately upon closing my eyes, I perceived a stony vault over my supine body. The vault resembled the bottom of a swimming pool; the Gunite-like surface of the vault could be aqua, white, or beige. Rarely, it resembled engraved obsidian, and sometimes it was of a gauzelike nature mixed with ice or glass crystals.

There were three categories of the formed visual imagery that I perceived on these surfaces.

In the first category, geologic forms, the imagery tended to be proto-morphic and crude but often gave way to the more elaborate structures of category two, sculptural forms. The most amusing of these (which occurred on the fourth night) were enormous Lucite telephone/computers. But there were also tables and tableaux in which the geologic forms sometimes took unusual and bizarre shapes. One that I recall is a TV-set-like representation of a tropical landscape. In the third category, the most elaborate forms assumed human anatomical elements, including long swirling flesh columns that metamorphosed into sphincters, nipples, and crotches, but these were never placed in real bodies. In fact whole body forms almost never emerged. Instead I saw profiles of faces, profiles of bodies (often inextricably mixed with penises, noses, lips, and eyebrows), and torsos that arose out of the sculptural columns of flesh and sank back into them again. My brain was cranking out primitive images, all right, but they were frag-mentary and not narratively integrated as they are in normal dreaming. There were scenes but there was no scenario. My vision was rather like a painting by the abstract expressionist Arshile Gorky.

The most fully realized human images included my wife and featured her lower anatomy. She was as beautiful in those visions as she is in real life. Amusingly, I saw a Peter Pan-like Robert Stickgold and two fairies enjoying a bedtime story. Though visual disturbances are quite common in Wallenberg's Syndrome, they have only been reported to occur in the awake state with eyes open. Blurring of vision, which I had, and oscillopsia (the tendency of objects to appear to move), which I did not have, are attributed by neurologists to disturbances of oculomotor and vestibular physiology caused by brainstem stroke. We are still woefully ignorant of these signs of damage to our brains.

Despite some relief from antihistamines, which I began to take on day 8, the severe suppression of my sleep continued for about two weeks. On February 15, 2001, I wrote the following:

Among the strange psychic phenomena is the continued sense that normal sleep and dreaming are impossible. Last night I had the image of the antihistamine sedatives that I was given working on my anterior hypothalamic sleep mechanisms but my lower brain stem system could not be definitively turned over.

Added to the ironic insult of paralyzing the swallowing mechanism of a gourmand was the injury of sleep deprivation in a sleep and dream scientist. If I didn't know better, I would say that these losses of function were gotten up to punish me for my excessive indulgence. But by whom? As with apparently precognitive dreams, I assume that chance, not a purposive agency, was at work. You may think differently. My assumption is that the damage to my brainstem, which is at the very center of my interest in brain science, was also a chance occurrence. That grants me an opportunity to move knowledge forward rather than fill me with regret for the loss of my energetic work and play.

Vertigo and Lateropulsion

Immediately after the stroke, my hallucinatory experiences involved the vestibular as well as the visual domain. These vertigo variants consisted of the vivid impression of being launched through space like a missile. They were never associated with the protomorphic visual images I have already described; they were accompanied by their own specific imagery. They could be precipitated by forced ambulation (when I was awake in the daytime), or they might occur spontaneously (while I was lying motionless in bed at night trying to sleep). The first and most violent episode occurred on the first night of my hospitalization in Monaco. Here is my journal account of that episode, which occurred immediately after I vomited my breakfast:

I suddenly felt as if the bed were rotated 90 degrees in a counter-clockwise direction and catapulted downward toward the front of the hospital and into the sea. The illusion that I was actually moving at very high speed through space was so completely convincing—and so terrifying—that I said to myself, "So this is what death is like." To my amazement, these sensations abated as rapidly as they had begun but they made a very lasting impression on me.

Less dramatic variations on this experience occurred three times during the acute phase of my illness. They were sometimes associated with sneezing attacks. I have always been a convulsive sneezer (as was my father).

Since my stroke, clusters of up to nine sneezes can occur at any time of day; they lack the normal inspiratory wind-up of sneezes, consisting instead of entirely of explosive short expiratory phases. My sneezing tendency thus continues as before, but the length of each sneeze is cut in half. However, these half-sneezes are about twice as violent as my previous full snorts.

In the acute post-stroke phase, and for 10–30 days thereafter, I was prone to the illusion of falling, or even hurtling, to the right when well-meaning attempts were made to help me ambulate. In these instances, which occurred after I had stood up, I suddenly felt that I was being propelled through space parallel to the ground. I was incapable of righting myself despite frantic and powerful muscular efforts. These involuntary movements are called lateropulsions in the neurological literature, where they are reasonably attributed to vestibular and/or cerebellar damage. They became less frequent and less intense but could still be provoked until about thirty days after my stroke. Since then I have had a milder but still annoying tendency to lurch to the right.

The release of such unwelcome behavior after a stroke favors the concept that the brain is spring-loaded, like a jack-in-the-box, and thus prone to go off in a startling array of tics if these are not actively suppressed, presumably by inhibition of the offending circuitry. My brain is full of tricks that can be called upon when needed. This is a variation of the theme of virtual reality that I emphasize in my protoconsciousness hypothesis.

Dreaming Returns as I Learn to Walk

Between days 8 and 15, I began to have more dreamlike imagery associated with fitful sleep. During this period there was still no dreaming of the REM-sleep type, with elaborate, rapidly evolving plots, movement through dream space, cognitive bizarreness, and emotional intensification. My brainstem was unable to generate the physiological conditions necessary for dreaming. Here are two descriptions of such fragmentary images recorded on day 8:

I have the sensation of having paper all over my body which cannot be removed because there is a computer program that instantiates equal and opposite commands each time I try to remove one of them. This fruitless struggle goes on for hours and gradually replaces the alternating state of lucid thinking and lush visual hallucinations of the preceding 6 nights.

I see a female monkey whose head and paws are made out of silver foil containing brown flower petals. The monkey mama is floating in the air in front of me like a comical beatific protector.

On day 10, I had a brief perception of a human character and the beginnings of dreamlike narrative structures:

Ed (Schott, my coworker in Boston) is filling in brain drawings for people who want to know how the brain works. He has made a huge quilt out of about thirty or forty drawings all of which were in color and connected together in a scrupulous way. I said 'Look Ed, you don't need to do all this for the other people, why don't you keep this one for us and just send them a copy.

Such mentation, which is formally similar to my dreams, was not sustained, and the loss of typical REM-sleep dreaming persisted for 30 days.

On day 31, at Brigham and Women's Hospital, I had the following experience:

Before I woke up I had a prolonged and interesting dream experience in which I imagined that I was being treated by a woman or two women (possibly nurses) who were giving me a magical fabric to put on my skin. This fabric released a kind of coolness and produced a pleasurable sensation over my skin which I relished and I kept enjoying it as the fabric was moved from place to place on my hands, my chest, my belly, and my face. It was a little bit like the coolness that emanates from the ice packs that I used in waking to counter facial paraesthesias but the feeling was very gentle and not like any other sensation that I have ever experienced. Nor was this dream like any other I ever had because it just continued on and on and on in this wonderful analgesic almost narcotically pleasant mode.

I remember wondering what the mechanism of the heat release and simultaneously perceived cool pleasure might be, and being unable to come up with any reasonable explanation. I knew that I couldn't reason well, but even that recognition didn't lead me to think that I was dreaming. Instead I attributed it to warmth of the women who had obviously made an important discovery on how to comfort people. I would guess this went on for about thirty or forty minutes until I gradually woke up and then I could go back and forth in and out of this dreamy state for about five minutes. But by 5:30 a.m. I was too wide awake to do anything else but remember it well, contemplate it, and vow to tape record its contents. To this report I added an interpretation:

This "dream" means that something is changing in my brain. I hoped it meant that my spontaneous sleep mechanisms were recovering to some degree. I hasten to emphasize however that this was nothing like any REM sleep dream I ever had.

My First Post-Stroke Dream Recollection

My first post-stroke recollection of an elaborate and sustained dream occurred on day 38. Still in the Spaulding Rehabilitation Hospital, I had begun to learn to walk again. I recognize that the content of the dream is emotionally salient. I am also impressed that its occurrence coincided with the beginning of active recovery of my motor brain. I began walking, in the awake state, at the same time I resumed dreaming, in sleep. My brain was healing. Here is my description:

It took place in a foreign country, which I thought might be Yugoslavia or Hungary. Lia and I were on a trip and we were crossing a bridge with a lot of other people. It was a high arched bridge of a medieval sort. The bridge suddenly separated from the land and became a boat swimming across a very small river to get to a village on the other side. We had plans to stay in an old fashioned inn.

There was already some discomfort and difficulty finding each other as the boat got near to the shore. I caught glimpses of Lia. She was talking to someone else, a man. At one point, either before or just after we got off the boat, I noticed that she had given or sold to him a half-inch bit used with my large brace to drill holes in wood in Vermont. I was very surprised and somewhat hurt by this. I noticed also that the bit had been used to make a very perfect hole in the shoulder bag, which the man wore. It was a shoulder bag very much like mine.

In the dream, Lia explained to me that she had sold the drill but would give me the money. It still seemed odd to me that she would give a stranger one of my most precious tools without asking me. I was feeling very vexed and apprehensive. We got on the land, we walked around looking for the inn and we were separated from each other on several occasions. During one of the times that we were together, she made it clear to me that she needed to have a secret life.

When I was asking her about this man, it was clear that she meant that she needed to be free to have an affair with him if she wanted to. I found that very odd and very disquieting and tried to express my concerns. When we finally got to what appeared to be the inn, there was a strange scene in which she was again difficult to find. But I found her in what looked like a kitchen and she was preparing to cook some food, which struck me as odd, since this was such a flimsy excuse. I asked her when she would be finished and she looked at her watch and she said 45 minutes, to which I agreed knowing that this was all the time she would need to make love with whichever stranger she had selected.

I then walked around the inn, which had a very peculiar structure. On one side, there was a row of seats roofed over as in a theater and beside each of the seats were exotic bouquets of flowers. I walked down from one level of this improbable architecture to the next, finally getting to the bottom, and wondering in which room Lia and her lover were situated and how I could get to the window to see it. But by going down, I was of course descending from the bedroom level as if to avoid my curiosity. I wandered all the way around the other side of the building, admiring the ancient medieval architecture, all of which was quite exotic and entirely impossible. When I came back to the place where I thought I might find Lia, and there indeed was her coat, the brown coat with the fur trim and hat that she wears so often and that I like so much, but no sign of her and no sign of whatever man she might be with.

Here was an REM-sleep dream if there ever was one. The report ran to 603 words, whereas NREM dream reports rarely exceed 100 words (if there is any recollection at all). We don't need Freud's help to discuss its meaning: cognizant of the damage inflicted on me by the stroke, I am especially vulnerable to feeling rejected by the woman I love, the most important person in my life. I have always thought that the meaning of dreams was transparent. This is a good example.

Intimations of Mortality

I have always been quite resigned to the idea of my own death. Everyone dies, and I will die. And I have always hoped that I would not outlive my brain (as my mother did) or my body (as my father did). From what I have seen, life beyond age 80 usually isn't easy. And although I recognize many notable exceptions of people who transcend the ravages of age, even 75 years strikes me as quite enough of life.

Now that I am 77, it is not clear to me whether 80 is worth a try. I have almost died twice already. Both experiences were clear and dramatic harbingers of my mortality. They were also instructive with respect to the subject of my scientific interest in the mind and its relationship to the brain. In the case of my brainstem stroke in February 2001, I experienced changes in sleep and dreaming that were new to me and had not been previously described in the scientific literature.

The next chapter describes my experiences of pneumonia and heart failure in October 2001, which made my stroke symptoms worse and added new handicaps to my already limited capacities. All these phenomena have been described before, but never by a trained observer, the experimental animal that is me as both patient and scientist. I hope they will give scientific weight to first-person accounts of normal and pathological brain states. Without subjectivity, the quest for mind-brain integration is doomed to failure. When subjectivity is taken into account and objectified, success is closer at hand than we recognize.

12 Heart Failure

Between April 15, 2001, when I was discharged from Spaulding Rehabilitation Hospital, and October 5, when I was readmitted to Brigham and Women's Hospital, I had enjoyed a pleasant summer. Quite satisfyingly, I had been able to resume a relatively full range of activities. On June 16, I traveled to Sicily with my wife, and we stayed in our apartment in Messina until about August 15. In late June and early July we had a wonderful vacation in Stromboli with our twin boys, then 5 years old. I thought I was out of the woods. My consciousness was unimpaired and I was ready to resume an active life. My brain had taken a hit, but the part of it that sustained my external self was unchanged.

In retrospect, I may have made a great mistake in trying to recover my swallowing so completely and so quickly. I was pleased to be able to have the gastric tube taken out of my stomach in mid May. By that time I relied entirely on orally ingested normal food instead of the canned pabulum I had been taking through the tube. Flushed with success in this, I ate everything I pleased that summer and early fall, including a huge tray of fresh sea urchins I had after an already sumptuous seafood dinner at a restaurant in Messina called Anselmo's. Such gourmandizing inevitably led to increasing aspiration and probably contributed to the pneumonia that brought me down in early October.

Before I went to Sicily, home-based rehabilitation and nursing had helped me regain mobility. Once the gastric tube was out, I was able to eat nearly anything I wanted. I was still on coumadin to slow blood clotting and prevent embolic phenomena. Wanting to avoid a fall and a bleeding accident, I didn't ride bicycles or garden with my usual freedom, but I was able to drive, to cut the grass, to go to work every day, to review my grant resubmission, and to enjoy the press reception of two books: *Out of Its Mind: Psychiatry in Crisis* (which I had written with Jonathan Leonard) and *The Dream Drugstore*. Together with the publication of "Dreaming and the

Brain" in *Behavioral and Brain Sciences*, the publication of these books was a deeply satisfying sign of my continued productivity. My scientific brain-self was alive and well.

In Messina that summer, I was able to complete a first draft of a short book on *Dreaming* for Shelley Cox at Oxford University Press. Shelley had been after me to do a book for the last couple of years, but I had declined her invitation until the two other books had been published. It was fun to write that little book, and especially to be able to show that I could function as I had before, writing in the morning either in my office in Messina or on the dining porch at the Hotel Miramare in Stromboli. Lia and I had a very full range of social activities, having dinner with friends, even spending long weekends with several of them. Taormina was a particularly exciting venue that year, with a concert by the always fresh, always relevant Bob Dylan. In general I was feeling very good about the future. I was completely unprepared for what was going to happen to me in October.

Warning Signals

There were, however, some important premonitory signs. One was that my attempt to get off the 20-milligram daily dose of Ritalin that I had been taking since early April was unsuccessful. Ritalin had been prescribed to get me going at Spaulding Hospital. Three months later, I simply could not make the reduction from 10 to 5 milligrams of Ritalin without finding that my motor system had begun to behave in a very Parkinson-like manner. For instance, it was practically impossible for me to initiate movement without the help of the 20-milligram dose. I reasoned that I needed the dopaminergic chemical push from Ritalin to reach the telephone in our hallway, which might ring as many as four times before I could even get out of my chair in my adjoining office.

Ritalin mimics the action of naturally released stimulant molecules in the brain. For this reason it is called sympathomimetic. The brain chemical Ritalin imitates is dopamine. Dopamine is involved in motivation and reward as well as in activation of the motor system. That is why amphetamine is so popular. Amphetamine has similar actions to Ritalin on the dopamine system but is a much more dangerous drug. Ritalin is less likely than amphetamine to produce psychosis, and it is less addicting. That's why it was prescribed for me at Spaulding. It did help me get out of bed, to remain alert during the daytime, and to learn to walk again. During the summer in Messina, I continued to need it to keep me mobile.

Dopamine is an aminergic neuromodulator, like norepinephrine, serotonin, and histamine, but, as has already been noted, dopamine does not undergo the same cessation of release in REM that is evinced by the other three neuromodulators. This surprising fact may indicate a persistent role for dopamine in the mediation of all brain states, a role in the persistence of movement (be it real or virtual), and a role in the persistence of consciousness (be it waking or dreaming). As will be said again in chapter 18, it may also mediate psychosis.

When I got back to Boston that September and saw my doctor, James Winshall, it was clear that I had gone back into atrial fibrillation. The electric-shock defibrillation that had been administered before my transfer from Brigham and Women's to Spaulding on March 15 had not held. My heart had reverted to the abnormal rhythm at some point during the summer. I don't know exactly when. But there was already evidence that two processes were at work whose causal connection had to be considered. I had become dependent on Ritalin, and my brain and body couldn't get along without the aminergic stimulant boost. In order to try to reduce my propensity to cardiac arrhythmia, Dr. Winshall had strongly urged me to get off the Ritalin. By the time I did so, my motor and cardiorespiratory systems had acquired a major vulnerability which may have set the stage for the strange and sudden attack of heart failure that I experienced in October.

I probably was wise to resist taking Ritalin in the first place. But I had been persuaded by my doctor to try it in small doses to overcome my lassitude and inability to help me stay awake during late March and early April at Spaulding. Ritalin certainly helped me to wake up and to get out of bed. The dose was therefore increased to 20 milligrams. I was discharged from Spaulding on April 15 and was able to enjoy my twin sons' fifth birthday party the next day. My discharge made the medical and insurance people happy, but was I really ready for such rapid rehabilitation?

I wonder if my cardiovascular and cardiopulmonary systems had become dependent on the externally applied dopamine-like agent. It also seems possible that my withdrawal campaign was too vigorous. Complete withdrawal was occurring in four steps—from 20 to 15 milligrams, from 15 to 10, from 10 to 5, and from 5 to 0—over the course of two weeks. The second time around I didn't notice any of the withdrawal symptoms, so it is not at all clear how Ritalin and/or its withdrawal contributed to the dramatic clinical episode I will now describe.

Heart Failure

On Friday, October 2, eight months to the day after my initial stroke symptoms in Monte Carlo, I drove with my twin sons to Vermont. We left in the early morning, a time when I would normally feel extremely refreshed. Instead I felt dangerously drowsy. I had to stop for naps three times to avoid going off the road. In Vermont, I met my administrative assistant and friend Nick Tranquillo. We had had a lovely Friday afternoon and evening together. We enjoyed Saturday too, as many of our lab friends came from Boston to join us in the country. This was the annual Columbus Day weekend retreat for the staff of the Laboratory of Neurophysiology. Our ritual outing had been neglected for the past two years owing to the deaths of Lia's parents in Sicily. In the fall of 2001 it was particularly exciting to renew the retreat. I felt as if I had been granted a second

Members of the Laboratory of Neurophysiology team outside the sugar house at my North Star Farm in October 2001. This was our last Columbus Day outing; it occurred two days before my readmission with heart failure to Brigham and Women's Hospital. It was during my recovery for delirium that the Thalamosaurus episode (described in the text) was recorded. Standing: Mercedes Atienza, José-Luis Cantero, Alexandra Morgan, Magdalena Fosse, Lili Kocsis, me, Bernat Kocsis, Emese Kocsis, Roar Fosse. Kneeling: Nicholas Tranquillo, Matthew Hobson, Luca Di Perri, David Kahn, Andrew Hobson.

life. Work was going well at the lab, and the Vermont foliage was at its lustrous peak.

I had hoped to recruit the visitors to do some picking up and burning of small branches from the woodlots that had been recently thinned by Roger Laramee and his brother Roland. But when I walked out through the fields to the woods, I was very aware of feeling not only too tired to walk, but tired in a very particular way. There is something distinctive about the fatigue you feel when the heart is the culprit. You know you don't have energy. You sense that your cardiovascular system is so starved for oxygen that it says No when asked to deliver more work.

When my father had developed cardiovascular problems (including arrhythmia and fatigue), about two decades earlier, he had sat down two or three times in the field while climbing the hill behind our Vermont house on one of his daily walks. In October 2001, I felt better only when seated on the ground, asking almost nothing of either my cardiovascular system or my motor system. Were those genes of my father now speaking to me in the same voice in which they had spoken to him?

I quickly abandoned the idea of cleaning up the woodlot, knowing that I couldn't even supervise the job much less participate in the work. I went back to the house, determined at least to be a jovial host. This was an easy task for me because the guests were so delightful. Seventeen of my co-workers piled into my dining room for a magnificent dinner on Saturday night. I was feeling quite giddy and wonderful. In that welcome social context I did not feel a bit tired. It is true that I had a cough, but I had no fever, no malaise, and no chills. There was nothing to suggest that I was rapidly developing triple pneumonia.

Once the dinner was over, I retired to my bed early and slept extremely poorly. The next day, for the first time in my life, I really felt like I didn't want to get out of bed. In fact I couldn't get out of bed. When I went downstairs to look around and noticed that no one else was up, I went back upstairs to sleep and stayed there for most of the day. I ate no breakfast, fixed my guests a lobster bisque for lunch, and ate a token amount of it but skipped dinner altogether. For a gourmand like me, that was a very bad sign.

By then I knew I was very sick, but I couldn't correctly assess what was going on. On Monday, I was so weak that I couldn't drive my car back to Boston. I asked Ed Pace-Schott to drive. When we got back to Brookline, Ed called Dr. Winshall, who suggested that I go to Brigham and Women's the next morning in an ambulance. We got in touch with Lia in Sicily, and she made a hurried return to Boston.

Back to the Hospital

I was re-admitted to Brigham and Women's Hospital on the morning of Tuesday, October 6, 2001, via ambulance and the emergency ward. I was then put on massive doses of intravenous antibiotics because my chest film revealed that no less than three of the lobes of my lungs were infiltrated with pneumonia. The kind of pneumonia I had is called atypical because it is not isolated to a single lobe, because it does not develop quickly, and because it is not associated with chills, fever, and the sense of intense illness that patients with typical pneumonias evince. It was nonetheless malicious. My pneumonia probably was caused by multiple episodes of aspiration of food as my dietary indiscretions had increased.

I didn't mind being in the hospital, and after two days of the antibiotic treatment I was beginning to feel better. I thought I would be discharged within the week and that I would go home and resume my life. That was not to be the case. While asleep on the night of Thursday, October 9, I suffered an acute cardiovascular collapse. I did not respond to wake-up stimuli, and my blood pressure reading was 60/0 instead of the usual 110/60. In this emergency state, I was transferred to the intensive care unit, where I spent five days in critical condition.

When my heart failed, my brain failed too. Not only was my brainstem partially dead as a result of my stroke; it was now so deprived of oxygen that it could not support waking consciousness, much less dreaming. The self that was mediated by my activated conscious brain was gone.

Doctor Winshall describes my first two days in the ICU as a touch-and-go adventure, implying that he wasn't sure whether I was going to live. When I finally regained consciousness, in the morning hours of Tuesday, October 13, I found myself with my hands tied to the bedrails and a tube in my trachea. By then I was breathing on my own. The nurses told me they were waiting until dawn to remove the uncomfortable breathing tube. My sleep and my dreams were once again totally disrupted, and many of my earlier stroke symptoms were exacerbated.

The Heart and the Brain

I have no memory of those five days in intensive care, although informants tell me that I appeared conscious much of the time. My amnesia for those days probably was induced by the medication I received. Dr. Winshall thought I may have had an acute aspiration event, although since my admission to the hospital I had taken no food by mouth and had been fed only through intravenous tubes. Perhaps the acute toxic state of my pneumonia precipitated this major setback. None of these explanations is very convincing to me.

Why did my heart fail so precipitately? I will try to answer this difficult question shortly by advancing a novel theory based on my own understanding of the brainstem. Here my scientific brain self is trying to go beyond conventional explanations of its own difficulties.

Which came first: my heart trouble, or my brain trouble? No one knows. Most people favor the primacy of cardiac pathology. In my own account, I will emphasize the possible role of brain dysfunction. On this view, the cardiovascular symptoms are viewed as secondary to the dyscontrol that results when neurons of the brainstem subserving autonomic physiological functions are lost as a result of a stroke.

By autonomic physiology I mean the entirely unconscious but critical regulation of my heart, my lungs, my gut, and the state of the rest of my brain by my brainstem neurons. All of me requires continuous and well-coordinated functional maintenance in order to eat, breathe, sleep, and dream normally. My brain has to function well if I am to survive. My cardiac rate and rhythm, my blood pressure, my respiratory rate and rhythm, my gastric and other mucous secretions, and my sleep-wake cycles are all automatically regulated. I had lost control—or, rather, my brain's control of these crucial functions had been diminished by the neuronal death that was my stroke.

The hypothesis that my heart troubles were secondary to my brain damage must be considered, because the area of my brainstem that was killed by my stroke contains neurons whose normal job it is to regulate sympathetic and parasympathetic control of the heart, the bowels, the muscles, and the skin. Even my pulmonary difficulties are conditioned by the stroke, because my lungs no longer function normally. As my oropharynx hypersecreted and hypersalivated, it became more difficult for me to cough effectively and to remove the increased number of food particles taken into my lungs. This vicious cycle led to my pneumonia. In parallel with this insidious cycle of dysfunction was the collapse of my cardiovascular functions.

Why else would my heart fail? When I sat down in the Vermont field, my subjective feeling was that I was suffering limitations that were due to imminent congestive heart failure. Heart failure like mine is called congestive because fluid accumulates on the venous side of the circulatory system when the action of the heart muscle becomes too weak to propel the blood that is delivered to it by the veins back to the arteries. Ultimately, the increased venous pressure causes fluid to be forced out of the veins and into the organs and tissues of the body. Puffy ankles are an outward sign of this congestion. Since October 9, 2001, I have had more than my share of puffy ankles. The fluid that was evacuated from my right chest cavity that day had been exuded by my lungs because my heart hadn't been able to pump the blood returning to it from my chest.

My doctors favored the hypothesis that I had had an acute myocarditis associated with my pneumonia. There is no direct evidence for that diagnosis. According to my quite different model, the weakening of cardiac function could as well have been due to changes in the autonomic nervous system of my brain.

The most significant evidence bearing on these two theories was the completely negative cardiac catheterization that was performed on October 21, 2001. Although my cardiac output was poor, my coronary arteries were described by the physician who did the study as "superhighways large and wide open enough to drive trucks through." So there is no explanation of my defective cardiovascular function in terms of the most common culprit, arteriosclerotic heart disease. In view of my self-indulgent dietary proclivities, I certainly deserved to have plaques in my coronaries. I always feared that fate, but it was not mine.

My alternative "brain-first" hypothesis has no direct evidence either. But it has one enormous theoretical attraction: it ascribes all my troubles to one disease and not two. It thus conforms to the principle known as Occam's Razor. The medieval scholar William of Occam decried the invocation of complex and/or multiple hypotheses where simple and single hypotheses suffice. Of course it is possible that I had two or more interdependent ailments, in which case Occam's Razor would be dulled by hard fact. Unfortunately we'll never know. Meanwhile, another brain mischief was about to overtake me.

The Dream Drugstore Revisited

Writing *The Dream Drugstore* over the previous two years had made me wonder why I had never taken drugs. "Fear" had been my honest answer. Now that I was critically ill, I had a chance to take drugs for good clinical reasons. I was surprised by the intensity and variety of pharmacological effects on my brain caused by the medications that were prescribed to help me. My psychological experiences during this second hospitalization reveal the potent effects of drugs and my idiosyncratic reaction to them that had been hinted at by my intense reaction to the benzodiazepine that I had been given in Monaco. These experiments of nature were cooked up for me by circumstances I wanted to exploit and understand.

Femtomil-Induced and Midazolam-Induced Amnesia

I have no recollection of my five days in the ICU, during which I had been intermittently conscious, unconscious, and delirious. After I began to regain automatic control of my blood pressure and of my breathing, I had the same sort of insomnia that I had experienced during the original post-stroke period: total waking all through the night. It was for this reason that I began seeking relief through various sedatives. But instead of achieving restful sleep, I experienced many side effects that are relevant to my hypothesis that normal dreaming is formally akin to delirium.

Serax-Induced Hallucination

Serax, whose generic name is Oxazepam, is a short-acting benzodiazepine with sedative hypnotic properties. Over the years, I have often prescribed it for patients without recognizing that it might affect them as it affected me. Serax induced a somnolent confusional state during which I experienced a very specific symptom that troubled me greatly. Thinking myself to be awake, I would extend my left arm toward the bedside table, only to realize that the glass for which I was reaching did not exist. My hand would pass right through it. The same disturbing insubstantiality characterized numerous other objects on my hospital tray. This must have been due to my hallucinatory construction of an unreal glass that would vanish as I tried to grasp it. I have no insight into what causes this disturbing effect except to say that it occurred in a brain state that was neither normal sleep nor normal waking but rather a hybrid state with elements of both waking and dreaming. In short, Serax had drawn me into a microscopic but robust delirium. Delirium is the mental state of people with organic brain syndrome. I have discussed this condition before, but its analogy to dreaming is important enough to warrant recapitulation here. Delirium consists of four formal changes in conscious state that are not normally seen in either schizophrenia or major affective disorders. This syndrome, discussed earlier the book, is repeated here for emphasis.

1. Disorientation   Time and place senses are disrupted.
2. Recent Memory Loss   Current events cannot be committed to memory.
3. Confabulation   There is a tendency to make up stories to fill in the gaps of faulty memory.

Table 12.1
Formal distinction of three types of psychosis.

Symptoms	Schizophrenic	Affective	Organic
Disorientation	No	No	Yes[a]
Recent memory loss	No	No	Yes[a]
Confabulation	No	No	Yes[a]
Hallucinosis	Auditory	Auditory	Visual[a]
Delusions	Paranoid	Paranoid/somatic	Denial[a]
Emotion	Flat	Intensified[a]	Intensified[a]

a. Indicates a feature shared with dreaming.

4. Visual Hallucinations   Delirium is distinguished from other kinds of psychosis by its visual (in contrast with auditory) hallucinosis.

The paranoid and somatic delusions that are seen in schizophrenia and in major affective disorders rarely accompany toxic deliria. The differences between schizophrenic and affective psychosis (on the one hand) and organic psychosis and dreaming (on the other) are presented in table 12.1. Note how closely dreaming mimics organic delirium and how different it is from the so-called functional psychoses, from schizophrenia, and from major affective psychosis.

Once again, I point out the relevance of all these observations to protoconsciousness theory. Normal perception depends on the brain-mind to supply imagery that fits a given stimulus. The brain-mind is thus a catalog of images, and these can sometimes be released when there is no stimulus or when there is an ill-defined stimulus. Dreaming is a very clear, normal illustration of this principle.

Ambien-Induced "Dreams"

Ambien, whose generic name is Lorazepam, has been reported to cause confusion in the elderly. It certainly confused me. I took it twice, and on each occasion I had the same stereotyped reaction. I was convinced that instead of sleeping in my hospital bed, I was sleeping in an attractively designed summer camp. I was aware that there were other people present whom I might or might not know, yet it seemed that I should know them. Women in what I took to be a kitchen were talking about making provisions for the other campers.

The voices I heard were almost certainly those of nurses conferring outside my hospital room. The room that I thought was in a summer camp was in fact my hospital room. And the rooms that I thought were occupied by other campers were in reality the rooms of my patient colleagues on pod 10A of Brigham and Women's Hospital. At the time, my conviction that this was a very special camp was entirely convincing.

During these long episodes, I experienced a euphoric and sleep-like transformation of my consciousness. Instead of being in a hospital bed, I felt that I was atop a huge pile of mattresses, rolled and stacked on end but very soft and comfortable to lie on. Amazingly, I could sink down to whatever level I chose and then have my consciousness follow me down the lovely deep folds in the pillow-like surface of the bed.

In reality, of course, I was in my hospital bed during all this. It just didn't feel that way. So, as in a dream, I accepted the reality of the camp scenario as if it were fully explanatory. It was extremely pleasant and reassuring to hear the women talking outside my door, in part because so many of them spoke with accents that sounded Spanish. In fact, many of the nurses were Hispanic. And some were very good nurses who know how to deliver patient care in the same hands-on fashion that had so endeared the Monaco nursing staff to me. But most of them were either underqualified nurses' aides or overtrained physicians' assistants.

This "dream" had a clear motive: I wanted more intimate care. I wanted to be touched and bathed. My body and my mind were hurting.

My Idiosyncratic Reaction to Benadryl

"In the intensive care unit, sooner or later everyone becomes psychotic," said Dr. Daniel Loewenstein, the neurologist who spoke with me after my dramatic episode of delirium. I had already begun to experience visual hallucinations when I tried to sleep, but it is the more distinctive and stereotyped hallucinogenic effects of benadryl that I want to emphasize here. I was wide awake, but I saw projected onto the ceiling over my bed fully formed visual images of my own brain's making.

On Wednesday, October 15, 2001, the night after my recovery from shock and cardio-respiratory failure, I had been unable to sleep even after taking several sedative pills. On Thursday night, my nurse, Bob, reminded me that I shouldn't be taking any pills by mouth. In order to achieve sedation, he suggested giving me morphine via the intravenous line in my arm. Thinking it might provide an interesting opportunity to experience and describe the dreamlike effects of a narcotic, I assented. In *The Dream Drugstore* I had made much of the oneiric effects of morphine described by Robert de Quincey and Samuel Coleridge, but they were addicts who took huge, repetitive doses of opium before having their ecstatic visions. Sad to say, morphine had absolutely no effects on my perceptions or on my sleep. Even after a second 25-milligram dose I was still wide awake and lucid.

Bob then suggested that we try the antihistamine Benadryl. Benadryl has been a popular over-the-counter drug and has been used as a clinical sedative and as a motion-sickness medicine for years. I thought this was an interesting idea, especially since the specific arrest of histaminergic neurons in REM sleep had been described by the team of my neurologist colleague Cliff Saper. This discovery put histamine neurons in the same category as the serotonin-containing and norepinephrine-containing REM-off cells that Peter Wyzinski, Bob McCarley, and I had discovered 25 years earlier. As was detailed in chapter 6, we used this discovery to create a new model of sleep regulation and a new theory of dreaming. We said that the brain used norepinephrine and serotonin to guarantee waking by damping down the intrinsic dream generator system of the brain that was fully released normally only in REM sleep. From the experiment that now presented itself to me, I might learn, at first hand, about the sudden and acute effects upon perception of blockade of the histaminergic neuronal system in my own brain. The effects were spectacular.

It must be admitted that my inferences about this drug experience are tainted by the massively dirty chemical conditions of the experiment (especially my pre-treatment with Ambien, trazedone, and morphine), but the effects were nonetheless so potent and so stereotyped as to warrant detailed description. It is clear to me that, whatever the pharmacological factor may have been, my waking brain was suddenly made autocreative in a way that astounded even me. Before this experience, I had had such vivid and persistent visual imagery only in my dreams.

Thalamo-Saurus

One of the advantages of taking Benadryl intravenously is that, because it created a strong sense of warming of the vein into which it was being injected, I was immediately aware of the drug entering my circulatory system. No sooner had my antecubital vein begun to heat up than there appeared the first of a succession of stereotyped and fully formed visual images that recurred for almost an hour on the ceiling over my bed.

The visual images I beheld were animated sketches of imaginary reptiles. These wonderful cartoon drawings came complete with the title "Thalamo-Saurus" rendered in a very artistic computer-graphics design format. In the show there was a sequence of four characteristic reptiles. The one that I remember best was a blue-and-red crocodile. But there were several others. There was one green-and-yellow lizard that typically followed the red-and-blue fellow across my ceiling, and there were a couple of smaller ones. There were also some butterflies, some birds, and some fish, but mostly the four exotic reptiles. With my eyes open, and only with my eyes open, these images would form. I saw them first on the right side of the screen over my bed. They then proceeded from the right to behind my left head as I watched and wondered.

By and large these were friendly little beasties, and I quite enjoyed them—especially when I found that I could alter their speed and location to some degree by making voluntary eye and head movements. Their trajectory was otherwise consistent, their appearance repetitive and clear, and their artistic characteristics quite internally harmonious and even beautiful. This was a "waking dream" if there ever was one. I was completely lucid in that I knew that these perceptions were illusory. But that did not detract from their vividness or from their entertainment value. Amazingly, there also appeared a detailed description of the studio in Tokyo that had made this animation sequence. It was in Japanese, which I read quite easily in the dream, despite the fact that my knowledge of the language is rudimentary and my recognition of the pictographic Kanji characters non-existent. The very apt and imaginative title "Thalamo-Saurus" suggests imaginary reptiles conjured up by my own drug-soaked thalamus. As far as I know, I had never before heard this neologism. This suggests that my aminergically demodulated brain-mind was autocreative in a very specific way. It wrote (in a foreign language) and it drew (in a very fetching style) as it composed and projected a work of art onto the ceiling above my bed.

But occasionally the beasties became distinctly unfriendly. I was frightened when the ceiling assumed a wave-like filamentous character and appeared to float down toward the bed like a parachute in a light wind. Then the images would become distorted on the falling ceiling and sometimes would even appear to separate from it. One particularly menacing goldfish-butterfly combination threatened to fly off the projection surface and enter my room space. It was the lack of boundaries that made me anxious and fearful of these perceptions.

Only artistic drawings could convey the exotic abstract patterning of these forms. Now that I am awake, I am incapable of drawing them. But you may be able to see them for yourself if you simply imagine that every animal was composed of geometrically organized body parts each of which was defined by two color outlines. In the case of the red-and-blue reptile, these figures were highly stylized, the red outlined around the blue. The pattern was repeated over and over again. The color blocks that formed the various components of the animals were fascinating and beautiful to look at. They were also very stereotyped and didn't change from the start of the show to the end.

To explain these effects, I offer a very specific and testable hypothesis. My capability of hallucinating visually is normally held in check by histamine, as well as by norepinephrine and serotonin. That inherent capacity is physiologically enhanced in sleep, when the availability of all three of these chemical substances decreases in the brain. This effect is already significant in NREM sleep (when the neurons that secrete the chemicals discharge at 50 percent of waking levels), but the decrease is maximal in REM sleep (when the neurons stop firing altogether). The blocking effects of histamine on my thalamus and cortex are strong enough to trigger the hallucinatory phenomena of sleep even if they are not strong enough to trigger sleep itself. My own resistance to sleep could have been caused by an overactivity of these modulators.

I have never before, or since, experienced such clear evidence that my brain was capable of artistically elaborate creativity. The fact that my brain was damaged by stroke and besotted with drugs hardly matters. The impact of this discovery, like the discovery of REM-sleep dreaming itself, makes crystal clear the main point of this book: it is the brain that produces the self, and it is the brain that produces the art and the science that the self assumes it has produced. This insight is at once edifying and humbling.

MRI Hallucinosis
After my near-death adventure in the ICU, I once again developed double vision. I made the mistake of telling the neurologists at Brigham and Women's about it. The question of an extension of my lateral medullary infarct was raised, and I was sent down to the brain imaging unit for a new MRI. The results were reassuring: there was no evidence of anatomical spread. I am nonetheless convinced that my stroke symptoms have been made functionally worse by my heart failure. My stroke-weakened brain is unusually sensitive to anoxia.

The experience of having the MRI done this third time was particularly unnerving. The previous two sessions in Monaco were equally stressful but did not evoke the psychotic effects I experienced in the MRI at Brigham and Women's. I was convinced that a young boy and his mother were lying in the MRI machine with me! Lying quiet and still in the dark as MRI images are being collected is a special case of sensory isolation. After about 30 minutes of magnet whining and cranking, I was ready to get out. But the technician admonished me: "Please don't move, the session is almost over." She said this several times before admitting that we still had 10 minutes to go. By then, I was sure that the boy (who was whimpering) and his mother (who was reassuring him) were suffering more than I was. I began to reach out to them and to reassure them that our torture would soon end and we would all escape unharmed.

You don't have to be a psychiatrist to understand the emotional salience of this psychotic experience. As with most of my dreams, the psychological meaning of my hallucinations and delusions was crystal clear. A part of me was the frightened child; another part of me was his reassuring mother.

At one point my hallucinatory perception of voices convinced me that there were numerous other people—all standing up—under the magnet at the same time! As a physician, I know perfectly well that MRIs must be highly focused on one and only one subject's brain at a time. I knew that that one subject was me. And I knew that I was lying down, not standing up. But my brain-mind was still easily tipped over into the delirious mode—probably because it was still anoxic, still under the influence of many drugs, and, in addition, sensorially isolated in the magnet.

Brain, Heart, and Lung Dysfunction: My Dysautonomia Hypothesis

The most conservative scientific theory that accounts for my three problems is that they have no relationship with each other but are simply coincidental. In other words, I have a tendency to develop a stroke via embolic or thrombotic occlusion of my cerebrovascular system, I have another tendency to develop pneumonia, and I have a third tendency to develop heart muscle disease.

An alternative model, and the one that I prefer because it is more parsimonious, is that the problems of all three systems (my brain, my heart, and my lungs) are not only sequential but also causally interconnected. Here is how such a causal sequence might work.

As a first and initiating episode, there was a thrombus in my vertebral artery. This caused a partial occlusion of my posterior inferior cerebellar artery and produced my stroke onset syndromes. Twenty-four hours later there was anoxic destruction of many structures in the lateral medullary and pontine tegmentum region on the right side of my brainstem. The damaged structures included parts of my oculomotor system, the trigemi-nal sensory system of my head and face, and the seventh nerve innervation of my facial muscles. More specifically and more severely, there was damage to my vestibular, cerebellar, glossopharyngeal, and vagal neurons. These neurons are normally committed to the autonomic control of my brain, as well as of my lungs, my heart, and my other viscera. The vagus nerve arising from Cranial Nucleus X in the medulla is the source of cholinergic input to my heart. Acetylcholine, a neuromodulator responsible for REM generation, puts an important brake on heart rate. In fact, this breaking mechanism causes fainting when the system is overactive.

Now I have a problem with cardiac rhythm and rate. My heart beats too irregularly and too rapidly to be efficient. Why? The doctors say I had myocarditis, but they have no proof for this theory. They are making what is called an exclusionary diagnosis. When they can't find any other cause, they assume infection. I am unhappy with this reasoning. I prefer the fol-lowing line of thought.

The cell loss that occurred in my brainstem damaged many autonomic neurons as well as sensorimotor neurons. This could have set the stage for failure of autonomic systems innervating my heart and lungs as well as those controlling the state of my brain. Loss of autonomic control could have also contributed to the dramatic changes in sleeping, waking, and dreaming that I experienced.

My glossopharyngeal and vagal nucleus impairments may have led to a secondary impairment in pulmonary regulation. My ability to clear my lungs of fluid was compromised, and my propensity toward pneumonia was increased not only because of the swallowing defects (due to glosso-pharyngeal cell loss), but also because of a weakening of the reflex reactions to aspiration.

My excessive secretions of mucus are another result of autonomic imbalance. For the past nine years, I have had a constant tendency to hypersecrete mucus, which is made much worse by eating, talking, or exercising.

Admitting that my troubles began with atrial-fibrillation-induced thrombosis of a blood vessel in my brain, what could be the cause of the post-stroke cardiovascular effects? Should those effects, too, be considered primarily peripheral, or might they be centrally generated? Let me begin to answer this question by reviewing the pathogenesis of my stroke. Damage to my right vagus nucleus impaired my ability to speak because the recurrent laryngeal nerve, a branch of my vagus, was immediately rendered non-functional. Now my speech is practically normal, but I am still distinctly hoarse. I hear it even if no one else does. Right from the start, it has been clear that many autonomic functions previously controlled by my right vagus nerve have been impaired. The vagus nerve contributes to the control of secretion from the salivary glands and the stomach. And it contributes to the way in which these secretions are moved up and out of the lungs and then down to my gastrointestinal tract. Could it be that I developed pneumonia because this traffic was so badly snarled?

The vagus nerve doesn't just innervate the pulmonary system. It also has powerful slowing effects on the heart. It was this propensity that allowed Otto Loewi to demonstrate neurotransmission by a chemical substance. Loewi called the heart-slowing chemical "vagustoff." It turned out to be acetylcholine. I hypothesize that the cardiac arrhythmia that was first seen in Monaco was, in part, the acute effect of the thrombus in the brainstem, which caused a dampening of vagal output.

The vagus nerve is one of the major causes of my heart slowing. Now I can no longer slow my heart, and I can't keep its beat regular. My heart function is still very impaired. For that reason, I need cardiac medications—lots of them. I take digoxin (to strengthen my heart muscle), zestril (to lower my heart rate), and lazex (to help me get rid of excess fluid and avoid getting puffy ankles).

Even with this range of treatment, I can't maintain effective cardiovascular output. This is due in part to the arrhythmia, no question about it. But it may also be due to a loss of trophic function normally mediated by the neuromodulatory systems of the brain on the heart muscle. In other words, my heart muscle tone may depend on trophic effects normally mediated by those autonomic inputs that I am now missing. These trophic effects may well be phenomena mediated by the cholinergic neurons of my medulla and the sympathetic neurons of my pons. On this view, my heart muscle depends on active sympathetic and parasympathetic maintenance. But when the support neurons die, my heart not only loses its rhythmic control but fails altogether.

However fanciful it may be, I prefer this integrated model to no model at all. A speculative theoretical bent has always characterized my science, and I feel both impelled and pleased to apply it to myself now that I am a patient. In fact, having a model that is related to my life's work and which integrates such a wild concatenation of symptoms is, in itself, not only intellectually gratifying but also therapeutic. Even if it is wrong, I feel better for having made it.

13   Back Ache

In the following fantasy report, I attempt to portray my life's most traumatic life experience metaphorically:

On June 26, 2008, I walked into a sweet shop in Jerusalem to buy a dessert. I was admiring the lithe figure of the young Palestinian woman standing in line ahead of me, when I noticed that she was wearing a belt of bombs around her lissome midriff. Noticing my noticing, she smiled seductively, pushed on her left nipple and blew us all up to paradise!

When I woke up in Brigham and Women's Hospital, my surgeon, Dr. Gregory Brick, said the operation had gone well. He had performed an L2-S1 laminectomy and an L4-S1 vertebral fusion. I felt as if I had been hit by a truck (or blown sky high by a suicide bomber). Never have I had such pain or been so uncomfortable. Was all that trauma worthwhile?

I first developed low back symptoms in the late 1980s, when I was in my fifties. My left thigh pain was then attributed to a bulging disk. The pain was typically made worse by driving. I ducked the recommended surgery and used bed rest instead. The pain dissolved. I walked away.

I can date that first attack of sciatica with precision because my wife Joan was becoming disaffected with me just when I needed her most. I was in bed, in severe pain, the weekend she traipsed off for a rendezvous with a man she later would marry.

In 2003, two years after my brainstem stroke, I began to have difficulty standing after getting out of my car. After a struggle with weakness, but not pain, I could walk reasonably well. I walked so well, in fact, that no one who examined me (including some of the world's leading neurologists) thought anything was wrong. I had had a stroke, and I was lucky to be walking at all, they told me. Another sign that there was something wrong with my back was the audible (to me) clanking of my back bones when I bent over to make my rather low bed. Of course, my doctors couldn't hear that, and they looked at me cross-eyed when I reported this bizarre waking experience. In retrospect, I was probably hearing my disc-deficient vertebral column telling me that I should get an MRI.

I also knew something else was wrong because my leg weakness was slowly but definitely progressive. Only when I began to have shooting pains in my left leg did anyone take me seriously. For this clear-cut sciatica symptom, I was given intrathecal cortisone shots, which partially or completely eliminated the pain for two or three months. But the weakness persisted and the pain was recurrent.

After seeing some muscle specialists, who struck out as fast as the famous neurologists, I was sent to Dr. Gregory Brick, an orthopedic surgeon. After hearing my story, Dr. Brick told me I probably had spinal stenosis and ordered an MRI. The images of my spine showed marked narrowing of both the vertebral canal and the small holes through which the spinal nerves to the leg muscles pass. This MRI picture, which could have been taken three years earlier, was so clear that a junior high student could easily have seen the pathology in my lower back. I apparently had the degenerative arthritis gene that had earlier hobbled my father and which later hobbled my own son, Christopher. I was also a victim of medical neglect.

Dr. Brick did not press for surgery. However, he said "If you can't stand it anymore, I will operate." I temporized for 18 months and sought other opinions. Finally, a neurologist at Brigham and Women's, Allan Roper, said that he thought my symptoms, including the leg weakness, were classic signs of spinal stenosis and might well be helped by surgery. I decided to have surgery, and it was scheduled for May 6, 2008.

When I asked Dr. Brick if he was sure I would be well enough by June 9 to give the keynote address at the Sleep Research Meeting in Baltimore, he suggested postponing the surgery. That indicated that I was in for a longer recuperative haul than I had anticipated. It is now nearly two years since my operation, and I have not yet fully recovered. In fact, I find myself more disabled than before the surgery.

How happy I was to go to that Sleep Society meeting in Baltimore! I had prepared a talk that integrated my old work and my new thinking under the title "Dream Consciousness." What I meant by that title was that dreaming, contrary to what Freud had led us to believe, is not an unconscious mental state at all. On the contrary, it is a rich and vivid conscious experience that occurs in sleep and can be recalled if an awakening occurs during or immediately after the dream. Dreams are otherwise difficult to remember it is true. But amnesia, implying organic causation, is one thing. Unconscious mental experience, implying psychodynamic repression, is quite another.

My work and that of others showed why it is amnesia, and not repression, that is responsible for dream forgetting. In REM sleep, the brain is activated (A) but put off line to external inputs and outputs (I) and—most important—aminergically demodulated so that memory (M) is disenabled. About three days before my talk in Baltimore, it suddenly occurred to me that I could go a step further and suggest that REM-sleep dreaming was not only not unconscious but "protoconscious."

By "protoconscious" I meant that REM-sleep dreaming was both ontogenetically prior to and foundational of waking consciousness. This idea negated Freud's view of dreaming as the enemy of waking consciousness, with the unconscious lying in wait for the ego to let down its guard in sleep so that a sneak attack on consciousness became possible. I replaced Freud's mutually antagonistic model with the hypothesis that the two states of consciousness, waking and dreaming, are mutually enhancing.

Whether or not this theory can be developed, tested, and upheld remains to be seen. But it certainly cleared the air in Baltimore. The audience, estimated at 6,000, gave me a standing ovation as I clutched the lectern to support my feeble legs. As I have continued to recover from my surgery, I have enjoyed beginning to develop my theory. I am grateful for that scientific opportunity whether I continue to improve or not.

Drug-Induced Psychosis

After my surgery on June 26, 2008, my pain was so intense that I learned, the hard way, how to move—and how not to move—in my bed. I was fitted with a brace (on which I later painted the imaginary Jerusalem suicide bomber), and Dr. Brick offered me a pain killer (which knocked me out). My general pain level decreased because I was snowed. But whenever I woke up enough to move, my pain was every bit as intense as before.

The worst effect of the drug, however, was the dreadful psychosis it induced. Whenever I closed my eyes (and I did so often), I saw the faces of many of my scientific colleagues in Baltimore. Most of them had three eyes, including a very large one in the center of the forehead. These grotesque faces went away when I opened my eyes and could again see the hospital surroundings and the medical staff.

The distortion of faces that I experienced when I closed my eyes was formally similar to an eyes-open vision that was reported to me by a psychotic patient, N.H. whom I used to see in my small basement office at the Massachusetts Mental Health Center in the 1960s. N.H. saw a single eye, right in the middle of my forehead. When I asked her to draw or paint that vision, she produced a very vivid image of an eye with a fish inside it. The faces of the colleagues that I saw when I closed my eyes on June 29, 2008 in Brigham and Women's were equally bizarre. Some had only one eye, but others had three. The hallucinatory eyes changed from singles to doubles to triples, and back again. This image shifting, which is typical of normal dreams, is called transmogrification by Martin Seligman, a well-known psychologist who worked in dream research in the 1980s.

The point here is that the brain—in normal dreaming, in psychosis, and in drug-induced delirium—is capable of producing visual hallucinations of a disturbing nature as well as psychedelic ones like my antihistamine-triggered reptiles. For me, the facial distortions were disturbing because they were emotionally salient: if my colleagues looked to other people as they looked to me, they would lose all credibility. If others believed, as I did, that they were all psychotic, too, my new dream theory had no chance of being accepted.

My patient N.H. must have felt that way, too. If she told me how my face changed during our therapy sessions, maybe I wouldn't see her again. But since I was a devoted and well-coached Semradian psychotherapist, I suspected that she was telling me not to probe so deeply and so fast because her hold on reality was shaky. I backed off, at least for a while. Unfortunately, neither my fine-tuned psychotherapy nor any combination of phenothiazine drugs could help Nancy control her discomfort. Several years later, she became a successful suicide on her fifth try; she hanged herself.

To cure myself of my own little psychosis, all I had to do was stop taking those pain killers. Why did they make me psychotic, and why did I guess—correctly, I suppose—that my own visions were drug induced? I will try to answer the second question first. I was very much helped by the timing of my symptoms, which coincided with my taking a drug. It was also helpful (and informative) to be able to stop the horrible facial transmogrifications by opening my eyes.

I was a victim of "lucid" psychosis. I knew I was psychotic because I could control the visions. This is exactly what lucid dreamers do. They wake up enough to know that they are dreaming. And they test their theory by voluntarily changing their dream plots. I know that this is true because I had once learned to control my dreams. Just as I had been a lucid dreamer, now I was a lucid psychotic. I knew that when I closed my eyes I would become crazy, and that when I opened them again I would be sane.

My switching from normal awake-state vision to eyes-closed psychosis may have been caused by tipping the balance between internal and external input, by voluntarily changing what I call Factor I in my AIM model. My patient N.H. learned to control her visions, too. After she was well enough to leave the hospital, she told me that she could stop the visions by counting the filigree indentations in the ceiling molding of her apartment. She found, as I did, that the mind was sensitive to input source (I), and that input source is state dependent. By shifting her attention from one form of processing (counting), she aborted another processing mode (visual hallucination). During that time, N.H. was employed as a fact checker by a company that published a city directory. She was very good at picking up typographical errors, and that ability helped to hold her psychotic symptoms in check.

These stories help us to get a firmer fix on factor I in the AIM model. The mind will process any information that is fed to it. In the awake state, it is preferentially tuned to external sources of information. We call these inputs sensory stimuli. But the awake mind is also sensitive to internal inputs: stimuli that arise in one part of the brain and influence another part. It is enough to open and close one's eyes to appreciate this interaction. When my eyes were closed after my back surgery, my vision was invaded by internally generated stimuli: the representations in my memory of the faces of my colleagues in Baltimore, whose positive appraisal I very much wanted and needed. When I opened my eyes, the hospital room stimuli took over and my three-eyed Baltimore colleagues disappeared.

Why doesn't this always happen to me as it did with N.H.? Why am I not always as prone to psychosis, as she was? The answer to this question is disappointingly vague but may help us to better understand factor M (chemical modulation) in the AIM model. All narcotics, including the drug I was taking for my post-surgical pain, block the receptors of the aminergic neurons of the brainstem, particularly the noradrenergic receptors of the locus coeruleus. The thorazine that failed to keep N.H.'s visions from taking over her mind is a dopamine receptor blocker. Thorazine is also an antihistamine, and I have elsewhere described the hallucinogenic effects on my brain of antihistamines. Maybe that's why the newer drugs are more effective: they are not antihistamines.

Facts such as those just recounted have convinced many psychiatrists that modulation (M) is a powerful force in regulating the balance between external and internal information (I) and, as a result, in helping the mind's capacity to focus on external reality in the awake state. Having a good M system helps to keep us all out of loony bins. How the M system goes bad is a matter of unresolved scientific controversy. Some are persuaded that M is genetically determined. But exactly how that might be true is not yet clear. Others say that whatever genes may contribute to M, environmental factors are important in shaping how it works.

If anxiety, elation, and anger are built-in states of the brain-mind, then their regulation is important and learning almost certainly plays a role in the shaping of M. Whatever the ultimate answer to this nature-vs.-nurture controversy might be, the role of M in determining the state of the normal brain-mind stands out like a lighthouse beacon to ships lost at sea. Whether I am dreaming or awake is an M function for sure. You can hang your hat on it (whether your wife mistakes you for that hat or not).

So I knew that I was psychotic after my surgery. But that blessed insight didn't make me like it. My discomfort was related to the fact that my three-eyed colleagues seemed to be just as crazy as I was. How, under the circumstances, would I ever be able to convince the rest of the scientific community of the utility and validity of my protoconsciousness hypothesis? I felt devastated. The only thing I had going for me was the thought of my apparent success in Baltimore. Without that, I was really lost.

I therefore decided that pain was preferable to psychosis and immediately switched from the more potent pain killer to Tylenol. Within 24 hours, both my colleagues and I were cured of our madness, and those polyphemous faces no longer appeared. What a relief! I was lucky to recognize what was going on and, even if I was wrong in my self-diagnosis, to make an experimental change in my treatment regime.

On July 1, I got myself transferred to Spaulding Rehabilitation Hospital. I had done well there after my stroke in 2001, and I had been impressed by the care my father had received there in 1990. I needed more time to recover than I gave myself, but I wanted to be in Vermont on July 10 so the twins could go to camp and I could enjoy the country.

I needed more time to recover my ability to walk and my ability to urinate when I wanted to. Four days was not enough time to get my bladder to obey my commands. That would take six days. The Foley catheter came out early, but I needed direct catheterization to empty my bladder properly (and it was a long time before I was completely continent).

When I finally recovered my ability to urinate I knew I would make it to Vermont as scheduled, on July 10. And, with Nick Tranquillo's help, I did. The small back bedroom on the first floor of my farmhouse was heaven. No TV. No cell phone. No catheterization. Instead, I had a lovely view of the romantic ice house and the pasture hill behind. I needed two ski poles, then one, then none as I made frequent trips to the barn to see the wondrous progress Bob Limlaw was making on my new gallery, the Museum of the Art of Life.

Mitogio, our country house in Sicily, is every bit as ideal a place to recuperate as Vermont. Salvatore Sgarlatta found screens for my bedroom windows, bought a powerful floor fan, and fitted the bed with extra cushions for reading. For about two very hot weeks, I lived in that room, venturing out only for meals and for the occasional brief sunbath. I read, with considerable disappointment, Friedrich Schiller's Philosophy of Aesthetics, sent to me by my German colleague Ursula Voss. Both Schiller and Goethe, whom he so admired, strike me as hypertheoretical and hypoempirical. Maybe that is an eighteenth-century disease, but it seems to affect Germans more than French or English authors. I think of Jonathan Swift, who seems 100 times more skeptical and realistic than either Goethe or Schiller. Funnier, too. I conclude that empiricism is essential to scholarly life.

With a stroke, heart disease, and spinal stenosis, I was more attractive to an undertaker than to a physician. But if I had not cheated death so often, I would never have had the ultimate pleasure of adding a functional component to my dream theory. In the summer of 2009, I was considering writing a major theoretical paper for Nature when I received an email message from Leonie Welberg, an editor at Nature Neuroscience Reviews. "Would you consider writing a paper on REM sleep and dreaming?" she asked. I said that I would be happy to oblige if my paper could be subtitled "Toward a Theory of Protoconsciousness." Documented with more than 150 references, the paper was published in the November 2009 issue. I will detail its claims in chapter 16, when I also will discuss the scientific implications of my work. As a corollary of my reframing dreaming as an organically determined state as well as a psychologically meaningful one, I theorized that REM sleep was as much a brain program for the future as it was a reaction to the past. The idea that the brain (my brain and your brain) has within it a virtual-reality machine that automatically cranks out models of the world and our place and time in that fictive world is deeply appealing to me.

In fact, it is difficult not to be self-congratulatory about this seductive concept. My conceit fades, however, when I wonder why it took me so long to arrive at this stunning hypothesis. Why was I so tied to the stimulus-response paradigm, and to Freud's decrepit dream model, that I persisted in believing that dreaming was a defensive reaction to life rather than an offensive preparation for it? Now it seems to me obvious that something like this must be true.

Lying in bed, reading and reflecting, may have helped. Certainly lecturing and teaching made me realize that the mechanistic story, beautiful as it was, suffered from incompleteness. I needed a functional hypothesis to finish the revolution. I needed a new and radically different way of reading the biological and psychological evidence. So complaints about my hardships and grousing about my medical shortcomings pale in the light of protoconsciousness theory. As a dying man, I am happy to have had this golden opportunity, whether my new theory is right or wrong and whether it is provable or not.

14 Sleep Strangulation

Can you choke yourself to death in your sleep? Yes, you can. Just as a sleepwalker may commit murder without conscious awareness, it is possible to kill yourself by strangulation. Breathing is controlled by neurons in the medullary brainstem. In fact, the neurons that constitute the respiratory center are an integral part of the same reticular formation that my research showed to be important to the state of the brain in control of behavior and of consciousness.

The changes in respiration that occur in sleep have been known since Aserinsky and Kleitman's original description of REM in 1953. A decade later, Fred Snyder and I published a more elaborate analysis of this effect, which we attempted, unsuccessfully, to relate to dream content. In the course of our work, we discovered that respiration might be increased in rate or blocked altogether during REM sleep. In the case either of an increase (called hyperpnea) or a cessation (called apnea), the transfer of oxygen to the bloodstream was reduced. The body, and especially the brain, needs oxygen in order to function properly. Even small drops in oxygen supply are noticed, and the respiratory center responds by trying to increase ventilation. Sometimes it fails to do so. This failure can cause sleep strangulation. By the time the normal impairment of breathing in sleep becomes pathological as what we then call sleep apnea, a person can literally choke himself to death. I know, because breathing impairment in sleep has threatened my own life. When an apnea sufferer attempts to breathe, the airway may collapse, making inspiration as physically impossible as when it is compressed by an assailant.

Sleep Apnea

How long ago did I begin to experience sleep apnea? Because the syndrome is subtle, subjective experience is not much help in answering this

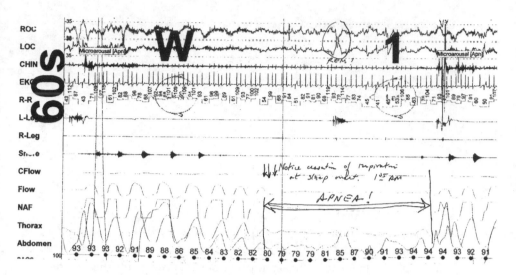

Sleep apnea. Having observed that cessations of breathing occurred in the sleep of healthy young males, I later failed to recognize that my own excessive daytime sleepiness (which led to three automobile mishaps) could be due to sleep apnea. In 2008, my doctor, Charles Morris, referred me to the Framingham Sleep Disorders Center. My polysomnogram revealed severe sleep apnea, which was counteracted by Continuous Positive Airway Pressure. I have been using my CPAP machine ever since, despite some difficulties tolerating the treatment.

question. But my stroke, in 2001, did destroy many neurons in my right medulla. Some of them may have been "respiratory" neurons, the loss of which may have diminished my drive to breathe—especially during sleep, when so many medullary reticular cells stop telling our lungs to expand and contract. The need for oxygen normally is reduced during sleep, when the musculature is relaxed or inhibited. Hence, many neurons that are respiratory in the awake state are on holiday during sleep.

I may even have begun to set up the sleep-apnea scenario in the early 1990s, when I gained 30 pounds. I attributed the ballooning of my body to the licentious engorgement of gourmet food during the years 1990–2000, when I was a member of the Research Network on Mind-Body Interactions. My colleagues and I tried, in vain, to spend down the MacArthur millions by meeting, five times a year, in hotels with the most glorious restaurants. We worked hard at science all day and ordered from exotic menus every night. I was happy to be a gourmand, but was I gradually obstructing my airway with fat globules?

In addition to giving my back a chance to heal, I am now conscientiously trying to lose weight. In Italy, where pasta is king, this is not easy.

I must simply refuse all carbohydrates, including bread. I don't miss bread. And I don't miss wine at the table either. As guests bring tempting bottles to me, my wine cellar is growing apace. I can't yet see any change, but it must be true that calories in equal calories out. I have not yet given up my ritual aperitivi. Not only do I enjoy those delicious drinks, but the symbolic division of night and day is important to me. I shut down my computer and close my journal every day at 6 p.m.

After dark falls, I might continue to read either a novel or a back issue of *Nature*. Dusk on the patio of our house in the Alcantara Valley of Sicily is very dynamic as the light begins to fade. Out come the bats; swallows dive vertiginously; pigeons and doves coo. The air cools and the hills become silhouettes against the dark but still luminous sky. Just this week, the moon rose, full, at sunset. We saw the moon rise again, but 40 minutes later the next evening, and another 40 minutes later the evening after that. As I watch this magical transformation, I sip a negroni, or perhaps a gin and tonic, and munch cheese and salami. There are so few pleasures left to me that I refuse all suggestions of dietary abstinence.

I sometimes experience irresistible sleepiness in the daytime. If I am reading, such dozing is benign. But if I am driving my car, it can be malignant. In fact, I have gone off the road twice while driving to Vermont. And once, while driving to Connecticut (alone) on the Massachusetts Turnpike, I lost control of the car and swerved wildly across two lanes of southbound traffic and back again. That time, I was sure I was a goner; however, I came to a stop safely in the breakdown lane.

In the spring of 2009, my tendency to fall asleep while reading in my armchair became irresistible. I would wake myself up by snoring loudly. I slept poorly at night, too, and occasionally I woke myself up by hearing my own voice giving elaborate lectures. My wife wisely moved to another room. She has heard me lecture many times, and she is a sound enough sleeper to ignore my symptomatic self-strangulation.

Suspecting that the neurontin I was taking for pain was overly sedating, I stopped taking it altogether. The facial pain was bearable, but my sleepiness was unabated. When I asked my new doctor, Charles Morris, if he thought I should take an arousing drug (perhaps Cephalon's Provigil), he said No. Instead he suggested that I should go to a sleep lab to rule out sleep apnea. I laughed at that idea, but in late May I checked into the Framingham Sleep Health Center. (Dr. Morris had taken the place of Dr. Winshall, who had been killed by a truck while riding home on his bicycle at night.)

At the Sleep Health Center, within three hours, I generated more than 200 central sleep apneas and showed oxygen desaturations of 65 percent.

The diagnosis of sleep apnea was thus made. During the second "split half" of the night, I used a Continuous Positive Airway Pressure machine and slept like a baby. I took my new CPAP machine with me to Baltimore, and I have used it faithfully ever since except when the mask makes it impossible for me to fall asleep. A text has to be really boring to put me to sleep now, and I am tempted to try driving again. Motorists beware: the driver of that white Mercedes station wagon may be me!

Why did my sleep improve dramatically when I began to use the CPAP machine? The mask over my nose and mouth made it possible to apply positive pressure to my airway. This positive pressure held my airway open and helped to counteract its tendency to collapse during sleep. I took the CPAP machine with me to Sicily in the summer of 2008. After a while, the mask became so irritating that I could not sleep at all, and I stopped using it. I immediately had difficulty staying awake in the daytime. Now I have reconciled myself to the use of the CPAP machine. The nocturnal discomfort is a small price to pay for daytime vigilance.

As I have noted, my excessive daytime sleepiness returned when I was not using the CPAP machine. When I sat up and wrote in longhand in my journal or edited on my computer, I felt quite alert. But when I lay down, or when I tried to read while sitting up in a chair, I had a tendency to doze off. This drowsiness was obviously incompatible with driving. I nonetheless renewed my Massachusetts driver's license. I did not tell the nice woman who passed me despite my marginal performance on the eye test about my excessive daytime sleepiness.

During the summer of 2009, I developed Cheyne-Stokes respiration. Persons sleeping with me in the same bed, and even family members or friends sleeping in the next room, were treated to the gasping that followed my periodic cessations of respiration.

I discovered this alarming condition for myself with the help of a German film crew that came to Sicily in September of 2009 to make a documentary about sleep and dream science. We mounted a film camera over my head and a microphone on the bedstead. The microphone picked up my breath sounds and recorded them on a digital device. Now I could see and hear my own respiratory arrests and compensatory gasping and choking. Recognizing that I had advanced to an alarming stage of the sleep-apnea syndrome, I resolved to resume use of the CPAP machine. I kept that resolution after returning to Boston in October of 2009.

I fell asleep easily with the mask on and usually slept long and deep. I even began to recall dreams again. Here are two amazing examples from my journal:

A Dry Wet Dream 11/16/09

I am making love to an attractive and responsive woman (I have no idea whom!). We are standing up and thrusting vigorously. After a while, I decide to climax but it is not possible. I wake up disappointed but amused.

Whereas sexual dreams are not uncommon, I rarely dream of famous men.

Berlusconi Dream 12/1/09

I woke up are about 4 AM with definite recall of a dream about Silvio Berlusconi. I was eating at a café restaurant with a group of unidentified people. Suddenly, it became clear (to me) that a short, dark-skinned man sitting behind me to the right was none other than Silvio Berlusconi. Although he didn't really look like Silvio Berlusconi (whom I can see very clearly when I am awake!), there was no doubt in my mind that it was he! I even noticed, in the dream, that his appearance was peculiar but it didn't make any difference to my belief that it was Silvio Berlusconi.

I was also surprised to find myself in a conversation with the Italian premier. I asked him some tough questions which he answered confidently and clearly. I thought to myself "He is certainly politically adept."

When he had finished his coffee, SB said goodbye and left with his coterie. I wanted to go too because I said to myself, "I will probably never see SB again" but he urged me to stay, have a coffee, and then come alone in a taxicab! I was disappointed but agreed with this suggestion.

I can't remember (at all) what we talked about but the image is very clear and (now) was very clearly not Silvio Berlusconi!

I was pleased to be dreaming again and to find that my capacity to dream bizarrely was unimpaired. Maybe my sleep apnea was now under control.

I had discovered sleep apnea in 1962 while working with Fred Snyder at the National Institutes of Health. A healthy-appearing young man, whom I had recruited as a subject in my study of respiratory activity and dreaming, stopped breathing for 45 seconds during one of his otherwise normal REM periods. I was so astonished and puzzled by this unexpected observation that I did not awaken the subject, nor did I inform him of his propensity to stop breathing as he slept.

Most embarrassing to admit, I was not aware that I had stumbled onto something much more important than what I was looking for. My oversight clearly demonstrates the power of expectancy to influence observation. That young man wasn't supposed to stop breathing for 45 seconds during his sleep. Therefore, to my naïve mind, he didn't stop breathing. I denied the obvious, the manifest, the truth.

When the Neuroscience Society was still young, my mentor, Edward Evarts, hosted a special-interest dinner at which the topic of discussion was "My Most Important Mistakes." This was a brilliant and unusual invitation to reveal the errors that are not supposed to be made in science. In fact, errors usually are covered up. The net goal of this subterfuge is to make us all look better than we really are.

In admitting my own failure to recognize the normal tendency of males to stop breathing in sleep, I wish not only to apologize for my own error, but also to underline the strong tendency we all have to believe what we believe and to ignore even dramatic evidence that we are wrong or that our knowledge is woefully incomplete. This principle extends, of course, to self-observation. I hope that the examples I have provided here will convince you that by looking more closely at your self you will discover something of importance to the world. I am not referring here to the narcissistic navel gazing that characterized the psychoanalytic era. That era is over. I invite you to share in the far more interesting and promising phase of self-understanding provided by neuroscience.

That a sleep expert should develop sleep pathology is as ironic as the earlier dream disorder following my stroke and the psychosis following my back surgery. I see two morals to this story. One is that afflictions of breathing and of mental illness itself are very common. The second is that describing these problems carefully helps to advance the brain-mind agenda and the brain-body agenda. We are living in an age of true renaissance. For the first time in history, we have the opportunity of integrating our experience with neuroscience. The scientific psychology that Freud could only dream of is well within our grasp.

V   Implications of My Work

15 Philosophical Implications

My brain is a subjective object. It is a physical thing that can see, can feel, and can represent its experiences to the self that it creates. The states of my brain are objective subjects. The brain creates my subjective states, and those states have structurally fixed formal characteristics. Research on sleep and dreaming illustrates how and why both of these two symmetrical principles apply and what light they shed on the elusive mind-brain question. In this chapter I will try to elaborate these principles.

My brain was formed with its own means of producing subjectivity. In utero, it was already capable of self-activation and thus theoretically capable of generating emotional primordia. In early life, this capacity was visible in the outward signs of REM sleep as well as in awake-state behavior. Long before I could have learned to express emotions, I was an REM-sleeping infant's brain that moved its eyes behind closed lids, collapsed its muscle tone, and made flexor movements of its hands, fingers, and legs. I evinced highly specific facial expressions. These include smiling (denoting pleasure) and grimacing (denoting fear or displeasure).

Because as an infant I could not yet speak, I cannot know with certainty that these fetal and neonatal activation states were associated with feelings or other conscious-state accompaniments. But as soon as my speech developed, I could have told my parents that I felt strong emotions when my outward behavior signaled REM. By that time, at the very latest, my brain had become a subjective object. As a four-year-old, I was already capable of creating a rich internal world of conscious experience and of elaborating a self that was increasingly capable of reflective thought and deliberate decision making.

It seems reasonable to suppose that primordial subjectivity arises much earlier than we suppose, even in utero, but we need not press this controversial claim to understand the first principle: The brain becomes a subjective object very early in life. It retains that capacity as long as certain of its parts remain healthy. Thus, I am capable of writing this book because my upper brain is intact and functions well despite horrendous damage to my cerebellum and medulla.

Since brain activation in REM sleep causes universal and stereotyped forms of consciousness that we all experience as dreaming, we can be sure of the second principle as well: Brain states such as REM-sleep dreaming are objective subjects. That is to say, brain activation states, including REM sleep, have formal features which are deeply built in. These features guarantee our lifelong experiential capacity for dreaming and the stereotyped formal nature of those dreams. This is what I call objective subjectivity. But, you may well ask, how can subjectivity be objective? To further explain this apparent contradiction in terms, consider the facts presented in the next section.

Brain States as Objective Subjects

When I see the outward signs of sleep, and when I notice with my eyes and observe with electronic instruments signs of what I see, which are unequivocal evidence of internal brain activation in another person, I can be sure that that the person's brain, a subjective object, has moved to a state of objective subjectivity. That is, I can predict that the reports of the state of consciousness described by a subject I rouse from that brain state will be characterized by rich and detailed sensorimotor perception, intense involvement in bizarre scenarios and behaviors, strong emotion, a distinct inability to think reasonably, and a dramatic failure to achieve insight into their true state of consciousness. My subjects believe themselves to be awake and suppose that they are behaving in the outside world when in fact they are asleep in their beds and dreaming.

These conclusions have deep and wide-ranging implications for philosophy and psychology. They also force major paradigm shifts upon psychiatry, upon medicine, and even upon the humanities. For 100 years, Western thought struggled to incorporate Freudian dream theory into the center of its conception of consciousness. Because that theory is so clearly wrong, the twentieth century's long struggle was a fool's errand. Now a truly revolutionary and liberating moment is at hand. When dream interpretation is relieved of the impossibly onerous responsibility of explaining objective subjectivity, it finds that the mental content of dreams is not so much defensive as it is hyperassociative and hyperemotional. In dreaming, our associations and emotions fit together in a clear and informative manner.

Freud's famous self-analysis is mocked in this double-exposure photograph of me lying on the couch and seated behind the couch in a chair. The photos were taken in front of a Tudor-style fireplace in the library of the Massachusetts Mental Health Center in the early 1990s. Behind me are portraits of Elvin Semrad, Jack Ewalt, Harry Solomon, and Freud himself. The influence of Freud was very strong in the early 1960s, when the disguise-censorship dream theory was still a widely accepted standard. I like to think that my work has updated dream theory by means of the brain science Freud knew was necessary to a truly scientific psychology.

How I reached these radical conclusions has been the main subject of this book. To tell the story as it evolved in the development of my awake mind, I have presented a memoir whose aim was to reveal what I take to be a deep and very probably innate skepticism about popular explanations of natural phenomena. I have also showcased my companion penchant for experimentalism, my yen to try things out to see if I could transcend conventional modes of thinking, modes of being, and modes of behaving.

Self-Observation via Journal

In 1973, when I reached the age of 40, I began to contemplate my mortality and to consider how I might transcend it. Having been trained as both a psychiatrist and an experimental neurobiologist, I began to cultivate a deep interest in my own consciousness, my own feelings, and my own behavior. It was then that I decided to begin keeping a journal that could help me to integrate my private experiences with my public achievements.

Now, at 77, suffering from what feels to me like a fatal illness, I have returned to my journal with a view to examining certain aspects of dreaming—aspects which I believe to be still beyond the reach of science but which seem to me to be robust evidence of personal truth. One outcome of this review is my book *13 Dreams Freud Never Had*, in which I contrast my own brain-based approach to dream interpretation with the speculative approach taken by psychoanalysis.

My journal now fills 150 volumes and contains more than 600 detailed reports of dreams. It also contains notes from meetings, ideas for papers and experiments, accounts of amorous adventures, poems, drawings, and photographs. Two things motivated me to keep this journal. One was the recognition that most of my written records were professional papers. They were filed by date of submission and publication; there was no evidence of what I was doing, thinking, or feeling at the time they were written. As my interest in building a science of subjectivity grew stronger and stronger, I felt obliged, privileged, and even eager to track my own conscious experience and to record, in one place, what I was doing, thinking, and feeling in parallel with a narrative account of my scientific activity. By including dream reports in the journal, I was setting them down in the context of life activities to which they might be related.

The other thing that motivated my keeping a journal was the recognition that air travel provided "time windows" that were ideal for it. Since I always carried the current volume with me, so as to be able to take notes of presentations, make sketches of colleagues, and jot down scientific ideas, I was able to turn the discomfort of waiting in airport lounges for delayed or canceled flights into the pleasure of writing in the journal. Before the events of September 11, 2001 made such things subject to seizure, I often took scissors and rubber cement in my carry-on bag so as to be able to incorporate photographs in the journal.

Since I travel a lot, my journalizing impulse was frequently realized. This was especially true when I went abroad. Even when flights weren't delayed, there were both long layovers in airports and long times in the aircraft where the only other options were poor sleep, hard-to-read books, and second-rate movies. I had always been a vivid dreamer, and my recall of dreams increased sharply whenever I traveled—probably because my sleep was lighter and I had more frequent awakenings when sleeping in unfamiliar bedrooms. It is also possible that the novelty that travel always brings stimulated my dreaming, though only rarely do I dream of a new place that I am visiting.

As time went by, I found that there were several other advantages to keeping a journal. The first advantage is that the journal serves far better than a drawer in a desk or a chest as a repository of photographs that make up the visual record of a life. By combining visual images with stories about personal experiences, my journal, like my dream reports, constitutes a scenario of my life. The second advantage is that, owing to my cutting, placing, and pasting of the photographs, the journal is an expression of craftsmanship, even if it is not, as some of my more friendly colleagues have suggested, a work of art. Whatever its artistic quality, it is certainly an engaging aesthetic indulgence. The third advantage of keeping a journal, and by far the most important, is to combat time's erosive effect on memory. The journal corrects for the inevitable distortions of the retrospectroscope.

By reading my journal, I am able to have some idea of my life experience at various important times. The journal is thus an extension of my visual, emotional, and intellectual memory. In short, it is an adjunct to my brain akin to Karl Popper's "third world" of consciousness. Popper so designates the books, libraries, and archives that facilitate recollection of collective human experience. In no category is this memory enhancement more striking than in the record of my dreams. So poor is my recollection of these dreams that it often seems impossible to me that I had them. And yet there are the reports recorded in my own journal, in my own handwriting. If I had not troubled to write them down, they would certainly have been irretrievably lost.

Sometimes I wonder what will happen to my journal after I die. Will it be lost, or perhaps thrown away by descendents who want the bookshelf space that it takes up? It now occupies about 20 feet of 12-inch-high book-shelves. My heirs, who may be quite embarrassed by the narcissistic musings of a self-styled hero of scientific investigation, may well choose to junk the whole thing. I have good reason to fear such a fate. The dream journal of "the Engine Man" (discussed in my book *The Dreaming Brain*) was sold off with the author's other books at 15 cents a pound and came into my hands only because a dealer of antique medical books recognized the value of the uninterpreted dream reports and the unusual drawings. But the extensive dream journal of Saint-Denys, which he claimed to have illustrated profusely with drawings, has never been found. It probably was thrown out with his papers. What a shame!

The present book thus serves to memorialize my journal. It was written for the same reason that I kept the journal: to document the facts of a private and public life in a way that might allow the correlation and revela-tion of interactions between them. In discussing the dream reports in *13 Dreams Freud Never Had*, I have tried my best to do this. In twin interests of fair play and of transparency, their publication together with some important facts of my life may give others a chance to make such correla-tions on their own.

Memory and Emotional Salience

In *13 Dreams Freud Never Had*, I focused on my then-current preoccupation with memory. I used my conscious recollection of my life, my journalistic records, and the dream reports to expose the peculiar way in which dreams make use of memories. I also emphasized that memory is not only evanes-cent for dreams after we have waked up but also remarkably limited within the dreams themselves. So limited is memory during dreaming that we usually aren't able to recreate a complete narrative after awakening. Nor can we use narrative memory to correct the obvious impossibilities of our dream plots, such as the appearance in dreams of people we know, when we are awake, to be dead. Even writing down detailed reports doesn't help me remember my dreams unless I carefully read and study the reports. No amount of professional diligence allows me to recall the many details that were so vivid when I first awakened from the dreams.

In my recent work on dreams, I have emphasized the transparency of their emotional salience. Unfortunately, I didn't start recording dreams until I was 40 years old, and I didn't record many until I was in my fifties.

During that period, both my love life and my work life expanded exponentially. Therefore, the dreams of that period are relevant to the major
lines of force in my life that contributed to the processes of turmoil and
growth. Their content may not be typical of what I have dreamed before
or since, nor are they likely to be like the dreams of others, even people
my age. Over the years, the only aspects of my dreams that have been
constant are their formal properties and their emotional salience. They are
always a bit nutty, and they always make some strange kind of emotional
sense. Consider a dream I had in which I was serving pasta—a dream I
recalled in exquisite detail because I woke up in the midst of its frustrating
action.

Pasta Dream—Wednesday, February 4, 2004

The dream took place in an 18th century, Amadeus Mozart-like interior, with men
and women all gotten up in elaborate finery and seated at long banquet tables where
they waited to be served their dinner.

My job was to serve the pasta which was coated with gobs of drippy tomato sauce.
I did not reason critically that the suspension of pasta on coat hooks behind the
diners' heads was unlikely, if not impossible. Instead, I dutifully struggled to get the
pasta servings off the hooks and on to the plates without spattering the sauce or
spilling the pasta on the guests' elegant clothes.

I clearly recall serving the pasta from a coat hook just above the right shoulder of
a gentleman who was sweating so profusely that he had taken off his white military
jacket. I thought that he might be worried that some of the pasta would fall on him.
I assured him that he was safe despite the obvious fact that even with the utmost
care I could not untangle the pasta without some spillage. This task was made more
perilous by the fact that I had to reach out, across the table, to reach the pasta hung
on the coat hook behind him and put some on his plate.

In my anxious struggle to succeed, I woke up, relieved that my anxious
conscious experience was only a dream. Never once during the dream itself
did it occur to me that this absurd situation could not be occurring in real
life. So vivid was the sensorimotor experience that I was sure I was awake.
But the minute I awakened, I knew with certainty that I had just been
asleep and dreaming. This unwilling suspension of disbelief is related to
my hypothesis that dreaming is an altered state of consciousness that in
many important ways simulates awake-state consciousness. I insist that
dreaming is not just a poor copy of the awake state but that it is also a
remarkably good predictor of that state.

What is the form of this dream, and what does its content mean?

Formal Analysis

My sensory and motor systems were both strongly activated and fully engaged in this dream scenario. I could see the palatial interior, the many dinner guests, and their formal dress as clearly as in the film *Amadeus*. Of course I had never witnessed an eighteenth-century banquet at first hand, but the hallucinatory experience was so vivid in its sensorimotor details that I took it to be real. I moved through the scene trying my best to fulfill my assigned role of pasta server.

The suspension of disbelief transformed my role (I am not a servant in any literal sense) and my place (I live in America, not Vienna), and transported me back 200 years. This three-way disorientation is itself bizarre, but not as bizarre as the incongruity of the pasta on the coat hooks. I had never seen pasta hung on coat hooks in any movie, nor had I ever imagined it in any fantasy or dream. It was a comic and creative image that directly served an essential purpose.

My emotional state in the dream was a mixture of intense elation (I loved the scene because it was so splendid) and mounting anxiety (I could not see how to avoid spilling pasta on the nobles).

Most emphatically, my critical judgment was non-existent. I did not question either the improbability of the scene or the impossibility of my task. The conviction that I was awake and behaving perfectly reasonably was total. Never once did I suspect that I was dreaming. The delusion persisted until I woke up. My pasta dream had all the formal features of psychosis, and yet it was completely normal.

Content Analysis

I had this dream the night before I was to entertain my fellow members of the Brookline Thursday Club. My wife and I had decided to serve bruschetta and pasta because we knew that the subject of the essay preceding the supper was to be "Pain" (in the French sense of "bread").

My anticipation of pleasing this anachronistic bunch of men and the specific menu chosen by us to do so may have contributed to my dream banquet, to my difficulties serving the dream pasta, and to my fear of failing to please my fellow club members. Is that all there is to it? Maybe so. Isn't that enough?

The seed of this dream was my anxious anticipation of a dinner arranged to please a collection of cronies. That I anticipated the challenge to be a lot more difficult than it really was is typical of me—and of my wife. In the end, Lia and I always do well with our entertaining, and the real banquet evening went off without a hitch.

These transparent and strong psychological and emotional shapers of dream content have nothing to do with the hallucinatory, delusional, and cognitively deficient features of the dream which I call formal. Those features are determined by the distinctive nature of my brain activation in sleep.

A Formal Approach to Dreaming

I trust it is clear by now that by 'formal' I mean the experiential structure of all dreaming rather than the content of the individual dreams. This difference is easily understood by clinicians, who rely on the Formal Mental Status Exam to assess the mental functioning of patients, especially in relation to disease of the brain. The universal form of dreaming is set during sleep by the internal generation of perceptions, beliefs, thoughts, memories, and emotions. When we dream, we see things that are not there, we believe things that could not be true, we remember things that never happened, and we often have strong emotions. Despite these intense features of dreams, we have difficulty remembering them.

The form of conscious experience that characterizes dreaming does not usually occur in the awake state unless we are mad. Many psychoanalytic thinkers still believe that the algorithm for producing dreaming is the mind's need to disguise and censor the true (so-called latent) dream stimulus from the false (so-called manifest) dream content. This theory is the basis of dream interpretation using the psychoanalytic technique of free association. Its aim is to discover the dreamer's ideas in connection with the content. It relies on a codified form of dream symbol reduction to reveal to the dreamer the true nature of the instinctual drives that generate dreaming.

In contrast to psychoanalysis, I treat the formal aspects of dreaming as the undisguised products of the brain when it is activated in sleep. I have asserted that brain physiology is responsible for most of the apparent nonsense of dreaming. Therefore, these formal aspects need not be interpreted. But that leaves much of the content unexplained.

I have been misunderstood by many colleagues who attribute to me a nonsense theory of dreaming. This attribution continues despite 15 years of effort to set the record straight.

In my first book, *The Dreaming Brain* (subtitled *How the Brain Creates Both the Sense and the Nonsense of Dreams*), I put my theory on the line by discussing what I thought was an extremely revealing dream of my own: my much-discussed Mozart dream. I may have no more luck now in convincing those who are committed to psychoanalysis that I am a great believer in dreams as meaningful links between one state of my brain (the state that is activated in REM sleep) and another (the state that is activated in the awake state). In fact, my ideas on this subject are so similar to what most therapists who have been trained in psychoanalysis now believe that we could move forward together if only they would renounce Freud's now-outmoded Disguise-Censorship Model. But, as psychoanalysts have always strongly emphasized, resistance to change is deep and strong.

The best outcome I can realistically anticipate is that people will understand what I mean and what I don't mean by dream interpretation. The juxtaposition of my discussion of my pasta dream and my discussion of my own life experiences reveals the operating of another algorithm that I call emotionally salient memory reinforcement. Emotionally salient memory reinforcement is still poorly understood, but it is consonant with the now-mounting evidence that while we sleep the brain works to reorganize memory. Far from burying impulses and memories in a dynamically repressed unconscious, dreaming calls up distant memories and ties them associatively to current events, even if such ties are loose or incomplete and the dream stories representing them are nonsensical by the canons of awake-state consciousness.

Toward a Science of Subjectivity

My pasta dream was a product of my anticipation of a real-life task (my impending Thursday Club dinner) and my associative memory of the difficult or impossible social demands of living in Boston, an anachronistic city if there ever was one. It wouldn't really be possible for me to pull off an eighteenth-century banquet, but I might try. And if I did, a little pasta on the coat hooks wouldn't faze me in the least. I would simply reassure my guests that this was normal in the eighteenth century, and everyone would have a good time.

The real question posed by this book is "Will you settle for a limited but greatly improved and scientifically solid dream theory while patiently awaiting more details, or will you be seduced by more speculative dream theories—such as that of Sigmund Freud—that purport to give a complete understanding of dreaming and promise to uncover the truth underlying each individual dream?" I have tried to show that there is plenty of psychological meaning in dreams, and that by subtracting and discarding their nonsensical formal features we can see this meaning clearly without resorting to the decoding of symbols. I hold that dreaming, like all other phenomena in the world, is a natural event and should be approached and understood naturalistically.

I further hold that consciousness can now be studied scientifically. To make progress in developing a science of subjectivity, we should put more emphasis on detailed and interpretation-free accounts of exceptional mental states. To that end, one potent strategy is to compare the formal aspects of such mental states and the formal aspects of brain function that are associated with them. The visuomotor hallucinosis and emotionality of dreams may be due to the spontaneous activation of the brain centers underlying vision, motion, and emotion, and the amnesia, the disorientation, and the inability to think critically may be due to deactivation of the brain functions underlying executive aspects of cognition. We already possess abundant evidence in favor of these two powerful hypotheses.

Achieving even this relatively crude approximation of brain and mind requires not only technical brain research—brain imaging and quantitative EEG recording, in particular—but also quantitative analysis of carefully recorded reports of mental experience. This is essential for all aspects of conscious experience, including the vicissitudes of the normal awake state. We also should look more closely at the alterations of mental states induced by drugs and by strokes and other localized lesions of the brain.

When I first championed these strategies, I had no idea that I myself would become the subject of such a cruel experiment of nature as my brainstem stroke. But when it happened to me I was ready to learn from my adversity, as I have tried to show in chapters 10–14. My stroke produced alterations of sleep and dreaming that can be understood in terms of the damage to my medullary and pontine brainstem. It was ironic, to say the least, to find myself impaired in the same way as many of my experimental animals. But whereas they were mute, I could self-observe and report my conscious experience.

As a sequel to my stroke, I now find myself impaired in a cardiopulmonary way. This unfortunate fact had led to a new series of self-observations. I would prefer that my mishaps had not happened, but they did, and my account of them has been tied to a theory of the sequential nature of my disease. I feel strongly that self-observation is an indispensable tool in the scientific understanding of consciousness. I offer this record as a way of showing that the naturalistic approach remains valid—to the end.

Subjectivity is a great problem for science. Many think that subjectivity can never be objectified and is therefore outside the bounds of science. But, as I have tried to show, not only is it essential to accept subjectivity as a source of data to support any theory of consciousness; subjectivity is a valuable and indeed an indispensable source of such data. If the subjective aspects of dreaming had earlier been seen as clear and direct expressions of brain activity, we might have avoided the century of speculative folly that psychoanalysis visited upon us. My subjectivity is now telling me that there is something going on in my brain that we physicians and scientists should try harder to discover.

16 Scientific Implications

In 1895, when Sigmund Freud was trying to create a psychology that would be "perspicacious and free from doubt," he vowed to base his new theory on brain science. But modern neurobiology was then in its infancy. In 1890, Santiago Ramon y Cajal had enunciated his Neuron Doctrine, an epoch-making concept that has prevailed for more than a century. On the functional side, Freud had only Charles Sherrington's very rudimentary reflex model to build upon. Aware that his "Project for a Scientific Psychology" was grossly inadequate, Freud wisely put it aside. He then created psychoanalysis on what he claimed were purely psychological insights. In this assertion, as our 1977 paper pointed out, Freud was as psychotic as any patient.

Thomas Graham-Brown, working in Sherrington's lab in the decade before World War I, tried unsuccessfully to persuade Sherrington that neurons were organized not only as reflexes but also as oscillators (or clocks) whose job it was to set (and vary) the threshold of reflexes. Oscillators, not reflexes, were the fundamental functional units of the brain. This idea, which Graham-Brown published in 1912 in the Proceedings of the Royal Society (presumably with Sherrington's mixed blessings), is the intellectual forerunner of all that we have since discovered about the brain in relation to dream consciousness.

In this chapter, I will recast my story in terms of the conceptual framework from Graham-Brown's idea of oscillators, through W. Ross Ashby's definition of brain states, to my new dream consciousness theory. I will consider how these ideas influenced dream theory, sleep medicine, psychiatry, and medicine in general.

Reflexes, Clocks, and Oscillators

Graham-Brown wanted Sherrington to acknowledge that neuronal excitability changes. There is no such thing as a reflex with a constant threshold.

The brain is dynamic, not static. By postulating "paired half-centers," Graham-Brown was presaging on-off, flip-flop switches that could change and even invert reflex excitability. He argued that the spinal cord itself enjoyed dynamic properties. Sherrington's spinal reflexes were thus more or less excitable. In the brainstem, we now know, reflex responses regularly change sign, flipping from excitatory to inhibitory and back again to excitatory. It is just such a sign change in reflex excitability that is responsible for the inversion of muscle tonus from high (in the awake state) to low (in REM sleep). That is why we can move when we are awake but not when we dream. Had Freud known this, he might have been more easily able to model the motor paralysis of which some subjects are consciously aware when they dream. To his credit, Freud commented on the failure to execute dreamed motor commands, and he correctly guessed that this failure was caused by motor inhibition during sleep. But this was about the only brain mechanism that Freud predicted accurately, and his cavalier dismissals of the astute physiological theories of his predecessors (including Wilhelm Wundt) make us suppose that this was just a lucky guess. As far as we know, Freud never read Graham-Brown's papers. By 1912, Freud was busy promoting psychoanalysis, which, he insisted rather arrogantly, had nothing to learn from neurology.

That the chemically specific neurons we now call modulatory might be an important aspect of neuronal clocks, oscillators, and half-centers was not explicitly recognized by Constantin von Economo, who nonetheless attributed the somnolence of survivors of the 1918 influenza epidemic to loss of cells in the substantia nigra of the midbrain. Those cells contain and secrete dopamine, a neuromodulator now well known to play a role in alertness, motor control, and cognition. Everyone now knows that it is precisely these dopamine-containing cells that spontaneously degenerate in Parkinson's disease, and that many of the deficits of that terrible malady can be ameliorated by dopamine boosters such as levodopa.

Although we are still ignorant of exactly how dopamine works, we are sure that it is plays a major part in setting levels of excitability and modes of action throughout the brain. For example, we know that dopamine influences the hypothalamic circadian clock that controls our daily cycle of rest and activity, and therefore affects body temperature. Circadian-rhythm biology and sleep science rode along on parallel tracks for a long time, but now the two fields are conceptually and empirically unified. Recently, Cliff Saper has proposed that a flip-flop switch tells the circadian-rhythm clock when to turn on the pontine NREM-REM sleep phase oscillator and when to turn it off.

Takao Hensch, his parents, and his collaborators. In phase 2 (1977–1995) of our work in the Laboratory of Neurophysiology, we tested the reciprocal interaction model at the level of cells and molecules. A leader of this project was James Quatrocchi, a neuroanatomist who synthesized carbachol-flurescent microspheres so that REM sleep could be triggered from microscopic pontine brainstem loci. After retrograde transport of the microspheres, the pre-synaptic domain of the pharmachologically defined hot spots could be mapped. Quatrocchi was helped in this line of work by Takao Hensch and Oscar Hsu. Left to right: Meg Wilcox, Mr. and Mrs. Hensch (parents of Takao), Jim Quatrocchi, Ken Yamamoto, me, Takao.

The role of dopamine is complemented by that of acetylcholine, another neuromodulator, whose cell bodies lie in the lower brain and project to the thalamus and cortex, where they act to promote activation and consciousness. The work described in chapters 7–9 of this book shows how such neuromodulatory neurons may interact in the generation of the states of waking, sleeping, and dreaming. We have come quite a long way toward developing the brain science that Freud, in 1895, declared essential to the elaboration of a scientifically solid dream theory.

It would appear that the brain works, in part, by regulating and synchronizing its vast array of neurons by means of clocks composed of a relatively few well-placed and well-connected oscillators composed of modulatory cells. Thus neurons (á la Ramon y Cajal) are organized as reflex circuits (á la Sherrington) but are subject to spatial and temporal regulation by oscillators (á la Graham-Brown). A crucial detail of this formulation is the chemical specificity of many oscillatory neurons (á la von Economo).

To summarize our discoveries: The NREM-REM cycle of sleep is governed by a pontine brainstem oscillator consisting of interacting populations of

REM-on cells (which are cholinergic and glutamergic) and REM-off cells (which are noradrenergic, serotonergic, and histaminergic). This system, one sort of neuronal clock, is gated by the circadian oscillator controlling rest and activity. The go-to-sleep-and-dream messenger from the circadian clock in the hypothalamus to the NREM-REM clock in the pons appears to be the inhibitory neurotransmitter GABA, which actively shuts down the aminergic neurons essential to waking. Dopamine is secreted at high levels both in the awake state and in REM sleep.

There may also be a signal to the REM-off cells in the form of a decline in the level of hypocretin, a protein secreted by the hypothalamus, which normally sustains the aminergic modulation necessary for waking. Hypocretin is known to be deficient in narcolepsy, a rare but instructive sleep disorder characterized by a loss of alertness and by the unwanted occurrence of REM sleep in the daytime and at the onset of sleep.

The State Concept

It is important to note that although the excitability of the neurons that constitute brain clocks is continuously changing, the neuronal elements of the brain interact in such a way as to sustain activity within finite time limits, giving rise to enduring states such as the awake state, NREM sleep, and REM sleep. The positive correlation of the period length of the NREM-REM sleep cycle to brain size suggests that a phase-pulsed process (such as protein transport time) may play a role in setting the time constant of some long-term brain rhythms. States confer both temporal stability and functional versatility, two important adaptations realized in the behavior of higher animals. To wit, the awake state can be maintained for 16 hours or longer when a mammal reaches maturity.

When the sun is up by day and when electric lights are on in the evening, we function remarkably well in the awake mode. We walk, talk, work, think, and socialize in that state. At night, when the sun and the ambient temperature go down, we sleep. Sleep not only confers energetic efficiency; it also allows us to enter two other states—NREM sleep (about 5–6 hours) and REM sleep (about 1½–2 hours)—every night. Each of these sleep states has its own mechanistic signature and its own functional significance.

In this book, I have focused on REM sleep and suggested a new way of looking at its function as the brain's creator of a virtual world. Whatever value this protoconsciousness hypothesis turns out to have, it is critical that we recognize the unequivocal advantage of the brain's ability to regulate and differentiate its own states. From a general scientific point of view, this is a major conceptual advance requiring the rewriting of textbooks, many of which still suffer from the benighted notion that there is only one functionally significant state: the awake state. The sleeping brain can do many more things than we previously imagined, and we now think that the already long list of sleep functions will undoubtedly be extended and elaborated by future research.

The scientist who first advanced the state concept was W. Ross Ashby, whose 1946 book *Design for a Brain* was mathematically oriented. Ashby was ignorant of sleep and dream science, which didn't exist in 1946, but he developed several nonetheless useful quantitative guidelines. A state, according to Ashby, is the instantaneous value of all the parameters of a system. For a system as complex as the brain, this value cannot be determined. Fortunately, the values of certain brain parameters tell us a great deal about the brain's three cardinal states: the awake state, NREM sleep, and REM sleep. The restricted set of values that we now use is incomplete, but it is a reasonable proxy for the dauntingly large set of values of the whole system.

Ashby did not know that brain states are clamped. They do not spontaneously vary over all possible domains of the virtually infinite state space. (I will demonstrate this point when I take up the AIM model in the next section.) By 'clamped' I mean held or restrained so that, for example, our behavior is synchronized with cosmic energy (via the circadian clock system) and also obeys its own internal rules (set by the NREM-REM oscillator). Our research has, I think, helped to make these insights clear.

Later in this chapter, I will turn my attention to the psychological, psychiatric, and general medical instantiations of the state concept. For now, it suffices to say that the values of all the variables of a system (Ashby's definition of a state) are fixed within certain limits, so that states endure. That is the good news. The bad news is that every system of the brain (and the rest of the body) is state dependent, and thus our brains and our bodies are intrinsically prone to dysfunction. I have already offered the example of narcolepsy, which causes people to fall asleep at unwanted times. Breathing and heart action also are subject to state dependency and thus are subject to state-linked vicissitudes, which may be unhealthy. For example, breathing may cease or be impeded in sleep, and heart action may speed up or slow down to a dangerous degree.

State-Space (AIM) Modeling

It has been traditional since the dawn of sleep science in the 1950s to regard sleep variables as linear functions that change with time. The now-classical graph of sleep stages displays the fluctuation of one system variable or of multiple system variables. But the interaction of variables, their non-linearity, and their cyclicity are not well visualized by this graphic scheme. These two-dimensional sleep graphs are hold-overs of the smoked drum kymographs of the Sherringtonian era and the polygraphic data of the early sleep lab era.

Instead of being linear, and running in only one direction, brain state activity is often exponential and hence non-linear; it is always recurrent, and its cycles are often elliptical. The elliptical shape of brain state cycles is more like the orbits of planetary bodies than it is like the stairway of traditional sleep graphs. This makes me wonder if inner space (the brain) is more like outer space (the cosmos) than we have, until now, thought.

The periodic recurrence of elliptical brain cycles within sleep has a now-well-known neuronal and biochemical dynamism that two-dimensional graphs represent incompletely and inaccurately. Three or more dimensions are needed to do our knowledge graphic justice.

The AIM model plots the values of three functions—activation ($A = x$), input-output gating ($I = z$), and modulation ($M = y$)—as three dimensions of a state space. Time, t, is a fourth dimension of the schema. Such a model, though still admittedly inadequate, is a major conceptual advance because it recognizes both cyclicity and reflex inversion.

Furthermore the three variables A, I, and M have cellular and molecular determinants.

The AIM model thus plots deeper brain mechanisms than surface polygraphy could be expected to reach. By creating a multidimensional state space, the AIM model also leads to novel conceptualizations of normal psychophysiology, the pathophysiology of sleep disorders, and the pathogenesis of psychiatric diseases.

A still further advance of multidimensional state modeling is its compatibility with mathematical descriptions of state control systems. This scientific nicety was recognized as long ago as 1975 by my colleague Robert McCarley, who fitted the neuronal data from REM-on and REM-off cells to the theoretical curves mathematically engendered by the Volterra-Lotka equations describing prey-predator interactions in field biology. This approach is now being extended by Herrmann Prossinger, a mathematician at the University of Vienna, whose surprising and elegant graphics of the

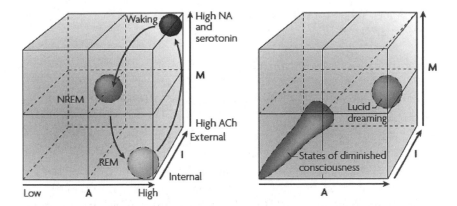

AIM model of brain-mind state control. Left: *State-space definition*. Three perpendicu-
lar dimensions are established as x = A (for activation), y = M (for modulation), and
z = I (for input-output gating). The instantaneous values of A, I, and M can all be
derived from the neuronal data of animal experiments. Factors A and I can be estimated in human sleep lab data, but as yet there is no way of measuring factor M
in humans. *Domains of the state space*. Waking (W), NREM sleep (N), and REM sleep
(R) occupy distinct loci of the space as defined above. Waking and REM are both in
the right-hand segment of the space, owing to their sharing of high activation levels.
But waking and REM sleep are quite distant from each other in the high-activation
segment of the space, owing to their very different I and M values. Thus the activated
REM sleep brain-mind is both off line (I) and chemically differentiated (M) compared
to waking. NREM sleep is positioned in the center of the space because it is intermediate in all quantitative respects between waking and REM. *Trajectories in the state
space*. The values of A, I, and M change constantly, but the changes are constrained.
Sleep and wake alternate in time owing to circadian influences. During sleep, AIM
values tend to follow elliptical trajectories through the state space. As sleep advances
in time, AIM values go less deeply into the NREM sleep domain and more deeply
into the REM sleep domain. Right: *Forbidden zones in AIM space*. The normal, cardinal
domains of Wake, NREM, and REM sleep occupy relatively limited zones of the
state space. Diseases, such as those neurological conditions producing coma and
minimally conscious states, are all arrayed in the left-hand segment of the space
owing to their low activation values. Also shown here is lucid dreaming. Lucid
dreaming is a hybrid state with features of both waking and dreaming. In AIM, it
is situated in the middle of the extreme right-hand side of the space, between waking
and REM toward either of which lucid dreamers are drawn (as suggested by the
arrows in the diagram). Other sleep and psychiatric disorders may also find their
place in the schema. Credit: *Nature Neuroscience Reviews*.

AIM model are as thought-provoking as they are aesthetically satisfying representatives of state cyclicity.

The Psychophysiology of Dreaming

State-space modeling is an important prelude to integrated brain-mind theorizing. Instead of saying simply that dreaming is highly correlated with REM but may also occur in NREM sleep, the AIM model may soon allow us to predict the probability of such a correlation precisely. On the assumption that, at some as yet unknown level, the state of the brain is the state of the mind, objectivity and subjectivity are two aspects of a single reality. In other words, the AIM model, being cellular-molecular at its root, may be closer to the deep level of brain-mind unity than the superficial measures of the clinical sleep lab.

As a thought exercise, let us assume that dreaming becomes more and more probable as brain activation increases together with input-output gate closure and declining levels of aminergic modulation. This concatenation of events turns the brain on, puts it off line, and stimulates it internally, while changing its mode of information processing maximally. It seems reasonable to expect that these profound physiological changes must be reflected in our conscious experience. The prediction of the probability of dreaming from physiology is more than a scientific footnote. It moves us a giant step closer to our goal as neutral monists. There is one system, the unified brain-mind, and we have access to two aspects of it. One aspect is objective (as expressed in the AIM model); one is subjective (as experienced by all of us in our beds). This bold conclusion is qualified by the limited claim that, for the nonce, we are predicting the formal aspects of dreaming, not each dream's particular content.

If psychoanalytic models of dream interpretation satisfy you, go ahead and spend your time and money on them. Nothing that I have discovered or discussed disproves Freud's dream theory definitively. But if, after reading this book, you are not more skeptical about Freud's Disguise-Censorship Model of oneirogenesis, then I have failed you and can only apologize.

Lucid Dreaming Revisited

As I have emphasized repeatedly in this book, neurobiologists and cognitive scientists are engaged in new efforts to establish the brain basis of consciousness. Progress in brain imaging and in quantitative EEG recording in humans and unit recording in animals have contributed to this movement. But progress has been limited by the relative poverty of the paradigms used in these studies, most of which do not take subjective experience into account.

One promising though problematic paradigm—lucid dreaming—has recently been employed with encouraging and complimentary results by my colleague Ursula Voss.

What is lucid dreaming? It is the rare but robust awareness that one is dreaming and that one is not really awake, as one usually assumes when dreaming. Lucid dreaming is thus paradoxical in containing elements of both awake-state consciousness and dreaming consciousness. We may thus hypothesize that the brain substrates of primary consciousness and secondary consciousness are co-activated and available for scrutiny.

The spontaneous occurrence of lucid dreaming varies across individuals and with age within individuals. It is also susceptible to pre-sleep autosuggestion. That is, its relatively low spontaneous incidence can be increased by training. Not only can young subjects learn to become lucid dreamers; they can perform intentional self-awakenings, and even institute plot control by introducing voluntary decision making into the normally involuntary dream experience. This plasticity makes lucid dreaming significant to clinical efforts to change the minds of patients.

Aside from its powerful psychedelic and entertainment value, lucid dreaming is an attractive phenomenon for scientific investigation within the area of consciousness studies. Lucid dreamers often claim that they can watch a dream evolve and alter its course as they see fit. If one believes these claims (and I will give my reasons for believing them), one can conclude that the human mind is capable of being in two states—waking and dreaming—at any given time. For the experimentalist, this means that it may be possible to measure in the laboratory the physiological correlates of three states: the awake state, non-lucid dreaming, and lucid dreaming. Since the three states are psychologically distinct, they must be physiologically distinct. If they are physiologically distinct, the physiological distinctions may be enlightening.

The History of Lucid Dreaming

One reason for taking the claims of lucid dreamers seriously is the distinguished company in which they find themselves. The first scholar to document lucidity extensively was Marie-Jean-Leon Lecoq, Marquis d'Hervey-Saint-Denys, whose very credible and well-written book *Les Rêves et les Moyens de les Diriger* was published in English in 1982 as *Dreams and*

How to Guide Them. Saint-Denys was a noted China scholar and a member of the Academie Française. Like many of his Parisian colleagues, he was experimentally inclined and concerned with the mechanism of dreaming (which he thought of as clichés souvenirs, or snapshot memories, in keeping with the development of photography in nineteenth-century France by Joseph Niepce and Louis Daguerre).

Saint-Denys was also concerned about the moral implications of a state of mind—dreaming—that was apparently involuntary. He wondered how a person could be held accountable for his behavior in his dreams. If we are not morally accountable for our dream actions, there must be a part of us that is intrinsically guilt-free. This concern has earth-shaking repercussions for jurisprudence because it extends the insanity defense indefinitely.

Mary Arnold-Forster was an English gentlewoman who described her own lucidity experiments in a book, *Studies in Dreams*, published in 1920 with a foreword by the respected Boston psychologist Morton Prince. Apparently not aware of the work of Saint-Denys, Arnold-Forster (a niece of the novelist E. M. Forster) was principally concerned with determining what she could and could not do when dreaming lucidly. Like many other lucid dreamers, she taught herself to fly and thus to enter, at will, all of the rooms of her house. She particularly enjoyed flying down the stairs. The phenomenological tradition of description and self-experimentation has now been taken up anew and described by Janice Brooks and Jay Vogelsong in their book *The Conscious Exploration of Dreaming*. Brooks and Vogelsong go further than their predecessors in their efforts to define the limits of lucid dreaming. Can one pass, like Harry Potter, through solid walls? Yes, one can, according to Brooks and Vogelsong.

After the discovery of REM sleep by Aserinsky and Kleitman in 1953, objective study of lucid dreaming was undertaken by Steven Laberge. Working at Stanford University, Laberge demonstrated that lucidity always arose from REM-sleep dreaming, and that subjects were able to signal out of REM sleep that they were lucid by making a series of voluntary eye movements. Laberge's insistence that lucid dreaming occurred within REM sleep invited criticism on the ground that the subjects were fully awake. It now appears that Laberge's subjects were both awake and dreaming at the same time. This makes the phenomenon appealing to sleep and dream researchers.

How can the brain be in two different states at once? The answer to this question is that state dissociations are, in fact, quite commonplace, as Mark Mahowald, the co-discoverer of the REM Sleep Behavior Disorder, has convincingly argued. One part of the brain may be asleep while another is awake, as in cases of sleepwalking where the gait generator and the navigational system of the brainstem may be fully functional while the cerebral cortex is still in stage IV of NREM sleep. Sleepwalkers, usually children or adolescents, are notoriously difficult to arouse, even though they navigate quite well. A dolphin, in order to keep its respiratory blow-hole just above the water's surface, sleeps with one side of its brain while the other side remains awake. Such impressive dissociations serve to estab-lish a potential physiological basis for dissociative personality disorders, for hysteria, and for otherwise puzzling clinical phenomena.

How can we be sure that an experimental subject is really asleep when lucidity is signaled by a set of voluntary eye movements? How do we know that the subject has not fully waked up? The answer to this question requires a conceptual leap. It is that the subject is both awake and asleep with different parts of the brain in different states at the same time. Mistakes can still be made, of course, and appropriate cautions and safe-guards must be taken, but the best proof that lucid dreaming is a third state of consciousness, between the awake state and non-lucid dreaming, is empirical. The results of two recent studies suggest that this is indeed the case.

Taking advantage of recent improvements in the resolving power of the human electroencephalogram, Ursula Voss and her colleagues at the University of Frankfurt have found that lucid dreaming is associated with an EEG power-and-coherence profile that is significantly different from non-lucid dreaming and the awake state but intermediate between those two states. Lucid dreaming is characterized by more 40-Hz power than non-lucid dreaming, especially in frontal regions. Since it is 40-Hz power that was correlated with awake-state consciousness in previous studies, it can now be suggested that enough 40-Hz power has been added to the non-lucid dreaming brain to support the increase in subjective awareness that permits lucidity, but not enough to cause full awakening. (I encour-aged and coached Ursula Voss in this study, for which she kindly made me a co-author of her paper, but the difficult empirical work was done by Voss and her Frankfurt-based team.)

By measuring the coherence between frontal and occipital EEG patterns, Voss demonstrated that subjects enjoyed more EEG coherence when lucid than when not lucid, and, again, less than in the fully awake state. A reasonable interpretation of this finding is that dreaming is the result of posterior brain activation whereas the awake state requires frontal activation as well. In lucid dreaming, subjects are between the two states and therefore on the edge of each. That may be why lucid dreaming often gives way to waking or is lost to non-lucid dreaming. Lucid dreaming is on the cusp of two states which are programmed to be all-or-none, winner-take-all, with ties improbable. That's why lucid dreaming is rare and evanescent.

Another German group, under the leadership of Michael Czisch in Munich, has used MRI techniques to study the activation of brain regions during lucid dreaming. The pattern of brain-region activation was markedly different in lucid dreaming from that seen in non-lucid dreaming. Lucid dreamers showed increased activation of the brain regions that distinguish humans from macaque monkeys. These areas are not only frontal, as might have been predicted from the findings of Voss et al., but also temporal and even occipital. This finding suggests that awake consciousness may consist of both primary consciousness and what Gerald Edelman has called secondary consciousness. I recently proposed that primary consciousness is characteristic of dreaming. Put another way, the awake state, by including secondary consciousness, is characterized by higher orders of insight, abstraction, and awareness of awareness—precisely the attributes that dreamers normally lack. Dreaming has strong primary elements, including a sense of self, a sense of agency, and a sense of movement through a space, all integrated with emotional salience. It may be that the primary/secondary distinction depends on the acquisition of language by humans, as Edelman has suggested. In any case, the language hypothesis is consistent with the findings by Czisch et al. that dream lucidity depends on activation of those brain regions that are distinctly human.

Lucid dreaming is an unusual state characterized by elements of both waking and dreaming. A rare but robust condition, it has attracted the attention of scientists interested in further specifying the brain basis of consciousness.

The Pathophysiology of Sleep Disorders

Sleep-disorders medicine is a burgeoning field. There are more than 1,000 sleep clinics in the United States, and many more around the world. The huge increase in the scientific study of sleep compensates for centuries of medical neglect of fully one-third of human life. Far from being the inert and peaceful state that most people once thought it to be, sleep is a dynamic and turbulent maelstrom that is unleashed whenever we close our eyes and set out on our nocturnal voyages.

The science described in this book is relevant to sleep-disorders medicine in several specific ways. The new science allows sleep physicians to understand how and why the establishment of set points and the timing of state transitions are so problematic. Two simple ideas help us understand why sleep is difficult for some people to achieve (insomnia), why the awake state is difficult for some people to maintain (hypersomnia), and why our motor systems are prone to go haywire when we sleep (the parasomnias).

Set points are fixed by oscillators whose chemically specific neuronal components are subject to extreme fluctuations. State transitions require synchronization of billions of neurons so that the whole brain flips (or flops) at the same time. Some neurons want to race ahead of the others; others choose to be stragglers.

The AIM model should help physicians to understand such dissociative disorders as narcolepsy (in which patients fall directly into REM sleep from the awake state) and sleepwalking (in which subjects navigate motorically but are cognitively unresponsive). In REM-sleep behavior disorder, people act out their dreams instead of having their movements be experienced only as dream fictions. An important scientific advantage of the AIM model is its heuristically valuable capacity to put all sleep disorders in a single state-space format. Not only does such plotting emphasize the dynamism of the brain-mind and the overlap between the various ailments; it also suggests more effective chemical interventions aimed at curbing undesirable and dangerous aspects of dissociation. For example, one drug (or the suspension of another) may immediately reduce the probability that a patient with REM-sleep behavior disorder will hurt himself or his spouse.

Psychiatric Implications

The very word 'dissociation' conjures up memories of Jean-Marie Charcot, Pierre Janet, and Sigmund Freud. It was their inability to model dissociative phenomena neurologically that led Freud to create psychoanalysis. Modern sleep science provides a dynamic neurological substrate for hysterical conversion. As my review (just above) of recent progress in understanding the brain basis of lucid dreaming suggests, it has also opened the door to the study of hypnosis.

In the following chapter, I suggest that a good way for a normal person to understand madness is to pay attention to his own dreaming state. That state is characterized by hallucinations, delusions, bizarre cognition, amnesia, and confabulation.

As I have already pointed out repeatedly, dreaming is, by definition, delirium. It is not just like an organic psychosis; it is an organic psychosis.

Portrait of me by N.H. (1966). When I was a psychiatric resident at MMHC in the late 1960s, one of my most severely handicapped patients was N.H. In my office one day, she told me that when I became too overbearing, she saw my face as a fish eye. I suggested that she make a picture of this image in Art Therapy. This is the painting that she made. In 2008, I myself became psychotic after surgery for spinal stenosis. Whenever I closed my eyes, I hallucinated three-eyed colleagues whom seemed to me to be insane. This caused me great distress because such colleagues could not possibly give credible support to my new dream theory. These hallucinations ceased when the Dilaudid that I was given for post-operative pain was discontinued.

This means that it is possible (perhaps even necessary) to go crazy when we are asleep in order to remain sane when we are awake. The devastating effects of sleep deprivation force us to take this idea seriously. Three to five days of selective deprivation of either REM sleep or NREM sleep lead inevitably to psychotic perceptual (hallucinatory) and conceptual (delusional) experiences.

A person need not have abnormal genes or qualitatively unique brain chemistry to become quite deranged. Of course, this does not mean that bad genes or bad chemistry do not contribute to mental illness. They probably do. But the brain-mind is capable of generating psychosis on its own. All it has to do is change state.

Madness may be the price we pay for our capacity to dream and for our protoconsciousness. The fact that there is really no good animal model for schizophrenia or for major affective disorder suggests that a well-developed mind is a prerequisite for insanity. One may have to have a highly developed mind in order to go out of it! Put another way, if you possess a virtual-reality projector in your head, that device can get out of its box when you sleep. It does so regularly when you dream. If pressed, by stress and/or genes, it can even make you quite nutty in the daytime. Consider the five examples of my own mental illnesses I gave in part IV of this book.

If this line of reasoning is correct (and it seems to me to be quite compelling), then we are not only autocreative but also autopsychotic. As I will try to explain in the next chapter, this hypothesis puts the art-insanity nexus into a tidy, naturalistic context.

A Word about Psychiatric Treatment

If the best cure for dream psychosis is simply waking up, what lesson can we draw from that? When we wake up from dreaming, our REM-off aminergic neurons resume firing and our brains are once again bathed in norepinephrine, serotonin, and histamine. It follows that drugs which enhance our REM-off neurons should be effective anti-psychotic agents. And they are. The biogenic amine reuptake blockers (of which Prozac may be the best-known example) are effective drugs. By blocking amine reuptake, the modulators stay longer in the synaptic clefts, where they work their wonders. These drugs are more anxiety reducing and mood enhancing than they are anti-psychotic, so there is something wrong with our model.

I said that we do not yet know what dopamine does to the brain-mind in REM sleep. We do know, however, that dopamine neurons, unlike the other aminergic neurons, do not turn off in REM sleep. In the absence of their co-modulators, dopamine and acetylcholine (also abundant during REM sleep) may tip the brain into its dream psychosis mode. The most potent anti-psychotic drugs block the dopamine D-2 receptor, hence interfering with dopamine's action. What happens to dreaming when patients load up on the old standby phenothiazine or the new atypical anti-psychotics (e.g., risperidol)?

Psychiatric diagnoses are still made in the daytime, thereby ignoring the night. Furthermore, psychiatric diagnoses are still made as if they were descriptions of forever-fixed disabilities. Yet spontaneous recovery is not unheard of, and mental illness may both remit and evolve, changing its character from thought to mood disorder as it does so. This suggests that psychiatric diagnosis is committed to the same outmoded two-dimensional schema as the sleep charts which brain science has rendered obsolete.

Disordered systems undergo complex interactions as the brain moves from one part of the state space to another. Thus today's schizophrenic is more like tomorrow's manic-depressive if the schizophrenic symptoms have not remitted entirely. Such plasticity does not surprise sleep scientists, who see it all the time. We do not like to admit it, but we are still very ignorant of the intrinsic dynamism of our brains, our minds, and our bodies. The research described in this book may help to sensitize us to these realities.

Medical Implications

The scientific implications of our new findings and theory extend beyond the narrow confines of sleep medicine and psychiatry to general medicine. One obvious implication is that all physiology is state dependent. There is not one system in the human body that does not undergo a significant change during sleep. This means that any medical exam conducted in the daytime must be considered incomplete. Even such a classical disease as diabetes, of which the crucial pathophysiology is insulin deficiency, is state dependent. Carbohydrate metabolism is variable, and normal subjects are rendered less able to regulate glucose if they are deprived of sleep. Sleep deprivation is thus diabetogenic.

My main point here is now increasingly recognized and indicates that medical and sleep science must progress together on a single track. Like the brain and the mind, their investigative efforts are strengthened by integration. Not only is diagnosis state dependent; as my Bellevue story clearly shows, the central diagnostic instrument—the physician's brain-mind—is susceptible to sleep deprivation and recovery from it. In other words, not only is diagnosis state dependent; diagnosticians are, too.

The caveat "Physician, heal thyself" falls on deaf ears if sleep is regarded as a waste of time. And patients may not want to hear that they should not consult or be treated by sleepy doctors. I am not aware of any hospital or any medical coverage system that has guaranteed sleep to its physicians. People become sick at all hours. It is hard to imagine how society can respond to this exigency without a huge increase in the cost of good care.

General Conclusions

Biological science is at a major crossroads, with a forced choice threatening to separate the microscopic investigation of cells and molecules from the macroscopic systems-level paradigms of more holistic integration. Both are needed, but economic and political forces combine to drive scientists to an isolation that weakens both approaches. In this book I have tried to show why the understanding of dreaming profits from recognition and exploitation of cellular-level and molecular-level analysis. Neurophysiology and psychology not only benefit from knowing each other; they are really two arms of the same body—ours.

In chapter 15, I examined the greatest integrative challenge confronting us: the mind-body problem. In chapter 17, I will explore the higher level of integration that I think links science and the humanities. It is my general conclusion that sleep and dream research is an inviting context for a both-and strategy rather than an either-or strategy. I hope that many of my colleagues and our government's funding agencies will agree with me. Without either peers or patrons, the sort of brain-mind science that I espouse cannot proceed. With both, it will flourish.

17 Dream Science and the Humanities

In my Wesleyan senior honors thesis on how nineteenth-century novelists influenced Sigmund Freud, I cited *The Brothers Karamazov* as a source of some of Freud's ideas. I cited the repressed patricidal impulses that caused Dmitri's epilepsy and were finally released in the murderous assault on his father, the ambivalence of emotion that characterized Ivan's sadomasochistic relationship with Gruzenka, and the idealism of Alyosha, of Father Zossima, and of Dostoyevsky (who yearned for the God whose existence Freud denied).

Because no brain science existed upon which he could build his dream theory, Freud had no choice but to speculate. In doing so, he drew heavily on contemporary artists' insights into human nature.

Now that we have a brain-based theory of dreaming, we might imagine a reversal in the direction of the flow of information between brain science and the arts. Indeed, recent books by Semir Zeki (*A Vision of the Brain*) and Margaret Livingstone (*Vision and Art*) link the neuroscience of vision to the visual art of painting. In this chapter, I will focus on how modern sleep and dream science might influence the humanities (which is not say that the humanities no longer influence science). Of the many themes that could be of interest to humanistic scholars, I will discuss three: autocreativity; automaticity; and anticipation.

Autocreativity

Because dreaming is both universal and universally synthetic, we all are naturally creative when we dream. Seeing things clearly in the absence of external stimuli is an analog of hallucination, and dreaming can be a model for psychopathology. Therefore, dreaming is of interest to psychiatry, a humanistic field of medicine currently striving to be more scientific.

But seeing things that aren't there can also be a model for visual imagination and, as such, can be quite useful to visual artists.

Believing things that cannot be shown to be true is something that we all do every day of the week, especially if we are religious. My colleague Jeffery Saver interviewed scientists and found that most of them held religious beliefs that were incompatible with their scientific knowledge. We are all believers, some more credulous than others. It is in our nature to believe what we see, hear, and feel; we have no choice in the matter. This human propensity is of great interest to students of divinity, but also to dramatists, who rely on us to suspend our disbelief every time we enter a theater. In dreams, the will is weakened and the suspension of disbelief is both spontaneous and strong.

In the absence of critical judgment, memory, and external space-time parameters, dreamers confabulate complex and interesting fiction. Robert Louis Stevenson regularly consulted with his dream fairies when he was

Dreamstage collaborators at the opening of the Carpenter Center for the Visual Arts show in April 1977. The Dreamstage exhibition (titled an Experimental Portrait of the Sleeping Brain) was conceived by me (second from left with glasses) and by the composer Paul Earls (far left) of the MIT Center for Advanced Visual Studies. Freelance photographer Ted Spagna (second from right) contributed his unique time-lapse studies (including the one shown here of Peter Pileski sleeping at home with his pet cat). Neuronal landscapes were the work of the Swedish graphics artist Ragnhild (then Karlstrom) Reingardt (right).

stuck for the resolution of a literary problem. In my dreams, I may ski skillfully with no evidence of having had the stroke that ended my awake-state skiing career some years ago. This is because my upper brain still skis quite well in an entirely fictive way. Our dreams are thus as wild as any novel we could read and as vivid as any film we could see. The brain theater is open every night, and it is free.

The great twentieth-century filmmakers Federico Fellini and Ingmar Bergman recognized the autocreative quality of dreams and used it when writing scenarios and when directing. *Juliet of the Spirits* is one of Fellini's most exuberant celebrations of the human imagination. Bergman's *Persona* is a classic annotation of his own autocreativity (and also a hint at proto-consciousness). We can look at our dreams in the private theater of our bedroom. We don't have to drive to the cinema, park, buy an expensive ticket, eat more popcorn than is good for us, and often be disappointed by what we see. All too often I fail to suspend my disbelief in a movie theater. This never happens in my dream films. We have a scenarist and a *metteur en scène* inside our heads. Our artist-self works for us skillfully and fools us every time.

The suspension of disbelief, which is essential to the success of behold-ing art when we are awake, is neither occasional nor fleeting in our dreams. It is so constant and so deep that we can call it a cognitive deficit and hope that its scientific analysis will benefit psychology. It probably will. But no matter how we analyze imagination and self-deception, we can also enjoy our momentary freedom from reductionism—our escape in dreams from what the Spanish playwright Pedro Calderon de la Barca disparagingly called "the grinding will of man."

How amusing it is to create chimeric mergers of people we know (and even of people we don't know)! The Chris Gates in the dream I had last night didn't look at all like my good friend Chris Gates. The film actor playing Richard Nixon doesn't really resemble Nixon but looks enough like Nixon for me to accept the impersonation uncritically.

Emotional salience holds dreams and great art together. We have a built-in capacity to assign meaning and to derive it from our experience. We use this interpretive talent in many ways. In the awake state as well as in dreaming, we would be lost without it. But we may be lost with it, too.

For example, consider three cardinal dream emotions: anxiety, elation, and anger. Recent evidence suggests that these emotions are existential elements. They are not only reactions to daytime experience, nor are they always symptomatic. They are, rather, integral components of our autocre-ative armamentarium. The interpretation of dreams must take this fact into account. Instead of viewing dream emotions as reactions to something, we must begin to see that they are primary parts of our selves. When fine-tuned, they allow us to use our senses and to decide between trust and distrust, between threat and safety, and between fight and flight. They are thus essential to what we call intuition. In dreams such primary elements may play an initiating role in dream plot selection. In my anxiety dreams, for example, the content often concerns what I call incomplete arrange-ments. I have forgotten to bring my slides to a lecture; I have no passport or ticket; I may not be dressed properly. In my view, these content items are reactions to emotion, rather than the other way around. Until recently, we had to depend on great works of art to tell us these things. Much as we had to go to a cinema to stimulate our visual imaginations, we had to go to a bookstore or a museum to experience emotional salience. Such outings may still be useful, but now we can begin to look at, remember, and record our own dreams as we seek to understand ourselves better. When I make an entry in my dream journal, I become a critic of my own productions. I usually rave and almost always chuckle.

I want to emphasize the last point: appreciation. Whether or not we like or understand our own dreams, we must, at least, marvel at our ability to have them. We can no longer say "I have no artistic talent." We may not be able to draw what we see in our dreams, and we may not be very good at either describing or understanding them, but the mere fact that we have them warrants a huge increase in our self-esteem. We are lowly creatures, sure enough. But when we dream, we transcend our humble origins. We fly, we defy, and we lie, all with impunity.

At the beginning of the twentieth century, when Freud was promoting his dream theory, artists were already explicitly accessing their dreams as inspiration or substantive material for their work. I refer, of course, to sur-realists such as Max Ernst, Salvador Dali, and Paul Delvaux, whose work constitutes a culturally accepted metaphor for dreaming. They regarded dreams as a hidden reality, a reality that they felt was superior to the awake state. I do not endorse that idea. But much as Freud's theories were pre-saged by Dostoyevsky and other novelists, the activation-synthesis hypoth-esis that I now espouse may have been anticipated by visual artists.

No surrealist painter surpasses René Magritte, especially when it comes to representing the formal aspects of dreaming. Magritte explicitly denied that his paintings represented dreams, claiming a more mystical source. But his canvases capture, better than any other work of art, such dream features as bizarreness, loss of space-time order, diminished self-awareness, and the hint of meaning beyond appearances. I will comment on this last, important formal property of dreams later when I discuss anticipation. The word 'anticipation' denotes two central aspects of my new theory: prediction and planning.

The autocreativity of the human brain-mind forces revolutionary changes in psychology, as I have already pointed out a number of times. At the same time, it stimulates revision in the social sciences. If I am not, as Locke suggested, a blank slate upon which the truth is written, but rather a brain-mind that, early on, creates its own truth, questions arise about the role of others in my development and in my emerging world view. If my proto-self develops in tandem with proto-others, the degree to which this population of proto-others is learned or innate is a paradox for sociologists as well as for psychologists to ponder. In any case, it is clear that dreaming is distinctly social. The cast of characters in our dreams often exceeds the number of people in the scenes of our waking life. I am almost never alone in my dreams. I may not know who all my dream companions are, but I know that they are there.

Schoolteachers know that a child brings a brain full of data to the classroom. John Dewey and Maria Montessori might have thought that schools needed only to be attentive, waiting like midwives for delivery of innate knowledge. On this view, the child, like Rousseau's noble savage, already knows the truth better than anyone could teach. Though it is true that educators should be aware of autocreativity so as not to squash that talent, its growth must be fostered just as the instruments of secondary consciousness, such as abstract mathematics, must be instructed.

Automaticity

That the brain programs its own states automatically is a discovery that offends the many people who are loath to admit the implied operation of randomness and self-organization. Most people prefer to think of themselves as having been created—and maintained—by some divine and faultless architect. Such people are so convinced of perfect divinity that they are willing even to accept genetically determined developmental disasters (e.g., Down Syndrome) as the inexplicable but nonetheless wonderful workings of mystery. Even for those few of us who have thrown off these quaint dogmas, it is difficult to accept the implication of randomness. As Albert Einstein famously asserted, "God does not play dice." The activation-synthesis dream theory faces this sort of resistance. Dreams must have hidden meanings, and people still pay good money to prophets who promise revelation. Yet we must take seriously Douglas Hofstadter's idea

that because dreams are unpredictable they must also be resistant to interpretation with anything approaching scientific confidence. The same
caveat applies to works of awake intellect—Eliot's poetry, Beethoven's
music, Leonardo's paintings, and so on. Not every detail of these works
was deliberately planned. Even to the extent that the details are deliberate,
there is an automaticity to the creative process that is transferred to the
product. We need this element of uncertainty, and we would be wise to
accept it and (I now suggest) to celebrate it.

We are very lucky to be, among other things, automatons, machines,
even Zombies. "Ugh," you may say. But suppose that you were not, in
many fundamental ways, an automaton. Suppose you had to plan every
aspect of your behavior deliberately. Suppose you had to remember to
breathe, to breed, or to believe. We wouldn't last long either as individuals
or as a species if many of our vital functions were not automatically
controlled.

Even our waking consciousness is automatic. We feel that we are in
control, but there is no scientific evidence that consciousness itself is
causal. In point of experimental fact, it now seems quite likely that our
brain (an automaton if there ever was one) decides for itself what it wants
us to do. It then becomes conscious of its own motive, but the conscious
experience of willing occurs long after the brain has set in motion the act
that we suppose, erroneously, that we have willed.

If we are troubled by our acts, we can reduce the probability of recurrent
impulsiveness by training our brains to behave properly. In that sense,
consciousness retains its vaunted monitoring function. "Free won't" is all
we need for moral control. We learn from our mistakes. If our brain tempts
us, we just say No.

The humanistic fields that have most to gain from the recognition of
automaticity are moral philosophy and jurisprudence. Scientific human-
ism holds that morality is self-evident, but some persons still rely on an
external authority, such as a church, to help them know right from wrong.
We all must obey laws. Even scientific humanists need police, judges, and
lawyers to help them navigate moral waters.

The legal system still is based on the assumption of free will, even
though it has progressed to a consideration of whether the perpetrator of
a crime suffered from a mental defect that precluded his making a rational
distinction between right and wrong. But what about a dreamer? Is any
dreamer in full possession of his cognitive faculties? Obviously not, and
we are very unlikely to prosecute dreamers for such fictive crimes as they
may commit in their dreams.

What about a sleepwalker? Is a person whose upper brain is in stage IV of NREM sleep guilty of a crime committed in that state? Courts are beginning to say "Not guilty" even to murder charges leveled against somnambulists. This precedent opens a floodgate to pleas of innocence from criminals with abnormalities in their EEGs or in their PET scans. It has even been suggested that criminality is always associated with cerebral dysfunction. How can anyone be held accountable for his brain's automaticity?

A deeper question, of course, is to what extent any awake-state behavior is automatic, with consciousness playing catch-up. Given this open question, a course in behavioral neurobiology could well become a prerequisite for admission to a law school. Law students might even be asked to keep dream journals to help sensitize themselves to the subtleties of state-dependent psychology.

Automaticity deeply offends our *amour-propre*. Freud opened a can of moral worms with his concept of a lawless unconscious. For Freud, every human act was the product of a compromise between an exigent id and a socially compliant superego. It may be worse than Freud imagined. There is no such compromise in our new model. Our brain is always exigent and always impulsive. We fit our notion of will down upon it as if it were in control whereas it is a mere explainer of what has already happened automatically. Even those explanations have an automatic character. This is what Freud meant by 'rationalization'.

When we are faced with works of art so radical as to defy rationalization or the naturalization that our built-in model of the world is designed to understand, we become very uncomfortable. Experimental art, after all, is motivated by a desire to overturn convention. When John Cage and David Tudor visited Wesleyan in 1957, their concert for prepared piano provoked delight in Norman Brown because it challenged traditional music structure. The brain and its auditory system are metronomic, which is one reason so many people love Mozart. The predictability and memorability of musical phrasing causes pleasant reverberations in our rhythm-governed brains. Not surprisingly, Mozart claimed that his pieces just came to him— that the music flowed freely out of his brain.

But there is much brain activity that is dysrhythmic, and unpredictable and uninterpretable meaning may be the very essence of modernity. Anxiety is the leading emotion in dreams, so much so that we are often relieved to wake up and discover that a dream was only a dream. So it was with the audiences who whistled at Stravinsky's *Rite of Spring*, then got up and walked out as if the new music were only a dream. Now I, for one, sit with delight on the edge of my seat as Stravinsky makes me anxious, just as often happens in my dreams. What I am saying is that the brain is both the creator and the appreciator of all art. Some of that art, like some of my dreams, is chaotic and anxiety provoking. Art, like our dreams, helps us know ourselves better—especially art that is admirably automatic.

Anticipation

Perhaps the most startling and novel aspect of the new Dream Consciousness paradigm is its insistence on a "prepare for" function as well as a "react to" function. This is what I mean when I say that REM-sleep dreaming is much more prophetic than a simple narrative replay model would predict. When I dream, I am not simply a storyteller doomed to repeat what I already know. Through the automatic autocreativity of my dreaming brain, I concoct entirely original scenarios, ideas, and experiences that point tantalizingly from my past to my future. When I dream, I am as much getting ready for tomorrow as getting over today. Of course I sometimes use today's data to map tomorrow's agenda, but I move forward in a new light with only a glance at the rear-view mirror. Views of human nature that ignore this futuristic orientation are doomed to erroneous incompleteness.

Incompleteness was a major shortcoming of Freud's pessimistic model, which understood the future only in terms of the past. Yes, the activation-synthesis model agrees that the past is real, and the repetition compulsion really does threaten us. But the future beckons, saying: "Change! Try something new!" Whatever you do may look and feel like your past, but it is certainly not completely predictable from your past. If psychoanalysts were really able to predict the future, we would know it by now, and we would be bound to take their scientific claims more seriously. But psychoanalysts wisely hedge their bets, always stating that the prognosis is guarded.

The activation-synthesis theory of dreaming does not pretend to predict exactly what will happen tomorrow. It recognizes both the open-ended quality of dream content and the unexpected effects of interaction with the waking world. It nonetheless prepares the individual for just such unpredictability by instantiating a multifaceted and versatile agenda. Dreaming advises "Be ready for anything; anticipate nothing with certainty." In my Vermont dream, my farmer neighbor says "I may be hard to find, but when you get there, you can count on my presence." This statement is more like a Buddhist koan than like a Western weather report. Come to think of it, dreaming is more like my favorite religion (Buddhism) than it is like the Protestant church I left behind when I refused to color the angels.

When I hypothesize that REM-sleep dreaming is a state of protoconsciousness, the prefix 'proto' is chosen to convey the temporal sense of "prior to" as well as the structural sense of "fundamental to" or "basic to." When I was a fetus aspiring to become an infant, I did not even attempt waking consciousness until I had logged as much as three months of simulation. And when I finally poked my head out, I quickly pulled it in again for an equal amount of virtual-reality time.

We anticipate the challenges that lie ahead by getting ready to meet them. We create, within our heads, a model of the outside world. No matter how erroneous that model may be, it is better than nothing. And, like our dream chimeras, it is not a bad copy after all.

Educational Implications

I have already emphasized how happy the John Deweys and Maria Montessoris of the educational world will be with protoconsciousness theory. They can be sure of an alliance with their students' brains. Those brains are actively reaching out for data to help them realize their potential. The educator has only to educate (or lead out) rather than beat in any truth. That learning is always a two-way street lightens the teacher's burden considerably.

Mothers and fathers are our first and foremost teachers. Their task is made easier by realizing how much their child brings to the mastering of tasks and to the challenge of socialization. That much of the child's contribution is enhanced by sleep is a big surprise. It puts a more positive value on a state that many parents still regard as downtime even if they urge their children to get a lot of it. Some people even regard sleep as an unwelcome waste of time. It is enlightening to note that the baby is making up its mind at the same time that it guarantees rest for the tired caretaker.

Schools should acknowledge the didactic power of sleep too. Instead of insisting that ostensibly lazy adolescents get up at 6 a.m. in order to be in school by 8, it may be worth trying a later start time (perhaps 9:30 or 10:00 a.m.) on the assumption that time spent asleep is at least as useful to the teenage brain as time spent doing homework. The school day might then continue until 4 p.m.

Curriculum Reform

How can educators take advantage of the new science of sleep and dreaming? A program for lower schools must begin by recognizing what is going on within the child's head. Brain science should therefore be an integral part of teacher training, not the very occasional add-on that it now is. After all, it is the brain that learns. Most teachers already know that. But how the brain uses sleep to learn is a topic that must be addressed when updating teacher training.

Resistance to recommended scheduling changes will be monumental. School professionals (including teachers), city traffic regulators, and authoritarian moralists will all dig their heels in as deep as hospital administrators do when failing to institute clearly indicated duty-shift changes. In this case, the woozy student is as cognitively impaired as the sleep-deprived agent of medical malpractice; the sleepy student thus suffers instead of the patient. In both cases, the administrator feels fine because he or she is older and has gotten enough sleep.

Whatever the policy regarding schedules, it should be easy to persuade educators that self-knowledge is as important as knowledge of ancient cultures, that learning to learn is as useful as learning to read, and that learning to take proper care of one's brain is the highest goal of all. Brain education must be a lifelong process. Being in school from age 5 through age 22 is already testimony to the length of brain training. Parallel to this useful practice is meta-education about the brain.

Yet brain education *per se* has only recently and haltingly entered school curricula, and almost never before the junior high level. A graded series of introductions to the science of the brain could be coupled with education about science as a process. A particularly seductive theme of this initiative is the concept of life as a laboratory. At no added expense, teachers could be encouraged to inculcate direct observation and self-study techniques, such as watching and describing a baby brother or sister sleep. Many families have pets that can be observed. The recording of dream reports is a joint exercise in writing and psychology that even 10-year-olds are likely to find interesting.

From the study of dreams, the step to a discussion of mental illness is short and direct. A good way to understand madness is to report dreams and talk about them. Do not interpret until you have first asked questions. What is it like to be crazy? If you dream, you know the answer. You see things that are not there, you believe things that are not true, your thoughts are jumbled, your feelings are intense, and you elaborate stories to hold it all together. What causes the brain to dream? Why does it stop when you wake up? In what way is waking up like a cure for madness? The chemistry of dreaming is now understood well enough so that preliminary answers to all these questions can be offered. Also well known are the effects of exogenous chemicals such as alcohol and recreational drugs. Mental health workers might also be the target of such instruction, which aims at self-control at a time of high risk. During adolescence and young adulthood, intoxication and late-night motor vehicle operation sometimes conspire to cause irreparable brain damage.

A severely injured brain is damaged forever. How many children, adolescents, young adults, or even parents really know that? Very few, I am afraid. Getting this message across is not helped by well-publicized experiments showing that some nerve cells regenerate. Most don't, however, so severe brain injury, be it toxic or traumatic, gives no second chance. The stupor associated with too many boxing blows, too many head-to-head football tackles, or too many nightcaps is not health-giving, as sleep is. But brain damage is the most tragic of illnesses because it is 100 percent avoidable.

Getting these principles into practice will be about as easy as the legislative passage of protective gun laws, but the universality and magnitude of the problem may help us to achieve something as unexpected as the ban on cigarette smoking. In only 25 years the United States has become almost completely "smoke free." In another quarter-century it should be possible to cut self-inflicted brain damage in half. That's progress, but it isn't good enough. We need to do better. No one who is spared the living death of irreparable brain damage need occupy a hospital bed or ride in a wheelchair until he or she dies.

The best antidote to the endless and fruitless arguments about euthanasia is prevention of brain death so that brain life can continue to confer its many blessings on us. You have a brain; protect it. Get all the sleep you feel you need, then get a little more. And don't forget to dream, even if you can't remember one dream in any detail.

REM sleep is not only good for the maintenance of well-being and health; it is also essential to life. Allan Rechtschaffen's sleep-deprivation studies of rats prove it. Then how can so many people consider sleep to be a waste of time? They are simply uninformed. They need to be educated. Recall that there was a long delay in the scientific recognition that sleep was not as quiescent as its outward calm suggested. None of us guessed that sleep would be such a rich ground for physiologists to cultivate. If sleep science and dream science are in late middle age, we may hope that wisdom is just around the corner.

In a culture that places a high premium on achievement, it is natural to overvalue the awake state and to undervalue sleep. We must begin to correct this imbalance through education. Knowing that sleep not only knits up the raveled sleeve of care but draws up the knitting plan is a helpful insight. We need not devalue the awake state to acknowledge that sleep makes it better by enhancing its planning and its execution.

The long and short of the story is that behavior and cognition both degenerate with sleep deprivation and improve with recovery sleep

Schools and Museums of Science

One way to promote sleep and dream science is by coordinating school curricula with visits to science museums. When my first wife, Joan Harlowe, worked with Kathy Kane of the Boston Bicentennial Commission, she contacted Boston's Museum of Science, which wanted to conceive, fund, and install an exhibit on the human brain. That was in 1975, when my own science was flourishing. I was then busy recording from individual brain cells in sleeping cats. I was enthralled by what I was seeing and hearing from the depths of the brain. It occurred to me that a good way to interest the public in brain science might be to invite people to visit my lab. That was impractical, but we could certainly set up a sleep lab in a museum. The emphasis of the Dreamstage exhibit, which I conceived and helped to create, was on the process of science rather than its product. I was satisfied if my exhibit could convey one (and only one) substantive point: that the brain is active in sleep.

A normal person slept in the museum's transparent bedroom with as many as 500 visitors looking on in wonder during a single day. A Dreamstage sleeper could stay awake if he or she was so inclined, but was required to agree to sleep nowhere else but in the exhibit. All the Dreamstage sleepers slept quite well, and they never resorted to sedatives.

How did we convey the central idea that the brain was active even during sleep? We connected the sleeper's brain to traditional sleep-lab instruments so as to demonstrate conventional recording. But we also fed the electrical signals along to a laser system, designed by Paul Earls, that displayed the sleeper's brain waves, muscle tone, eye movements, and heart action on the walls of the gallery. In addition, the photographer Theodore Spagna projected his time-lapse sequences of people sleeping at home to give a sense of the motoric dynamism of sleep, and the graphic artist Ragnhild Reingard created a three-screen slideshow of neuronal anatomy so that visitors could see inside their brains. The tour de force of this so-called Dreamstage Darkspace was a series of animated dream drawings from a journal kept by an insect specialist at the Smithsonian Institution in the summer of 1939. The drawings clearly conveyed the fictive movement of dreams. In the adjacent Dreamstage Light Space, we used conventional media to explain the darkspace phenomena.

After an experimental run at Harvard University in 1977, Dreamstage went on a national tour from 1978 to 1980, then returned to Boston's Museum of Science. In that museum and in every other museum we visited, I was impressed by the universal fascination of young and old visitors, and also by the complete disconnection of the exhibit visit from school or home-based science education. In my opinion, children see a day at a science museum as a day off from school. I am determined and committed to changing that disconnection.

In the year 2002, I recreated Dreamstage in the barn of my former dairy farm in Vermont. With the enthusiastic support of Caledonia County's superintendent of schools, Scott Graham, I helped several teachers to create units on Brain and Sleep Science for their eighth-grade students. The children study the brain in class before visiting the museum. They also record their observations of baby brothers and sisters, their pets, and themselves. I would say that at least half of the students get something out of the visit. They all remark on the real human brain that I keep in a jar outside the sleep chamber. It's the only brain they have ever seen. Competing with the hormones and the fantasies of adolescents is not easy, but sleep and dream science is attention-getting for those who are able to stay awake and maintain attention. High school students, especially those with career interests in health science, are much more receptive, as are college and medical school students. The enthusiasm of my professional colleagues assures me that Dreamstage is not "dumbed down." I have a hunch that younger children might like Dreamstage too.

The secret of Dreamstage is not so much that the exhibit is "hands-on" (the buzzword of the science museums) as that it is dedicated to demonstrating a process rather than showcasing a product. Seeing for oneself is the essence of science. Of course, not every child in the United States (or even in the small state of Vermont) can visit Dreamstage. Our lesson plans and DVDs can, however, visit them. And I am working on a virtual visit to the museum that will be available to anyone with access to a computer.

Science for Everyman

The most important point to be made about sleep and dream science is that it is work in progress at one of the last and most important scientific frontiers: human consciousness. Since consciousness and its sleep-related vicissitudes are universal, every living person has something to give and something to get from this enterprise.

The something to give is precious subjective experience. In the preceding two chapters, I argued that subjective experience is an essential datum of sleep and dream science. It is embarrassing to admit it, but after more than 50 years of laboratory work our inventory of dream reports is still very incomplete. Most sleep-lab subjects are young (of college age), but we need to look at dreams over a lifetime. With age, dreams are very likely to change in frequency and content. Do their formal properties change too? I doubt it, but I don't really know. Not everyone can write (or sleep) like Marcel Proust, but anyone who has completed eighth grade can helpfully describe his or her conscious experience.

Earlier in this chapter, I exhorted parents and teachers to foster self-reporting in children no later than age 14. Now I say to all of you: Keep a journal in which you note anything of interest about your conscious experience. Did you have a striking dream? Describe that dream in detail before you try to interpret it. In fact, if you dispense with interpretation altogether, you will probably do a better job with the description. I am inviting you to suspend not disbelief but belief. Welcome to science. In essence, it is the suspension of belief.

If reading this book has helped you to understand the difference between dream form and dream content, so much the better. Research is needed in both domains. Do your best to provide reports that will be useful to us. If you need guidance, send me your first ten reports and I will respond. My email address is allan_hobson@hms.harvard.edu.

Do not neglect waking consciousness. Do you daydream? If so, please describe your daydreams so that they can be compared with your nocturnal experiences. Do you have fantasies like those in "The Secret Life of Walter Mitty," or are your fantasies more banal, as mine are? Do you anticipate social interactions, prepare scripts for them, or review important life episodes? Believe it or not, waking consciousness is much less well studied than dream consciousness. That's paradoxical, because the awake state is much more accessible than dreaming. Or is it? Although I know that I have almost continuous fantasy when I am not concentrating on a task in the awake state, it is quite difficult for me to capture and describe my musings. For me, catching dreams is easier. What is your experience?

Is your consciousness a seamless stream, as William James supposed, or is it more choppy and discontinuous, as John Antrobus asserts? Does your mind flow, or does it jump unpredictably from one subject to the next? Or does it do a little of each? Is your day anything like Leopold Bloom's (in James Joyce's *Ulysses*), or is it less chaotic, less romantic, and less mytho-logically derived? We need to know, and only you can tell us what your experience is really like.

Do you have exceptional mental states? Do you imagine things so intensely that you actually perceive them? Do you see, hear, or feel things that other people cannot corroborate? Don't assume that such perceptions are symptoms of mental illness. They may well be, but instead of interpret-ing them, send their description to me. Do you ever have waking (lucid) dreams, as described in chapter 15? Laboratory research is ongoing in this area. You may be able to help.

Why a chapter on the humanistic implications of modern sleep and dream science should end with these appeals demands an explanation. Suffice it to say that I consider the distinction between science and art to be considerably less sharp than is generally assumed. To put it another way, I am convinced that brain science, including the study of sleep and dreams, is one of the humanities in the same sense that dreaming is delirium. Splitters will be unhappy with this assessment; lumpers will rejoice. Whether you are a splitter or a lumper, welcome aboard.

18 Functional Conclusions

What Is the Function of REM-Sleep Dreaming?

I have told my life story in terms of questions like this one. I believe that I was born with a predilection for biology and that biological forces shaped many of my most important life experiences. I have tried to show that the flow from biology to psychology and from psychology to biology is continuous and smooth. In advocating integration, I am not arguing for reduction, as many psychoanalytically inclined readers may fear. On the contrary, I am only taking up Freud's Project for a Scientific Psychology, abandoned in 1895 for want of data. Now, in 2010, we can begin a new to work again on the abandoned project. My life has been devoted to this goal.

Why Do We Have REM Sleep?

If we now know enough to understand that REM sleep and dreaming did not evolve to protect consciousness from invasion by noxious impulses arising from the unconscious mind in sleep, as Freud thought, then we must wonder why we have REM sleep and why we dream. Why do we have two kinds of consciousness, one in the awake state and the other in dreaming?

Protoconsciousness theory answers this functional question in a very simple way. Mammals and birds evolved REM sleep in order to achieve primary consciousness—a definite advantage over amphibians and reptiles, which have no discernible consciousness whatsoever. To achieve even the low-level perception and emotion that characterize primary consciousness, a considerable amount of brain growth was necessary.

To prepare and maintain the additional specialized brain tissue, it was advantageous to evolve an autoactivation mechanism that could turn on the system in sleep and to thereby simulate its awake-state operation.

At the same time, it was advantageous to achieve thermoregulation so that the animal could function in a wider range of environmental conditions. The more highly evolved brain was also a beneficiary of that thermoregulation. The mammalian brain functioned well only in a very narrow temperature range.

So demanding was the task of evolving even primary consciousness that it was useful to provide the mammalian brain with a simulation test pattern that could operate automatically, especially in early development but also later in life. One of the boldest claims of protoconsciousness theory harks back to Freud. It states not only that the brain network that supports primary consciousness and dreaming operates at full throttle during early life, and later in sleep, but also that it operates in a damped form throughout the awake state.

In its damped form, primary consciousness is like Freud's primary process. But instead of consisting mainly of exigent drives (the id) and needing repression (by the ego and superego), primary consciousness cooperates with secondary consciousness by providing the building blocks of waking consciousness. Waking consciousness is guided by the cortical networks that I call secondary, which are most highly developed in humans.

In the awake state, primary consciousness networks (which are subcortical) are not so much repressed as inhibited. When, for one reason or another, they become disinhibited (or greatly excited), they can take over consciousness. Then they may cause alarm. As a simple and entirely normal example, consider the startle response. An unexpected stimulus causes the subject to orient quickly ("I jumped a mile"), to feel fear ("You scared me to death"), and to interrupt the flow of cognition (be it fantasy or reading). It is not for nothing that we call this indulgence in background processing "daydreaming."

The more positive contributions of primary consciousness to the awake state are more difficult to demonstrate, because waking consciousness subjectively seems to be all of a piece. But protoconsciousness insists that primary consciousness networks participate actively in shaping perception and other aspects of cognition when secondary consciousness has the upper hand. Another commonplace example, akin to startle, is the filling in that occurs when a stimulus is partial but suggestive. My own favorite case of filling in involves my "seeing" my co-worker Bob McCarley when I left my office at the Massachusetts Mental Health Center and caught a glimpse of his Irish tweed hat on the rack beside my door. The hat was indeed Bob's, but Bob was not there, except in my mind. I projected his image to fill in a man under the hat.

Protoconsciousness theory states that such anticipatory projection (or anticipation) is going on all the time, though direct evidence for it is so fleeting and so short-lived as to be difficult to notice. This makes sense, because the most important tasks of awake-state perception are accuracy and speed or environmental object identification. The survival value of these attributes is self-evident.

Why do we have REM sleep? The answers to this question are now clear. We need to convert a necessarily limited set of genetic instructions into an active organizational program for the brain. That action program, I say, is REM sleep. It runs much of the time during the third trimester in utero, and it runs about eight hours a day during the first year of life. The infant, I say (now more facetiously), is making up its mind. By "mind," of course, I mean its protoconscious brain.

At the same time that it facilitates the brain circuit development that will ultimately come to underlie waking consciousness, REM guarantees homeothermy. Homeothermy not only confers on its possessor behavioral versatility; it also creates the stable internal temperature that is necessary to complex brain function. All mammals have REM, and all mammals and birds are homeothermic. Depending on the number and the connectivity of thalamocortical neurons, animals have a little cognitive capacity (primary consciousness) or a lot (primary plus secondary consciousness).

Humans have a lot more cognitive capacity than even monkeys. And primates have a lot more cognitive capacity than sub-primates, other mammals, or birds. But all of us mammals have primary consciousness, REM, and homeothermy.

Why Do We Dream?

We dream because our brains are activated during sleep. We dream most intensely during REM sleep because that is the stage with the greatest brain activation. Our dreams are strange because the activation is regionally restricted and not as widespread as it is in the awake state. In particular, the frontal brain, thought by neuropsychologists to be the seat of executive ego function, is not activated. Hence, we lack insight and control. Our memory is impaired because the activated brain is demodulated. The aminergic systems of the brainstem that are normally active in the awake state are turned off.

Does that mean that dreaming is epiphenomenal? Does it mean that dreaming is not really important? Perhaps. But it does not mean that dreaming is meaningless, or that studying it is useless. Dreams may be

instructive precisely because they are hyperemotional and hyperassociative. They are thus worthy of psychological attention if one abandons the
Freudian idea that their real psychological meaning is shrouded in symbol-
ism needing decoding. For protoconsciousness theory, dreams are as
revealing as they are creative. Dreaming is a glorious mental state worthy
of our respect, interest, and enjoyment. A life without dreaming would not
be life.

Bibliography

Allison, T., and D. V. Cicchetti. 1976. Sleep in mammals: Ecological and constitutional correlates. *Science* 194 (4266): 732–734.

Aschoff, J. 1965. Circadian rhythms in man. *Science* 148: 1427–1432.

Aserinsky, E., and N. Kleitman. 1953. Regularly occurring periods of ocular motility and concomitant phenomena during sleep. *Science* 118: 361–375.

Ashby, R. 1952. *Design for a Brain*. Chapman and Hall.

Aston-Jones, G., and F. Bloom. 1981. Activity of norepinephrine-containing locus coeruleus neurons in behaving rats anticipates fluctuations in the sleep waking cycle. *Journal of Neuroscience* 1: 876–886.

Baghdoyan, H., R. Lydic, C. Callaway, and J. A. Hobson. 1989. The carbachol-induced enhancement of desynchronized sleep signs is dose dependent and antagonized by centrally administered atropine. *Neuropsychopharmacology* 2 (1): 67–79.

Berger, H. 1929. Über das Electrenkephalogramm des Menschen. *Archiv für Psychiatrie und Nervenkrankheiten* 87: 527–570.

Bizzi, E., and D. Brooks. 1963. Functional connections between pontine reticular formation and lateral geniculate nucleus during deep sleep. *Archives Italiennes de Biologie* 101: 666–680.

Birnholz, J. 1981. The development of human fetal eye movement patterns. *Science* 213 (4508): 679–681.

Bowker, R., and A. R. Morrison. 1976. The startle reflex and PGO spikes. *Brain Research* 102 (1): 185–190.

Braun, A. R., et al. 1997. Regional cerebral blood flow throughout the sleep-wake cycle. *Brain* 120: 1173–1197.

Bremer, F. 1935. Cerveau isolé et physiologie du sommeil. *Comptes Rendus des Séances et Mémoires de la Société de Biologie* 118: 1235–1241.

Brooks, D., and E. Bizzi. 1963. Brain stem electrical activity during deep sleep. *Archives Italiennes de Biologie* 101: 648–665.

Buzsáki, G. 2007. The structure of consciousness. *Nature* 446 (7133): 267.

Calvo, J., S. Datta, J. Quattrochi, and J. A. Hobson. 1992. Cholinergic microstimulation of the peribrachial nucleus in the cat. II. Delayed and prolonged increases in REM sleep. *Archives Italiennes de Biologie* 130 (4): 285–301.

Card, J., L. Swanson, and R. Moore. 2008. The hypothalamus: An overview of regulatory systems. In *Fundamental Neuroscience*, third edition, ed. L. Squire et al. Academic Press.

Cartwright, R. 1996. Dreams and adaptation to divorce. In *Trauma and Dreams*, ed. D. Barrett. Harvard University Press.

Chase, M., and F. Morales. 1983. Subthreshold excitatory activity and motor-neuron discharge during REM periods of active sleep. *Science* 221 (4616): 1195–1198.

Chugh, D., Weaver, T., and Dinges, D. 1996. Neurobehavioral consequences of arousals. *Sleep* 19 (10): S198–S201.

Cooper, J., F. Bloom, and R. Roth. 1996. *The Biochemical Basis of Neuropharmacology*, seventh edition. Oxford University Press.

Czisch, M., R. Wehrle, C. Kaufmann, T. Wetter, F. Holsboer, T. Pollmächer, and D. Auer. 2004. Functional MRI during sleep: BOLD signal decreases and their electrophysiological correlates. *European Journal of Neuroscience* 20 (2): 566–574.

Dahlstrom, A., and K. Fuxe. 1964. Evidence for the existence of monoamine-containing neurons in the central nervous system. I. Demonstration in the cell bodies of brain stem neurons. *Acta Physiologica Scandinavica* 62: 1–55.

Datta, S., J. Calvo, J. Quattrochi, and J. A. Hobson. 1992. Cholinergic microstimulation of the peribrachial nucleus in the cat. I. Immediate and prolonged increases in ponto-geniculo-occipital waves. *Archives Italiennes de Biologie* 130 (4): 263–284.

Datta, S. 1995. Neuronal activity in the peribrachial area: Relationship to behavioral state control. *Neuroscience and Biobehavioral Reviews* 19 (1): 67–84.

Datta, S. 2000. Avoidance task training potentiates phasic pontine-wave density in the rat: A mechanism for sleep-dependent plasticity. *Journal of Neuroscience* 20 (22): 8607–8613.

Datta, S., and R. MacLean. 2007. Neurobiological mechanisms for the regulation of mammalian sleep-wake behavior: Reinterpretation of historical evidence and inclusion of contemporary cellular and molecular evidence. *Neuroscience and Biobehavioral Reviews* 31: 775–824.

Datta, S., V. Mavanji, J. Ulloor, and E. Patterson. 2004. Activation of phasic pontine-wave generator prevents rapid eye movement sleep deprivation-induced learning impairment in the rat: A mechanism for sleep-dependent plasticity. *Journal of Neuroscience* 24 (6): 1416–1427.

Dawes, G., H. Fox, B. Leduc, G. Liggins, and R. Richards. 1972. Respiratory movements and rapid eye movement sleep in the foetal lamb. *Journal of Physiology* 220 (1): 119–143.

Dement, W. 1958. The occurrence of low voltage, fast, electroencephalogram patterns during behavioral sleep in the cat. *Electroencephalography and Clinical Neurophysiology* 10 (2): 291–296.

Dement, W. 1960. The effect of dream deprivation. *Science* 131: 1705–1707.

Dement, W., and C. Fisher. 1963. Experimental interference with the sleep cycle. *Canadian Psychiatric Association Journal* 257: 400–405.

Dement, W., and N. Kleitman. 1957. Cyclic variations in EEG during sleep and their relation to eye movements, body motility, and dreaming. *Electroencephalography and Clinical Neurophysiology* 9 (4): 673–690.

Dresler, M., M. Kluge, L. Genzel, P. Schüssler, and A. Steiger. 2007. Synergistic effects of age and depression on sleep-dependent memory consolidation. *Pharmacopsychiatry* 240: 238–239.

Dresler, M., M. Kluge, L. Genzel, P. Schussler, and A. Steiger. 2010. Imparied sleep-dependent memory consolidation in depression. *European Neuropsychopharmacology* 20 (8): 553–561.

Edelman, G. 1992. *Bright Air, Brilliant Fire: On the Matter of the Mind.* Basic Books.

Epstein, A. 1977. Dream formation during an epileptic seizure: Implications for the study of the "unconscious." *Journal of the American Academy of Psychoanalysis* 5 (1): 43–49.

Flanagan, O. 2001. *Dreaming Souls: Sleep, Dreams and the Evolution of the Conscious Mind.* Oxford University Press.

Foote, S. 1973. Compensatory changes in REM sleep time of cats during ad libitum sleep and following brief REM sleep deprivation. *Brain Research* 54: 261–276.

Fosse, M., R. Fosse, J. A. Hobson, and R. Stickgold. 2003. Dreaming and episodic memory: A functional dissociation? *Journal of Cognitive Neuroscience* 15 (1): 1–9.

Fosse, R., R. Stickgold, and J. A. Hobson. 2002. Emotional experience during rapid-eye-movement sleep in narcolepsy. *Sleep* 25 (7): 724–732.

Fosse, R., R. Stickgold, and J. A. Hobson. 2001. Brain-mind states: Reciprocal variation in thoughts and hallucinations. *Psychological Science* 12 (1): 30–36.

Foulkes, W. 1962. Dream reports from different stages of sleep. *Journal of Abnormal and Social Psychology* 65: 14–25.

Foulkes, W. 1982. *Children's Dreams: Longitudinal Studies*. Wiley.

Freud, S. 1895. Project for a scientific psychology. In *The Standard Edition of the Complete Works of Sigmund Freud*, ed. J. Strachey et al. Hogart Press and Institute of Psychoanalysis, 1953–1974.

Freud, S. 1900. *The Interpretation of Dreams*. Basic Books.

Gazzaniga, M., and K. Baynes, eds. 2000. *The New Cognitive Neurosciences*, second edition. MIT Press.

Genzel, L., M. Dresler, R. Wehrle, M. Grözinger, and A. Steiger. 2009. Slow wave sleep and REM sleep awakenings do not affect sleep dependent memory consolidation. *Sleep* 32: 302–310.

Gerashchenko, D., T. Chou, C. Blanco-Centurion, C. Saper, and P. Shiromani. 2004. Effects of lesions of the histaminergic tuberomammillary nucleus on spontaneous sleep in rats. *Sleep* 27 (7): 1275–1281.

Graham Brown, T. 1912. The factors in the rhythmic activity of the nervous system. *Proceedings of the Royal Society of London, Series B* 85: 278–289.

Henley, K., and A. Morrison. 1974. A re-evaluation of the effects of lesions of the pontine tegmentum and locus coeruleus on phenomena of paradoxical sleep in the cat. *Acta Neurobiologiae Experimentalis* 34 (2): 215–232.

Hensch, T. 2005. Critical period mechanisms in developing visual cortex. *Current Topics in Developmental Biology* 69: 215–237.

Herman, M., S. Denlinger, R. Patarca, L. Katz, and J. A. Hobson. 1991. Developmental phases of sleep and motor behaviour in a cat mother-infant system: A time-lapse video approach. *Canadian Journal of Psychology* 45 (2): 101–114.

Hobson, J. A. 2009. REM sleep and dreaming: Towards a theory of protoconsciousness. *Nature Neuroscience Reviews* 10: 803–814.

Hobson, J. A., and M. Brazier, eds. 1980. *The Reticular Formation Revisited*, volume 6. Raven.

Hobson, J. A., S. Hoffman, R. Helfand, and D. Kostner. 1987. Dream bizarreness and the activation-synthesis hypothesis. *Human Neurobiology* 6 (3): 157–164.

Hobson, J. A., and D. Kahn. 2007. Dream content: Individual and generic aspects. *Consciousness and Cognition* 16 (4): 850–858.

Hobson, J. A., R. Lydic, and H. Baghdoyan. 1986. Evolving concepts of sleep cycle generation: From brain centers to neuronal populations. *Behavioral and Brain Sciences* 9: 371–448.

Hobson, J. A., and R. McCarley. 1977. The brain as a dream state generator: An activation-synthesis hypothesis of the dream process. *American Journal of Psychology* 134 (12): 1335–1348.

Hobson, J. A., R. McCarley, R. Pivik, and R. Freedman. 1974a. Selective firing by cat pontine brain stem neurons in desynchronized sleep. *Journal of Neurophysiology* 37: 497–511.

Hobson, J. A., R. McCarley, R. Freedman, and R. Pivik. 1974b. Time course of discharge rate changes by cat pontine brain stem neurons during sleep cycle. *Journal of Neurophysiology* 37: 1297–1309.

Hobson, J. A., R. McCarley, and P. Wyzinski. 1975. Sleep cycle oscillation: Reciprocal discharge by two brainstem neuronal groups. *Science* 189 (4196): 55–58.

Hobson, J. A., R. McCarley, and J. Nelson. 1983. Location and spike-train characteristics of cells in anterodorsal pons having selective decreases in firing rate during desynchronized sleep. *Journal of Neurophysiology* 50 (4): 770–783.

Hobson, J. A., E. Pace-Schott, and R. Stickgold. 2000. Dreaming and the brain: toward a cognitive neuroscience of conscious states. *Behavioral and Brain Sciences* 23 (6): 793–842.

Hobson, J. A., and E. Pace-Schott. 2002. The cognitive neuroscience of sleep: Neuronal systems, consciousness and learning. *Nature Reviews Neuroscience* 3 (9): 679–693.

Hofstadter, D. 1999. *Gödel, Escher, Bach: An Eternal Golden Braid*. Basic Books.

Hong, C., Harris, J., Pearlson, G., Kim, J., Calhoun, V., Fallon, J., Golay, X., Gillen, J., Simmonds, D., van Zijl, P., Zee, D., and Pekar, J. 2008. fMRI evidence for multisensory recruitment associated with rapid eye movements during sleep. *Human Brain Mapping* 30 (5): 1705–1722.

Ioannides, A., M. Corsi-Cabrera, P. Fenwick, Y. del Rio Portilla, N. Laskaris, A. Khurshudyan, D. Theofilou, et al. 2004. MEG tomography of human cortex and brainstem activity in waking and REM sleep saccades. *Cerebral Cortex* 14 (1): 56–72.

Ito, K., and R. McCarley. 1987. Physiological studies of brainstem reticular connectivity. I. Responses of mPRF neurons to stimulation of bulbar reticular formation. *Brain Research* 409 (1): 97–110.

Jackson, J. 1998. *Evolution and Dissolution of the Nervous System*. Thoemmes Continuum.

Jouvet, M. 1962. Research on the neural structures and responsible mechanisms in different phases of physiological sleep. *Archives Italiennes de Biologie* 100: 125–206.

Jouvet, M. 1973. Essai sur le rêve. *Archives Italiennes de Biologie* 111: 564–576.

Jouvet, M. 1999. *The Paradox of Sleep: The Story of Dreaming*. MIT Press.

Jouvet, M., and F. Michel. 1959. Electromyographic correlations of sleep in the chronic decorticate and mesencephalic cat. *Comptes Rendus des Seances de la Société de Biologie et de ses Filiales* 153 (3): 422–425.

Kahn, D., and J. A. Hobson. 2005. State-dependent thinking: A comparison of waking and dreaming thought. *Consciousness and Cognition* 14 (3): 429–438.

Kahn, D., E. Pace-Schott, and J. A. Hobson. 2002. Emotion and cognition: Feeling and character identification in dreaming. *Consciousness and Cognition* 11 (1): 34–50.

Kahn, D., R. Stickgold, E. Pace-Schott, and J. A. Hobson. 2000. Dreaming and waking consciousness: A character recognition study. *Journal of Sleep Research* 9 (4): 317–325.

Katz, L., and C. Shatz. 1996. Synaptic activity and the construction of cortical circuits. *Science* 274 (5290): 1133–1138.

Kihlstrom, J. 1987. The cognitive unconscious. *Science* 237 (4821): 1445–1452.

Knutson, K., K. Spiegel, P. Penev, and E. Van Cauter. 2007. The metabolic consequences of sleep deprivation. *Sleep Medicine Reviews* 11 (3): 163–178.

Kollar, E., R. Pasnau, R. Rubin, P. Naitoh, G. Slater, and A. Kales. 1969. Psychological, psychophysiological, and biochemical correlates of prolonged sleep deprivation. *American Journal of Psychiatry* 126 (4): 488–497.

LaBerge, S. 1990. Lucid dreaming: Psychophysiological studies of consciousness during REM sleep. In *Sleep and Cognition*, ed. R. Bootzin, J. Kihlstrom, and D. Schacter. American Psychological Association.

Laureys, S., and G. Tononi. 2009. *The Neurology of Consciousness: Cognitive Neuroscience and Neuropathology*. Academic Press.

Laureys, S., A. Owen, and N. Schiff. 2004. Brain function in coma, vegetative state, and related disorders. *Lancet Neurology* 3 (9): 537–546.

Libet, B., C. Gleason, E. Wright, and D. Pearl. 1983. Time of conscious intention to act in relation to onset of cerebral activity (readiness-potential): The unconscious initiation of a freely voluntary act. *Brain* 106 (Pt 3): 623–642.

Lin, Y., B. Bloodgood, J. Hauser, A. Lapan, A. Koon, T. Kim, L. Hu, A. Malik, and M. Greenberg. 2008. Activity-dependent regulation of inhibitory synapse development by Npas4. *Nature* 455 (30): 1198–1204.

Llinas, R. 2001. *I of the Vortex: From Neurons to Self*. MIT Press.

Llinás, R., and D. Paré. 1991. Of dreaming and wakefulness. *Neuroscience* 44 (3): 521–535.

Loomis, A., E. Harvey, and G. Hobart. 1935. Further observations on the potential rhythms of the cerebral cortex during sleep. *Science* 82 (2122): 198–200.

Lu, J., D. Sherman, M. Devor, and C. Saper. 2006. A putative flip-flop switch for control of REM sleep. *Nature* 441 (7093): 589–594.

Lydic, R., R. McCarley, and J. A. Hobson. 1983. The time-course of dorsal raphé discharge, PGO waves, and muscle tone averaged across multiple sleep cycles. *Brain Research* 274 (2): 365–370.

Magoun, H., and R. Rhines. 1947. An inhibitory mechanism in the bulbar reticular formation. *Journal of Neurophysiology* 9: 165–171.

Maquet, P., J. Péters, J. Aerts, G. Delfiore, C. Degueldre, A. Luxen, and G. Franck. 1996. Functional neuroanatomy of human rapid-eye-movement sleep and dreaming. *Nature* 383 (6596): 163–166.

Marshall, L., and J. Born. 2007. The contribution of sleep to hippocampus-dependent memory consolidation. *Trends in Cognitive Sciences* 11 (10): 442–450.

McCarley, R. 1982. REM sleep and depression: Common neurobiological control mechanisms. *American Journal of Psychiatry* 139 (5): 565–570.

McCarley, R., and J. A. Hobson. 1975. Neuronal excitability modulation over the sleep cycle: A structural and mathematical model. *Science* 189: 58–60.

McCarley, R., and J. A. Hobson. 1975. Discharge patterns of cat pontine brain stem neurons during desynchronized sleep. *Journal of Neurophysiology* 38 (4): 751–766.

McCarley, R., and E. Hoffman. 1981. REM sleep dreams and the activation-synthesis hypothesis. *American Journal of Psychiatry* 138 (7): 904–912.

McGinty, D., and R. Harper. 1976. Dorsal raphé neurons: Depression of firing during sleep in cats. *Brain Research* 101: 569–575.

Merritt, J., R. Stickgold, E. Pace-Schott, J. Williams, and J. A. Hobson. 1994. Emotion profiles in the dreams of young adult men and women. *Consciousness and Cognition* 3: 46–60.

Mori, S., H. Nishimura, and M. Aoki. 1980. Brain stem activation of the spinal stepping generator. In *The Reticular Formation Revisited*, volume 6. ed. J. A. Hobson and M. Brazier. Raven.

Moruzzi, G. 1966. The functional significance of sleep with particular regard to the brain mechanisms underlying consciousness. In *Brain and Conscious Experience*, ed. J. Eccles. Springer.

Moruzzi, G., and H. Magoun. 1949. Brainstem reticular formation and activation of the EEG. *Electroencephalography and Clinical Neurophysiology* 1: 455–473.

Moskowitz, E., and R. Berger. 1969. Rapid eye movements and dream imagery: Are they related? *Nature* 224 (5219): 613–614.

Nelson, J., R. McCarley, and J. A. Hobson. 1983. REM sleep burst neurons, PGO waves, and eye movement information. *Journal of Neurophysiology* 50 (4): 784–797.

Nielsen, T. 2000. A review of mentation in REM and NREM sleep: "Covert" REM sleep as a possible reconciliation of two opposing models. *Behavioral and Brain Sciences* 23 (6): 851–866.

Nielsen, T., and R. Levin. 2007. Nightmares: A new neurocognitive model. *Sleep Medicine Reviews* 11 (4): 295–310.

Nofzinger, E., M. Mintun, M. Wiseman, D. Kupfer, and R. Moore. 1997. Forebrain activation in REM sleep: An FDG PET study. *Brain Research* 770 (1–2): 192–201.

Pace-Schott, E., and J. A. Hobson. 2002. The neurobiology of sleep: Genetics, cellular physiology and subcortical networks. *Nature Reviews. Neuroscience* 3: 591–605.

Parmeggiani, P. 2003. Thermoregulation and sleep. *Frontiers in Bioscience* 8: s557–s567.

Pompeiano, O. 1967. The neurophysiological mechanisms of the postural and motor events during desynchronized sleep. *Research Publications - Association for Research in Nervous and Mental Disease* 45: 351–423.

Porte, H., and J. A. Hobson. 1996. Physical motion in dreams: One measure of three theories. *Journal of Abnormal Psychology* 105: 329–335.

Raichle, M., and M. Mintun. 2006. Brain work and brain imaging. *Annual Review of Neuroscience* 29: 449–476.

Rasch, B., Pommer, J., Diekelmann, S., and Born, J. 2008. Pharmacological REM sleep suppression paradoxically improves rather than impairs skill memory. *Nat Neurosci*; advanced online publication.

Rechtschaffen, A. 1978. The single-mindedness and isolation of dreams. *Sleep* 1: 97–109.

Rechtschaffen, A., and A. Kales, eds. 1968. *A Manual of Standardized Terminology Techniques and Scoring System for Sleep Stages of Human Subjects*. Brain Information Service/Brain Research Institute, University of California at Los Angeles.

Rechtschaffen, A., B. Bergmann, C. Everson, C. Kushida, and M. Gilliland. 1989. Sleep deprivation in the rat. X. Integration and discussion of the findings. *Sleep* 12 (1): 68–87.

Resnick, J., R. Stickgold, E. Pace-Schott, J. Williams, and J. A. Hobson. 1994. Self-representation and bizarreness in children's dreams. *Consciousness and Cognition* 3: 30–45.

Revonsuo, A., and K. Valli. 2008. How to test the threat-simulation theory. *Consciousness and Cognition* 17 (4): 1292–1296.

Roffwarg, H., W. Dement, J. Muzio, and C. Fisher. 1962. Dream imagery: Relationship to rapid eye movements of sleep. *Archives of General Psychiatry* 7: 235–258.

Roffwarg, H., J. Muzio, and W. Dement. 1966. Ontogenetic development of the human sleep-dream cycle. *Science* 152 (3722): 604–619.

Sanes, D., T. Reh, and W. Harris. 2006. *Development of the Nervous System*, second edition. Academic Press.

Sanford, L., A. Silvestri, R. Ross, and A. R. Morrison. 2001. Influence of fear conditioning on elicited ponto-geniculo-occipital waves and rapid eye movement sleep. *Archives Italiennes de Biologie* 139 (3): 169–183.

Saper, C., T. Chou, and T. Scammell. 2001. The sleep switch: Hypothalamic control of sleep and wakefulness. *Trends in Neurosciences* 24: 726–731.

Sastre, J., and M. Jouvet. 1979. Oneiric behavior in cats. *Physiology & Behavior* 22 (5): 979–989.

Saxvig, I., A. Lundervold, J. Gronli, R. Ursin, B. Bjorvatn, and C. Portas. 2008. The effect of a REM sleep deprivation procedure on different aspects of memory function in humans. *Psychophysiology* 45: 309–317.

Scarone, S., M. Manzone, O. Gambini, I. Kantzas, I. Limosani, A. D'Agostino, and J. A. Hobson. 2008. The dream as a model for psychosis: An experimental approach using bizarreness as a cognitive marker. *Schizophrenia Bulletin* 34 (3): 515–522.

Sherrington, C. 1906. *Integrative Action of the Nervous System*. Constable.

Siegel, J. 2001. The REM sleep-memory consolidation hypothesis. *Science* 294 (5544): 1058–1063.

Siegel, J. 2005. Clues to the functions of mammalian sleep. *Nature Insight* 437 (27): 1264–1271.

Silberman, E., E. Vivaldi, J. Garfield, R. McCarley, and J. A. Hobson. 1980. Carbachol triggering of desynchronized sleep phenomena: Enhancement via small volume infusions. *Brain Research* 191 (1): 215–224.

Singer, J., and J. Antrobus. 1965. Eye movements during fantasies: Imagining and suppressing fantasies. *Archives of General Psychiatry* 12: 71–76.

Singer, J., and J. Antrobus. 1972. Dimensions of daydreaming: A factor analysis of imaginal processes and personality scales. In *The Function and Nature of Imagery*, ed. P. Sheehan. Academic Press.

Singer, W. 2001. Consciousness and the binding problem. *Annals of the New York Academy of Sciences* 929: 123–146.

Smith, C., and L. Lapp. 1991. Increases in number of REMs and REM density in humans following an intensive learning period. *Sleep* 14: 325–330.

Snyder, S. 1986. *Drugs and the Brain*. Freeman.

Solms, M. 1997. *The Neuropsychology of Dreams: A Clinico-Anatomical Study*. Erlbaum.

Stickgold, R., L. James, and J. A. Hobson. 2000. Visual discrimination learning requires sleep after training. *Nature Neuroscience* 3 (12): 1237–1238.

Stickgold, R., E. Pace-Schott, and J. A. Hobson. 1994a. A new paradigm for dream research: Mentation reports following spontaneous arousal from REM and NREM sleep recorded in a home setting. *Consciousness and Cognition* 3: 16–29.

Stickgold, R., C. Rittenhouse, and J. A. Hobson. 1994b. Dream splicing: A new technique for assessing thematic coherence in subjective reports of mental activity. *Consciousness and Cognition* 3: 114–128.

Sutton, J., C. Rittenhouse, E. Pace-Schott, R. Stickgold, and J. A. Hobson. 1994a. A new approach to dream bizarreness: Graphing continuity and discontinuity of visual attention in narrative reports. *Consciousness and Cognition* 3: 61–88.

Sutton, J., C. Rittenhouse, E. Pace-Schott, J. Merritt, R. Stickgold, and J. A. Hobson. 1994b. Emotion and visual imagery in dream reports: A narrative graphing approach. *Consciousness and Cognition* 3: 89–99.

Tononi, G. *Psi*. Unpublished manuscript.

Vertes, R. 2004. Memory consolidation in sleep: Dream or reality. *Neuron* 44 (1): 135–148.

Vogel, G., F. Vogel, R. McAbee, and A. Thurmond. 1980. Improvement of depression by REM sleep deprivation: New findings and a theory. *Archives of General Psychiatry* 37 (3): 247–253.

von Economo, C. 1930. Sleep as a problem of localization. *Journal of Nervous and Mental Disease* 71: 249–259.

Voss, U., Holzmann, R., Tuin, I., and Hobson, J. A. 2009. Lucid dreaming: A state of consciousness with features of both waking and non-lucid dreaming. *Sleep* 32 (9): 1191–2000.

Walker, M., T. Brakefield, A. Morgan, J. A. Hobson, and R. Stickgold. 2002. Practice with sleep makes perfect: Sleep-dependent motor skill learning. *Neuron* 35 (1): 205–211.

Walker, M., T. Brakefield, J. A. Hobson, and R. Stickgold. 2003. Dissociable stages of human memory consolidation and reconsolidation. *Nature* 425 (6958): 616–620.

Wegner, D. 2004. Précis of the illusion of conscious will. *Behavioral and Brain Sciences* 27 (5): 649–659.

Wehrle, R., M. Czisch, C. Kaufmann, T. Wetter, F. Holsboer, D. Auer, and T. Pollmächer. 2005. Rapid eye movement-related brain activation in human sleep: A functional magnetic resonance imaging study. *Neuroreport* 16 (8): 853–857.

Wehrle, R., C. Kaufmann, T. Wetter, F. Holsboer, D. Auer, T. Pollmächer, and M. Czisch. 2007. Functional microstates within human REM sleep: First evidence from fMRI of a thalamocortical network specific for phasic REM periods. *European Journal of Neuroscience* 25 (3): 863–871.

Wiesel, T., and D. Hubel. 1963. Effects of visual deprivation on morphology and physiology of cells in the cat's lateral geniculate body. *Journal of Neurophysiology* 26: 978–993.

Williams, R., H. Agnew, Jr., and W. Webb. 1964. Sleep patterns in young adults: An EEG study. *Electroencephalography and Clinical Neurophysiology* 17: 376–381.

Williams, J., J. Merritt, C. Rittenhouse, and J. A. Hobson. 1992. Bizarreness in dreams and fantasies: Implications for the activation-synthesis hypothesis. *Consciousness and Cognition* 1: 172–185.

Wundt, W. 1874. *Grundzüge der physiologischen Psychologie.* Engelmann.

Wyzinski, P., R. McCarley, and J. A. Hobson. 1978. Discharge properties of pontine reticulospinal neurons during sleep-waking cycle. *Journal of Neurophysiology* 41 (3): 821–834.

Index